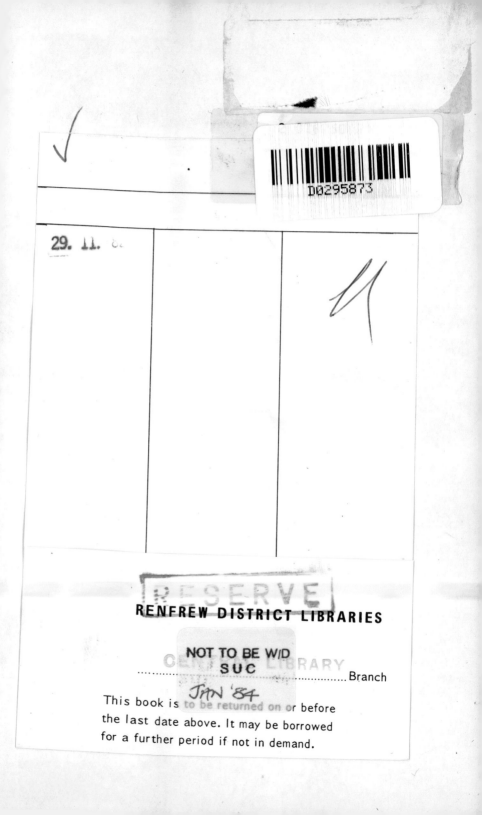

THE CHAINLESS MIND

TWENTIETH CENTURY THEMES

General Editor: JAMES L. HENDERSON

The Chainless Mind

A STUDY OF RESISTANCE AND LIBERATION

BY

JAMES L. HENDERSON

AND

MALCOLM CALDWELL

Eternal spirit of the chainless mind!
Brightest in dungeons, Liberty! Thou art,
For there the habitation is the heart—
The heart which love of thee alone can bind;
    BYRON: *The Prisoner of Chillon*

HAMISH HAMILTON
LONDON

First published in Great Britain, 1968
by Hamish Hamilton Ltd.
90 Great Russell Street, London W.C.1
© *1968 by James L. Henderson and Malcolm Caldwell*

SBN 241 91337 3

Printed in Great Britain by
Western Printing Services Ltd, Bristol

Contents

Acknowledgements

THE authors and publishers are grateful to the following for permission to reproduce copyright material in this book: Curtis Brown Ltd., for the extract from *How the Resistance Worked* by Ronald Seth; George Bell & Sons Ltd., for the extract from *The Chinese People and Chinese Earth* by K. Buchanan; Thames & Hudson Ltd. and Frederick A. Praeger Inc., for the extract from *The East German Rising* by Stefan Brant; Weidenfeld & Nicolson Ltd., for the extract from *Tito Speaks* by Vladimir Dedijer; Pergamon Press Ltd., for the extract from *European Resistance Movements*; Mrs. W. A. Bradley for the extracts from *Resistance, Rebellion and Death*; Mr. W. B. Yeats and Macmillan & Co. Ltd., for the quotation from W. B. Yeats; Penguin Books Ltd., for the extract from *The Crisis of India* by R. Segal; Ernest Benn Ltd. and Frederick A. Praeger Inc., for the extract from *Malaya* by J. M. Gullick; Hutchinson Publishing Co. Ltd., for the extract from *Who Lived to See the Day* by Philip de Vomecourt; Methuen & Co. Ltd., for the extract from *Nationalism and Communism Essays* by H. Seton Watson; The Clarendon Press, for the extracts from *Latin America* by H. Blakemore; The *Western Morning News* for the article on page 49; *The Times* for the article on pages 13–14; *Daily Telegraph* for the articles on pages 171, 190–1, 195, 199, 218; *Time and Tide* and Robert Speaight for the articles on pages 51–2.

Preface

THE four volumes in this series are written around eight words: Poverty, Affluence, Discovery, Invention, Resistance, Liberation, Art, Belief. Each and all of them may be regarded as nodal points of contemporary world history. They do not tell the story of the twentieth century, but they do claim that that story is meaningful and that its essential significance can be discovered through reflective scrutiny of these topics. It is assumed that the study of world themes such as these must form a vital part of modern man's education for survival.

The gist of this volume on Resistance and Liberation is that the spirit of man cannot be quenched, that his mind is chainless. Examples of that fact are taken from the struggle against oppression in Europe during the Second World War and from other regions of the world where liberation against various forms of imposed government has been sought and in some degree attained. The book attempts to study how men may turn oppression into liberty without being seduced on the way by the lust for power.

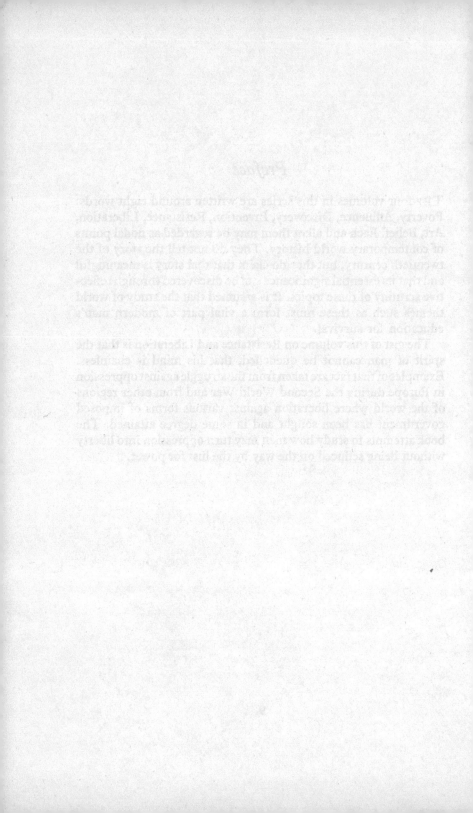

Introduction

THE word 'Resistance' has a resonance that is both specific and profound. It applies particularly to the struggles against oppression and imposed government in Europe during the Second World War and also to certain events elsewhere, which, although different in kind, share some of its distinctive quality. The word Resistance has acquired a special mystique, indicating a spirit of heroic protest.

Liberation has to do with the early stirrings of modern nationalism, especially in Asia, Africa and the Middle East. It is a phenomenon to be observed as appearing among and sometimes as part of the great ideological rivalries of the twentieth century. It is a larger theme than Resistance but the reason why the two can properly be associated is because of the big element of heroic protest that inspires them both and because of the inevitable shadow side of violence and horror by which both are accompanied.

Resistance can be violent or non-violent, and in many cases it is a combination of the two. In order to get the feel of our subject let us begin by taking two instances of it in the period before the Second World War.

1. The Easter Rising 1916

Our point of entry into the tangled and bloody history of Anglo-Irish relations is the publication in 1899 of Arthur Griffiths' *United Irishmen*. From it an excellent idea can be obtained of how the larger movement of Irish National Liberation had to bide its time for more than twenty years, while in the meantime various Irish resistance movements occurred. Griffiths' insistence that any kind of armed rising should be ruled out as impractical is especially interesting, as is also his insistence that they should limit themselves to passive resistance, a doctrine to which he gave the name *Sinn Fein—We Alone* (1906).

Just before the outbreak of the First World War a Home Rule
Bill was about to be passed at Westminster but at that critical
moment Ulster intervened, largely on the religious ground that
Home Rule constituted a threat from the Roman Catholic
southern part of Ireland to her northern part of the Irish Protes-
tant Ascendency. Sir Edward Carson led their resistance; Red-
mond started organizing a counter-resistance; British troops fired
on some of the latter's supporters but themselves threatened
mutiny at the Curragh. Then an Austrian archduke was assassin-
ated at Sarajevo and a local brawl got swallowed up by a world
war.

However, against the background of Britain's struggle with
Germany, 1914–1918, resistance of a kind continued against her
in Ireland. This was led at first by Patrick Pearse, who with his
followers still felt that Britain was the real enemy: their ardent
planning and speaking resulted in the Easter Monday Rising of
1916. After failing to capture the Castle in Dublin, they seized
the Post Office, proclaimed a Republic, but after a week's fighting
were forced to surrender—it was the Blood of the Martyrs:

> 'I have met them at close of day
> Coming with vivid faces
> From counter or desk among grey
> Eighteenth century houses . . .
>
> I write it out in a verse—
> MacDonagh and MacBride
> And Connolly and Pearse
> Now and in time to be,
> Wherever green is worn
> Are changed, changed utterly:
> A terrible beauty is born.'[1]

Immediately after the Armistice of 1918 their sacrifices began
to take effect: Irish candidates for election, after being elected,
refused to take their seats at Westminster but instead sat in Dail
Eireann or the Assembly of Ireland, with De Valera, actually at
the time in Lincoln gaol, as its President. Every day the underground movement gained in strength: as a result the Home Rule
Bill was amended so that Southern Ireland should become self-
governing, with Carson's Ulster excluded: this became law in the

autumn of 1921, but still in the South De Valera's followers refused to acknowledge it and an appalling civil war broke out between them and the 'Black and Tans' seeking to enforce the English constitutional settlement: in December, 1921 the Free State of Ireland obtained its independence as a Dominion within the British Empire. However, even this was not enough for extremists like Griffiths and Collins who encouraged further resistance; but the first died and the second was killed in action, and Cosgrave who succeeded them capitulated as the insurrection died away and accepted the original treaty arrangement. After De Valera succeeded him and with the passing of more years Eire eventually became fully independent.

This brief sketch provides a brilliant and dramatic miniature picture of a resistance movement within a national liberation one, its focal point being the Easter Rising of 1916—the gesture of heroic protest, which failed at the time but inspired subsequent victory. It was compounded of the following elements: religion— a devout if not fanatical Roman Catholicism; politics—the climax of revolt against centuries old foreign domination; economics—a cry of the poverty-stricken underling; culture—the Celtic revival; personality—leaders with magnetic power, like Pearse and Griffiths, Collins and De Valera. From all this 'a terrible beauty' was born.

In an article of April 7th, 1966 in *The Times*, entitled 'Ireland's Easter Blood Bath', it is suggested that the best explanation of the Irish impulse came from James Stephens who, publishing his eye witness account of the scene in Dublin at the time, summed up with:

'If freedom is to come to Ireland—as I believe it is—then the Easter Insurrection is the only thing that could have happened. . . . If after all her striving it came to her as a gift, as a peaceful present such as is sometimes given away with a pound of tea, Ireland would have accepted the gift with shame-facedness and have felt that her centuries of revolt had ended in something like ridicule.

The blood of brave men had to sanctify such a consummation, if the national imagination was to be stirred to the dreadful business which is the organizing of freedom, and both imagination and brain have been stagnant in Ireland this many a year. Following on such tameness failure might have been predicted, or, at least feared, and war (let us call it war for the sake of our pride) was due to Ireland before she could enter gallantly upon her inheritance. We might have crept into liberty like some kind of domesticated men, whereas now we may be allowed to march into freedom with the honours of war.'

Let us hold on to this psychological clue for future reference, particularly when dealing with the resistance movement in Yugoslavia.

2. *The Ruhr, 1923*

After the First World War as part of the Treaty of Versailles Germany was saddled with a huge reparations bill, which she had to pay the Allies. Partly because she could not and partly because she would not pay, France under Poincaré demanded coercive measures against her. In January, 1923, French and Belgian troops occupied the Ruhr, Germany's most valuable industrial area: occupation would continue until reparations were paid.

'The Germans could not fight; neither could they surrender. they resorted to passive resistance. All reparation payments were stopped, all German officials, managers and industrial workers in the Ruhr ceased work. They were fed by the German Government. A new war, bloodless but terrible, began.'[2]

With Germany in the throes of wild inflation, continued resistance of this kind became impossible; by September, 1923, the Government was bankrupt. However, this did not mean that the French got their reparations but rather that their intransigence had to give way before the hard economic facts, and so the American Dawes Commission was set up to devise a means of restoring Germany's solvency as a step to her eventual payment of reparations.

In November, 1923, as the old German mark was worthless, a new currency called the Rentenmark was invented, created in theory by a mortgage on German land and industrial plant. The reality contradicted this theory: a whole middle class had been wiped out; business was at a standstill. Revival, it was felt, could only be by means of a gigantic loan, recommended by the Dawes Commission, accompanied by a promise from France that she would get out of the Ruhr as a reassurance to German morale, and on October 31st, 1924, this plan went into operation.

What concerns us here, however, is what went on in the Ruhr during the French occupation of it; first there was the deliberate French incitement to German separatists to heighten their efforts to achieve a breakaway Rhineland province. Due partly to Britain's opposition to this policy and partly to the unsavoury character of some of the few German separatists, it failed. Secondly, there was the use of coloured troops by the French in the areas they occupied: this aroused passionate resentment among the German population.

> 'Before long, passive resistance became a state of undeclared war in which the weapons on one side were strikes, sabotage and guerilla warfare, and on the other arrests, deportations and economic blockade.'[3]

> 'The greatest attention was excited by the case of a certain Albert Leo Schlageter, who was arrested by the French criminal police in an Essen hotel on the night of April 7th, 1923, tried for espionage and sabotage by a French military court in Dusseldorf, sentenced to death on May 10th, and executed two weeks later.'[4]

Although as a person Schlageter may not have been attractive, his fate cast him for the role of national hero-martyr and the symbol of an active, as opposed to a passive, resistance movement. It is interesting to note for future reference in our study that the Communist Radek described him as 'a good soldier of the counter-revolution who deserves to be honoured by the Communists, soldiers of the Revolution, as an honourable man: let their future task be to make sure that men such as he become not wanderers into a void, but rather builders of a better future for the human race.' (Eyck, p. 238.)

In the instance of resistance in the Ruhr the following were obvious ingredients: politics—national resistance against foreign occupation shot through, often with contradictory impulses, by Rhineland separatist agitators; economics—a solidarity of workers and employers identifying with the political impulse to protest against the economic futility of reparations; religion and culture —nothing very much; personality—the individual Schlageter, of no great stature as a human being but useable at the time, and even more later on by the Nazis, as a symbol of the victimization of Germany by the French. Lastly it is worth noting the ambivalent connection of the Communists with the Ruhr resistance, for here is an element that is most persistent in our story, namely the tendency for Communists to support Resistance, in some cases even to provide its backbone, while at the same time criticising, or on some occasions betraying, its non-Communist associates in the movement.[5]

These two examples of resistance sufficiently illustrate the number and complexity of its ingredients: let us now turn to a more exact definition of our second term.

The word 'liberation' has been subjected in the modern period to a familiar process by which some narrower or more specific meaning is attached to a term of originally general denotation. 'Liberation' means the act of setting free—thus the liberation of the slaves after the American civil war. But in communist terminology, and now by extension and reaction more widely, 'liberation' has come to have a more definite sense. A 'national liberation struggle' is not just an anti-colonial struggle for political independence. It is also a struggle for the overthrow and supersession of the existing social structure—in practice, a struggle for socialism and economic autonomy in place of feudalism, capitalism and economic imperialism. It is a struggle for the radical transformation of the conditions of existence of the mass of the people, and not simply for the substitution of one elite group for another.

Understandably, the various world interests view the development of national liberation struggles in this sense from very different standpoints. Even inside the communist group of nations there are marked differences in interpretation and emphasis This is to be expected. There is no reason to suppose that two or more communist nations will be very much different in their intra-bloc relations from two or more non-communist nations. As long as there are nations, conflicting national interests will emerge. Of more direct relevance in the present context is the fact that the leaders of successful revolutions will naturally rationalize and generalize their own respective experiences. Since these experiences are bound to differ from one case to another, the resulting collections of generalized lessons and conclusions are also bound to diverge. Thus, both the Russian and the Chinese leaders claim to be dispensing Marxism-Leninism in their writings and analyses. But it is abundantly clear that the common body of Marxist-Leninist teaching has been filtered in each case through a unique complex of circumstances, resulting in two distinguishable solutions. We shall observe the practical implications of this when dealing with the unfolding liberation struggle in China and the role of the Russians at the time, influenced as they were by the genesis of the Soviet Union itself.

But let us start with the American attitude to national liberation struggles (an attitude which is shared by those in the most influential circles of the other Western capitalist countries). National liberation struggles by their very nature directly threaten the international economic and strategic interests of the West in general and the United States of America in particular. It is not surprising to find, therefore, the power of the West everywhere ranged against the liberation struggles of what has come to be known (rather misleadingly) as the 'third world'—a short-hand term for the poor, underdeveloped countries of Asia, Africa and Latin America. ('The two-thirds world' might be a better term, since the countries concerned account for roughly two-thirds of the population of the planet.) This opposition is justified by an interpretation of the origin and nature of liberation struggles which discounts their national and democratic character.

What is that interpretation? Briefly, it is that liberation struggles of the kind described above are not expressions of genuine indigenous aspirations but rather of the ideological and power aspirations of the existing communist countries. American intervention in South Vietnam, for example, is justified on the grounds that the National Liberation Front of South Vietnam is not an indigenous force, but an arm or tool of the communist government in Hanoi in North Vietnam. What appears to be a genuine civil war is thus, from the American point of view, actually an 'invasion' of the South by the North.

This interpretation informs the speeches and statements of the majority of Western statesmen, and is elaborated in a growing corpus of books by Western experts on 'subversion', insurgency, guerrilla warfare, and, a term of current popularity, 'unconventional aggression'. Dean Rusk, the US Secretary of State, argued as follows on a recent occasion:

'What is a "war of national liberation"? It is, in essence, any war that furthers the Communist world revolution—what, in broader terms, the Communists have long referred to as a "just war". The term "war of national liberation" is used not only to denote armed insurrection by people still under colonial rule—there are not many of those left outside the Communist world. It is used to denote any effort led by Communists to overthrow by force any non-Communist government.

'Thus the war in South Vietnam is called a "war of national liberation". And those who would overthrow various other non-Communist governments in Asia, Africa and Latin America are called the "forces of national liberation".

'Nobody in his right mind would deny that Venezuela is not only a truly independent nation but that it has a government chosen in a free election. But the leaders of the Communist insurgency in Venezuela are described as leaders of a fight for "national liberation"—not only by themselves and by Castro and the Chinese Communists but by the Soviet Communists. . . .

'In Communist doctrine and practice, a non-Communist government may be labelled and denounced as "colonialist", "reactionary", or a "puppet", and any state so labelled by the Communists automatically becomes fair game—while Communist intervention by force in non-Communist states is justified as "self-defence" or part of the "struggle against colonial domination". "Self-determination" seems to mean that any Communist nation can determine by itself that any non-Communist state is a victim of colonialist domination and therefore a justifiable target for a "war of liberation".

'As the risks of overt aggression, whether nuclear or with conventional forces, have become increasingly evident, the Communists have put increasing stress on the "war of national liberation". The Chinese Communists have been more militant in language and behaviour than the Soviet Communists. But the Soviet Communist leadership also has consistently proclaimed its commitment in principle to support wars of national liberation. . . .

'International law does not restrict internal revolution within a state or revolution against colonial authority. But international law does restrict what third powers may lawfully do in support of insurrection. It is these restrictions that are challenged by the doctrine, and violated by the practice, of "wars of liberation".

'It is plain that acceptance of the doctrine of "wars of liberation" would amount to scuttling the modern international law of peace which the charter (of the United Nations) prescribes. And acceptance of the practice of "wars of liberation", as defined by the Communists, would mean the breakdown of peace itself.'[6]

An academic exponent of the American doctrine, discussing the 'Communist search for a reasonably safe brand of aggression', writes:

'There is no denying that the small but disciplined cadres of the national Communist parties are extremely adaptable and effective tools of politics, and this is proving particularly true in the underdeveloped areas where shifts of attitude towards authority and traditional ways are likely to be the most sudden and explosive. These groups are well suited to identify with, and act on, popular grievances and to stir up considerable unrest even where the grievances are not pressing or serious. In most of the underdeveloped regions there have been plenty of ready-made grievances with which they have worked. These rebellious minorities have demonstrated that by exacerbating and exploiting existing tensions, they can, over time and with adequate assistance and support, build an aggressive military opposition that may finally destroy the government's ability to govern and thus reduce the country to a welter of confusion and civil war.'

A key phrase here is 'adequate assistance and support'. The author makes it plain that he means assistance and support from an outside Communist power. Thus:

'. . . unconventional offensives built round guerrilla operations and mounted against reasonably responsive and competent governments have little chance of gaining national victory
unless they receive sustained and large-scale support across a
contiguous border and can look to the Communist side of that
border as a sanctuary and base as well as a source of supply.'[7]

It is the purpose of the second section of the book to give something of the historical and sociological background to the unfolding drama of the emerging nations of Asia, Africa and Latin
America in the mid-twentieth century, and to probe into the real
character of the national liberation struggles which are so notice-
able and significant a feature of the current scene. The kind of
matters which will concern us in these coming pages are the
relationship between political independence and economic
autonomy, the extent of responsibility for present world poverty
to be allocated to colonialism and neo-colonialism, the role of the
communist powers in instigating, supplying and directing
revolutionary movements in other countries, and the proper
definition of 'liberation'.

Against the background of this twofold definition of Resistance
and Liberation, the first part of the book (Chapters I, II, III)
will deal with different kinds of Resistance Movements in the
Second World War and in the years since 1945. The second part
(Chapters IV, V, VI, VII, VIII) will trace the origins and growth
of liberation struggles in the non-European world.

REFERENCES

1. W. B. Yeats: *Easter, 1916.*
2. Sonntag: *European Diplomatic History 1871–1932*, pp. 356–7. The
   Century Company, 1933.
3. A. Bullock: *Hitler. A Study in Tyranny*, Odhams, 1952.
4. Erich Eyck: *A History of the Weimar Republic*, Vol. I, p. 237.
   Harvard University Press, 1962.
5. See Angress: *Stillborn Revolution*, Chap. XI—*The Communist Bid
   for Power in Germany 1921–23.* Princeton University Press, 1963.
6. Dean Rusk: 'American Foreign Policy and International Law', pp.
   349–51 in M. E. Gettleman (ed.): *Vietnam*, London, 1965.
7. J. E. Cross: *Conflict in the Shadows*, London, 1964, pp. 8, 10.

PART ONE

RESISTANCE

CHAPTER ONE

Resistance in France and Yugoslavia: A Comparative Study

BEFORE attempting to study two specific instances, an outline of the Resistance movements as a whole during the Second World War must be obtained.

There were Resistance Movements in the following countries: Albania, Hungary, Rumania, Czechoslovakia, Belgium, Denmark, Greece, Norway, Netherlands, Yugoslavia, France, Poland and occupied portions of the U.S.S.R., as well as within Italy, Austria and Germany. The last will be considered in Chapter Two, while with regard to Italy the vital date to remember is September 8th, 1943, when the King and then Marshal Bagdolio forsook the Mussolini Fascist régime and surrendered to the Allies, thus changing from enemy to Italian non-participants, with however a quite powerful anti-Fascist Resistance Movement operating as well. It is essential to understand how all these Resistance Movements, with of course the exception of Austria and Germany, stood in some kind of relationship to the three great Allied Powers, Great Britain, the U.S.A. and the U.S.S.R., and also, though not in all cases, to their own governments in exile, chiefly in London. Such governments existed in the case of the Netherlands, Norway, Belgium, Greece, Czechoslovakia and Poland, though in the case of the last three their authority was challenged from elements inside the borders of their own countries, while Denmark, although forced into nominal neutrality by the Germans, had secured vigorous representation in exile and eventually became an associate Allied Power. Perhaps a useful loose distinction to make is between internal resistance to Nazism and Fascism, an indigenous force aided to greater or less extent from without, and the external resistance of the Allied Powers'

23

grand strategy of war. It is to the attitude of the latter to the former that we must next turn our attention.

Beginning with Great Britain, it is useful to note a certain ambiguity which was to mark all her dealings with the various Resistance Movements. It is summed up in two quotations: the first, which undoubtedly continued to influence some senior British political thinking, is a remark of the Duke of Wellington in connection with the Peninsula War:

> 'I always had a horror of revolutionizing any country for a political object. I always said that, if they rise of themselves, well and good, but don't stir them up; it is a fearful responsibility.'

The second is a statement made by Winston Churchill in a letter to Mr. Dalton, the Minister of Economic Warfare whose office was to become 'The Ministry of Ungentlemanly Warfare', describing that office's function as being 'to set Europe ablaze'. Again on July 20th, 1941 Churchill remarked:

> 'The "V" sign is a symbol of the unconquerable will of the occupied territories, and a portent of the fate awaiting the Nazi tyranny. So long as the people of Europe continue to refuse all cooperation with the invader, it is sure that his cause will perish and that Europe will be liberated.'

To implement the Churchillian policy there was created a body known as 'Special Operations Executive' (S.O.E.), which, starting on a tiny scale in 1940 because of the British Government's heavy commitments in other spheres, gradually became the main instrument for Britain's cooperation with European Resistance Movements.[1]

Not unnaturally, S.O.E. to a major extent had to reflect official Foreign Office policy, and this, it cannot be too strongly emphasized, regarded final victory in terms of legitimist restoration rather than political revolution. As we shall be seeing this led to a whole series of confusions, contradictions and frustrations when the British actually came into contact with those sections of the Resistance Movements, generally the most dynamic parts of them, which were bent on political revolution.

'The original broad conception of S.O.E. activities was one of organizing as a first priority the sabotage of the German war effort, and only secondly that of encouraging subversion in an occupied Europe with which all touch had been lost.'[2]

When the whole course of the Second World War was transformed by the German attack on Russia, (January 27th, 1941) it became clear how diametrically opposed was the Soviet to the Anglo-U.S. attitude towards the Resistance Movements:

'The struggle against Germany must not be looked upon as ordinary war. It is not merely a fight between two armies. . . . In order to engage the enemy there must be bands of partisans and saboteurs working underground everywhere, blowing bridges, destroying roads, telephones and telegraphs, and setting fire to depots and forests. In territories occupied by the enemy, conditions must be made so impossible that he cannot hold out: those helping may well be punished and executed.'[3]

This was a far more extreme and ideologically definite view than that of the other two Allies, though by 1944/45 they had begun to learn about and have greater respect than previously for the active and passive sabotage which the Resistance could achieve.

The objectives of S.O.E. were: 'the organization and equipping of (a) systematic sabotage and intelligence, (b) secret armies in Occupied Europe'—aims which in many cases were to prove incompatible.

In summarizing the attitude of the U.S. Government to the Resistance Movements, the relevance of the following factors must be stressed: (1) the date of entry of America into the War, two and a quarter years after the Nazi invasion of Poland, (2) the U.S. isolationist tradition, which was ignorant and suspicious of European politics and tended therefore to leave that side of things to Britain, (3) U.S. links with the Vichy régime and French North Africa, the first of which had first put a brake on her enthusiasm for anything less conservative, the second of which fortified the American, and especially Roosevelt's, strong dislike and distrust of General de Gaulle. At and after the Allied invasion of Europe in 1944 the U.S. began to have a much closer concern, which, as the following episode illustrates, shows how even within the Anglo-American Alliance there could be serious differences of opinion as to the nature of Resistance Movements.

'The American Government, prior to the entrance of Anglo-American troops into Belgium at the end of 1944, had signed an Agreement with the exiled Government, under which Belgian areas liberated by Allied troops would be governed by a Belgian national appointed by the Government in London. When the Nazis were pushed out of Belgium left wing groups in the internal Resistance refused to accept the delegate of the Belgian Government-in-Exile, requesting instead the installation of an Allied military government. Churchill then ordered the British to use force to break down Belgian left wing resistance.'[4]

'Military advantages and human hope drew America into dealings with the European Resistance Movements. Once involved, American inexperience made the actual relations less fruitful than they might otherwise have been.'[5]

As for the third Allied Power, the U.S.S.R., here, as we have already seen, ideology is the clue to an understanding of the Russian attitude towards the Resistance Movements. Crudely stated, the U.S.S.R. regarded the war against Nazism as having become a just war only after the German attack on Russia, as compared with what previously had been the unjust "phoney" war of the Western Imperialist Powers against Germany.

'The Resistance was precisely a brilliant expression of the activities of the masses and their participation in the historical process. This fact alone is sufficient to recognize the Resistance as one of the most important elements in the victory of humanity and liberty over Fascist obscurantism.'[6]

In other words, the Soviet view was, understandably enough, that Resistance was logical and legitimate as the inevitable and just uprising of the workers exploiting a war situation of revolutionary potential.

Two constants would appear to emerge in the broad spectrum of the European Resistance Movements, patriotism and anti-Fascism. Yet these two factors, common to all of them, differed proportionately in strength in each and were often in conflict with one another. Again the methods of conducting Resistance were frequently similar, but they ranged from active violent assaults to passive resistance. A particularly effective example of the latter occurred in Denmark.

'One evening in November, 1944, Arne Hansen and his girl-friend Lotte Kjaers were rather bored, and decided that they would go to a cinema though they knew they would be made angry by the German film which they would be shown, and by the false news-reel which was a part of every programme. Nevertheless, they might get a good laugh, too, if there were a Danish wit or two in the audience.

'The main film was only half-way through, when it suddenly stopped, and the house-lights were turned on. To their amazement they saw men of the Resistance, armed with sub-machine guns, standing in the aisles, and forcing back into their seats the Germans in the audience who had jumped up when they realized that something unexpected was happening.

'When the Germans were cowed into silence, the leader of the Resistance party told the Danes in the audience not to be afraid.

"The cinema is surrounded by armed members of the Resistance," he said. "The doors are locked. No one outside can tell what is going on in here, and if the Germans do come, our party is sufficiently strong to hold them off while you all get away safely. Now, sit back and enjoy yourselves while you watch a film which has been sent to us from England."

'For the next two hours the audience, once they had got over their amazement, took his advice, and enjoyed one of the most famous of British War films, *In Which We Serve*, which had been written and produced by Noel Coward, who also played one of the leading roles. It was a patriotic and rather sentimental film about the British Navy, but one which appealed widely to British audiences wherever it was shown.

'The Danes enjoyed it no less, and when the lights went up at the end, they stood and cheered for nearly ten minutes. Then quietly and quickly they all left the cinema while the Resistance men kept the Germans in their seats, letting them go only when the last Dane was safely away.

'The daringness of this exploit raised the spirits of all Danes who heard of it in a way only equalled by the long applied Cold-Shoulder; and it upset the Germans in the same proportion.

'You might think that such a daring act could only be carried out once; that in future the Germans would put guards on cinemas to prevent it ever happening again. But it would seem that they could not spare the men to do this.

'The exploit was repeated again and again. Neither Dane nor German could ever be sure when he went to the cinema that he would see the advertised programme, or whether the Resistance might not take over the cinema and show an English film. In this way Danish audiences saw *The Moon is Down*, *Desert Victory*, *Donald Duck in Germany*, and the Russian film *The Fight for Stalingrad*, and many other English and Allied Films.

'Perhaps one of the best indications of how the occupied peoples kept up their spirits is the humour which was always bubbling out of some of them, and which, in its turn, raised the morale of others even higher.'[7]

It must never be forgotten that in the grand context of the world struggle, especially in the eyes of the chief combatants, Resistance played a minor role. Its real significance was for the people of those countries in which it took place and also, towards the end, in the degree of military assistance it was able to give the Allied invasion forces. Between 1940 and 1942 such Resistance as took place in Europe was entirely dependent on British support: between 1942 and 1944 the British lost this monopoly; from the spring of 1944 the British role grew relatively much smaller, a reflection of her decreased importance in the wider strategy which was now dominated by the Americans and the Russians.

As Monsieur Michel, one of the most distinguished writers on this subject has remarked:—'The post-war world was fashioned by the Allies. The Resistance did not leave its mark upon it.'[8]

Why? Because post-war Allied disunity shattered the delicate alliance of accommodation which had kept them together in an internal and external resistance to a common enemy during hostilities. Of the Resistance M. Michel remarks: 'Plus qu'une force, elle était un esprit, plus qu'une politique, une mystique.'[9]

Nevertheless, Liddell-Hart in his book *Defences of the West. Some Riddles of War and Peace*. (Cassell, 1950) asks the questions in Chapter Seven: 'Were we wise to foster Resistance Movements? Were their contributions to victory outweighed by their legacies of disorder?' Perhaps these questions will be more answerable at the end of our Franco-Yugoslav case study, but doubts are stirred when we reflect on some of the Resistance events not under study here, e.g. the tragic uprising in Warsaw, the internal strife in Greece, the tragic futility of so much of what happened in the Western Occupied Countries.

'Significantly, some of the most courageous members of the French Resistance now admit that the military effect of the Maquis or guerilla elements was outweighed by their cumulative ill effects, and wish that the Movement had been confined to the organization of non-violent Resistance.

'There is increasing evidence of the unmixed value of this form of Resistance as practised in Norway, Denmark and Holland, and of the Nazis' inability to cope with it. They were experts in violence, and knew how to meet it, but subtler forms of opposition baffled them.'[10]

To this theme, which raises the further question of whether it is true that the more violence there is in any society the less revolution or real change there can be, we shall return in our third Chapter.

We compare in order the better to define—in this case the nature of Resistance Movements in two very different countries: such definition as emerges from our study may also provide a useful gloss on the meaning of Resistance elsewhere. Our comparison will be of three things, French and Yugoslav connections with the Second War in general and the three chief Allied Powers in particular, the origins and growth of the French and Yugoslav ingredients of Resistance, and the final achievements of the two movements.

France declared war on Germany on September 3rd, 1939: then, after a period of 'phoney' war (drôle de guerre) in June, 1940 the German blitz invasion of France occurred. On June 22nd, 1940 Marshal Pétain, having taken over what was left of the French Government, agreed to an armistice with Germany. This involved the division of France into two parts, the Occupied

Zone of the north, north-east and a strip of the Atlantic west coast, and an Unoccupied Zone, the remainder of the country, with a nominally neutral French Government under Pétain and Laval situated at Vichy. The Armistice terms in fact established a stranglehold over the whole of France because they involved French payment of all the costs of the German occupation and German retention of the thousands of French prisoners of war until an actual peace treaty was signed.

For a year France lay stunned 'like a groggy boxer': then three momentous events began to make it possible for the seeds of internal resistance to Germany to grow. The first was the victorious outcome of the Battle of Britain, the second the German invasion of Russia in June, 1941, and the third the Americans' landing in North Africa in November, 1942 after their entry into the War as an ally of Britain and the U.S.S.R. two and a quarter years after the Nazis had attacked Poland. This triple development, together with the loathsome activities of the Vichy Secret Police and Darnand's French Militia and the dawning realization by more and more Frenchmen of all kinds that, contrary to their hopes and expectations, Marshal Pétain's plea for a resurgent, purged French sense of nationhood was being hopelessly perverted by the machinations of Laval and Darlan—all this meant that by the middle of 1943 the internal French Resistance really took on pace and meaning. One year more, and it was to prove itself strong enough to play an important, if still subordinate, role in the Allied invasion of Europe and the final defeat of Nazism. Before reviewing the origins and growth of that internal Resistance, it is necessary to identify two centres of external Resistance, which may for convenience be given the labels Giraudism and Gaullism.

After the collapse of Metropolitan France in June, 1940, most of the French Empire remained pro-Vichy, though there were those forces under the control of Generals Catroux and Koenig who gradually persuaded the reluctant and suspicious British Command in Egypt to accept their military support. Partly through their pre-belligerent contacts via their Ambassador in Vichy and partly from their own Intelligence, their temperamental inclinations and their distrust of de Gaulle, the Americans hoped to do a sufficient deal with the more or less pro-Vichy but semi-neutral elements in French North Africa to contrive an unopposed landing of their troops in North Africa. Thanks in part to the double-crossing by Admiral Darlan of his own Government and his subsequent assassination, military control passed into the hands of General Giraud, who by conviction and convenience was willing to declare his pro-Ally allegiance. The subsequent re-arming of the French in North Africa, largely by the Americans, and the somewhat less radical, more traditionalist outlook of Giraud and those around him led to many misunderstandings and disputes between Giraudists and Britain and the U.S.S.R. on the one hand and between Giraudists and Gaullists on the other.

Gaullism had grown up in London under the dynamic leadership of General Charles de Gaulle, who, rallying those French who escaped from France, founded the Free French and from the outset was determined on two things: first, that he and his followers were not to be treated as gallant French remnants enlisting in the Allied ranks but were to be regarded as the representatives of an undivided country, France; secondly, and following from the first, there could be no room for more than one centre of external Resistance and that was to be the Free French in London. Eventually, after the expenditure of much diplomatic ingenuity and continuing friction, Giraudism became submerged in Gaullism. Successful in gaining both of his objectives, de Gaulle naturally also sought to obtain supreme control of the French internal Resistance. At first he failed in this, due largely to the Anglo-American underestimation of the size and value of that movement, and even up to the invasion of Normandy the Allied plans did not reckon with a Gaullist establishment of French National Government in liberated France. Actually, this is what occurred, due to the vigilance and persistence with which de Gaulle had made and maintained his contacts across the Channel and in parallel with the British Special Operations Executive's liaison with the French internal Resistance. This question of who in fact controlled the internal Resistance was a vital issue, not least because if it had not been for de Gaulle's foresight and determination, that control would probably have been captured by the Communists. As it was, by establishing side by side with the National Council of Resistance another body called the *Délégation Générale*, under one of his own trusted men, Debré, de Gaulle avoided this. That body, the *Délégation*

Générale, acted as the organ representing the continuity of French statehood as such. Its existence was irrespective of, though obviously not necessarily inimical to, the Resistance, which was a merely temporary outcome of the wartime situation. Finally it must never be forgotten that without mounting Allied support, mostly British for the first two years, neither the internal nor external Resistance could have functioned at all. This is perhaps an appropriate place to draw attention to the excellent radio support given by the B.B.C. from London with its programme, *Ici Londres*.

With these two forms of external Resistance established, we may now turn to the origin and growth of the internal movement. A few of the seeds had been sown even before the outbreak of the War: they consisted of that small minority of Frenchmen in all walks of life, who had foreseen the menace of totalitarianism in general and Nazism and Fascism in particular but had been helpless in the face of it. After the defeat, individually, locally in groups, regionally and eventually nationally, they found their way to one another and recruited others to their ranks, though even at its height not more than six to eight per cent of the French population were actively involved. In any typical Resistance Group, united by nothing except a common hate of the German occupiers and a determination to get rid of them, there could be found the following assortment: a revolutionary syndicalist, a military man of the extreme Right, a Masonic professor, a Dominican father, a careers officer, a conscientious objector, a Communist worker, a Catholic university student and a Social-Democratic civil servant.[11]

These groupings cut across party, though the Socialist and Communist Parties maintained their separate identities throughout. Because of the Soviet-German Pact of 1939, French Communists had at first been anti-Ally: after the Soviet became an Ally they joined extremely actively in many of the Resistance Movements, especially in the *Maquis*, but in their own way, creating the *Front Nationale* and cooperating when convenient. This was the name (*Maquis*) derived from the wilderness country of Corsica where the first Liberation Movement by the Resistance had taken place in September, 1943, but which was then given to all those elements which trained and operated secretly from favourable districts, particularly the mountains, and on which the

morale of the military Movement depended. Such was the rigour
and discipline of the Communists that their influence far outweighed their numerical strength, and they even claimed, mis-
takenly and falsely, that they *were* the Resistance. To the above
list must, of course, be attached the support in different ways of
the Trade Unions and the Churches.

In January, 1942 a representative from the Free French in
London, Moulin, was dropped in France, and he began to organize the local and regional Resistance Groups into some kind of
central union: in May, 1943 the National Council of Resistance
was formed with Moulin in charge and, after his arrest and
murder, this office was taken over by Georges Bidault. This body
did something to integrate the efforts of widely dispersed groups
and even the different outlooks of those elements with left or
right wing tendencies and also, of course, to keep in being the
necessary liaison with the external Resistance.

What then were the content and method of the internal Resistance? First, there was Intelligence, the obtaining of vital information about the German Military, their movements and installa-
tions and then the communicating of this among the Resistance
Groups and more and more substantially to Allied Headquarters
both before and after invasion. Secondly, sabotage on both a
small and large scale of offices, railways and industrial plant was
steadily on the increase. Thirdly, there was assistance to those
threatened with forced labour and deportation. Fourthly, there
was help to Allied personnel, escaped prisoners of war and
baled-out airmen, and fifthly the more subtle, incessant harassing
of the Germans as people in their daily existence.[12] In addition
to all this there was, of course, the creation and maintenance of a
vast clandestine Press, the influence of which in sustaining French
morale can hardly be over-estimated.

Much of this work was carried out in cooperation with the
representatives of S.O.E., excitingly described in two books:
The White Rabbit by Bruce Marshall (Pan Books) and *Odette.
The Story of a British Agent* by Jerrard Tickell (Chapman &
Hall, 1949). From these and many other publications an idea can
be obtained of the heroic gallantry and fiendish cruelty displayed
by those involved: from them we can get some sense both of
what fun and excitement as well as horror and dreariness there
must have been in the enterprise. The following single example

gives some idea of the complex of motives and instincts at work.

'After a conversation on a train about British pilots eating carrots to improve their night-vision, I discovered from an oculist in Paris that heroin had the opposite effect. I asked London for a supply of heroin.

"What for?" they asked.

"Never mind what it's for," I replied. "I'll tell you when the operation is successful."

'The kilo of heroin which they sent to me must have taken a lot of argument and persuasion on their part to procure. It was sent by the American diplomatic bag from London and delivered to the Military Attaché of a then neutral embassy.

'Now I had to find a way of feeding the heroin to the German pilots. Who were the only people in regular contact with the Germans and able to administer the heroin to them secretly? The whores.

'There was a large concentration of German night-fighters around Tours, so I went to the people running the whore-houses there, and explained what I wanted to do. They agreed to gather together a number of the women, who were keen to work for the Resistance.

'A few of the Germans who patronized the brothels were already drug-addicts. To them, the whores sold the heroin; they promised they would not sell it to any but Germans. Other German pilots, who were often the worse for drink by the time they found themselves in a room with a whore, were tempted to try the heroin—"just a little sniff to see what happens." The result of course was a temporary feeling of well-being, which encouraged the young men to try a little more and so they were led into addiction. When a pilot refused to take the heroin, the women put some of the 'snuff' into cigarettes. Unknowingly, the Germans smoked the tainted cigarettes and were "hooked" in that way.

'It was an effective form of Resistance. A substantial number of night-fighter pilots, stationed in the Tours area, found their vision deteriorating. With each monthly medical examination they saw less and less.

'It was bound to lead to an investigation in the end. The

German doctors interrogated the pilots exhaustively about their habits, their movements, what they ate, what they drank, how much they smoked. By comparing all the answers to their questions, they found that the men whose eyesight had been affected had one thing in common: they all frequented the brothels. Among them were others who, it was clear, were suffering from drug addiction. All this took months, but more questioning brought the evidence about which whores at which brothels were handing out the dope.

'The Germans tracked down two of the whores, arrested them, and shot them. They were courageous women, who knew what they were doing and did it willingly. They were glad of the chance to revenge themselves on the Germans and to help their country at the same time.'[13]

Frequent occurrences, which inevitably resulted in mutual recriminations, were the falling into the hands of the Germans of arms and goods inexpertly dropped by Allied planes or parachute or inefficiently received by inadequately organized resisters: also the rash onslaughts by the Resistance which resulted in savage reprisals from the Germans and often the complete destruction of a whole piece of Resistance organization.

Up to the last moment of the Allied invasion there were doubts on the part of Churchill and Eisenhower as to the usefulness and reliability of that internal French Resistance Movement which was to play such a valiant part as the Free French of the Interior in the final military operations. Nevertheless, as the following extract makes clear, they need not have had such reservations.

'The response from the French Resistance is one of the epics of the War. The whole Organization was alerted on the night of 5th/6th June, 1944 throughout Belgium and France. Out of 1,055 railway demolitions planned, 960 were successfully carried out. By August there had been 2,900 attacks on the railways in France alone. The French Forces of the Interior had grown to over 100,000 armed troops. Seventy-six American Flying Fortresses with supplies of arms and ammunition were diverted in support of these operations on 25th June, and 400 again on 14th July. As a Supreme Allied Headquarters report put it, "The action of the Resistance Groups south of

the Loire resulted in an average delay of forty-eight hours in
the movement of reinforcements to Normandy, and even much
longer. The enemy was facing a battlefield behind his lines."
Similar action followed in Belgium, Holland, Norway and
Denmark. At the end of the War General Eisenhower wrote to
Major-General Sir Colin Gubbins, the Operational Comman-
der of S.O.E.: "While no final assessment of the operational
value of Resistance action has yet been completed I consider
that the disruption of enemy rail communications, the harassing
of German road moves and the continual and increasing strain
placed on German War economy and internal security services
throughout occupied Europe by the organized Forces of
Resistance, played a very considerable part in our complete
and final victory." '[14]

There is one man who can take us nearer to the inner meaning
of the French Resistance than any other: his name is Albert
Camus, and we shall conclude this first part of our comparative
study by taking a look at his significance. A French-Algerian,
born in 1913, Camus joined the Communist Party in 1934 as did
so many men of good will at that time, not chiefly out of any
ideological conviction but as a desperate protest against Europe's
drift towards totalitarianism and war. As is shown in *The God
That Failed*, disillusionment with the Communist cause followed
later. It was in December, 1941 that Camus crystallized his feel-
ings against the German occupation of France, and in 1942 he
joined the Resistance Movement *Combat* in the Lyons area; in
1943 he began to write for its paper and in 1944 became its
editor and contributed a number of anonymous articles. Camus
was clear that the Resistance and final Liberation Movements in
France must owe such integrity as they had to their working class
foundation: 'La France sera désormais ce que sera sa classe
ouvrière.', and of England he remarked: 'Ce peuple supérieur a
oublié de se plaindre.' However, in 1947 he withdrew from the
editorship of *Combat* and after further years of great literary
fame but ever-increasing disenchantment with the post-War
world he was awarded the Nobel Prize for Literature in 1957 and
was killed in a car accident in 1960.

Turning to his volume *Resistance, Rebellion and Death*, (Hamish
Hamilton, 1961) we find that many of his reflections reveal some-

thing of the spiritual essence of the Resistance, which was not only French.

'When the author of these letters says "you", he does not mean "you Germans", but "you Nazis". When he says "we", this does not always signify "we Frenchmen" but "we Free Europeans". I am contrasting two attitudes in two nations, even if, at certain moments in history, these two nations personified two enemy attitudes.'[15]

Speaking of the men of the French Resistance Camus wrote:

'We had much to overcome—and, first of all, the constant temptation to emulate you (the enemy). For there is always something in us that yields to instinct, to contempt for intelligence, to the cult of efficiency. Our great virtues eventually become tiresome to us. We become ashamed of our intelligence, and sometimes we imagine some barbarous state where truth would be effortless. But the cure for this is easy; you are there to show us what the imagining would lead to, and we mend our ways. If I believed in some fatalism in history, I should suppose that you are placed beside us, helots of the intelligence, as our living reproof. Then we reawaken to the mind and we are more at ease.

'But we also had to overcome the suspicion we had of heroism. I know you think that heroism is alien to us. You are wrong. It is just that we profess heroism and we distrust it at the same time. We profess it because ten centuries of history have given us knowledge of all that is noble. We distrust it because ten centuries of intelligence have taught us the art and blessings of being natural. In order to face up to you, we had first to be at death's door. And this is why we fell behind all of Europe, which wallowed in falsehood the moment it was necessary, while we were concerned with seeking truth. This is why we were defeated in the beginning: because we were so concerned, while you were falling upon us, to determine in our hearts whether right was on our side.'[16]

When Paris was liberated Camus wrote:

'Four years ago, men rose up amidst ruins and despair and calmly declared that nothing was lost. They said we had to carry on and that the forces of good could always overcome the forces of evil if we were willing to pay the price. They paid the price. And, to be sure, that price was heavy; it had all the weight of blood and the dreadful heaviness of prisons. Many of those men are dead, whereas others have been living for years surrounded by windowless walls. That was the price that had to be paid. But those same men, if they could, would not blame us for this terrible and marvellous joy that sweeps us off our feet like a high tide.'[17]

In *Combat*, 27th October, 1944, Camus mourns a hero of the Resistance.

'It was hard for us to speak of René Leynaud yesterday. Those who read in a corner of their newspaper that a Resistance journalist of that name had been shot by the Germans paid but fleeting attention to what for us was a dreadful, an atrocious announcement. And yet we must speak of him. We must speak of him so that the memory of the Resistance will be kept alive, not in a nation that may be forgetful, but at least in a few hearts that pay attention to human quality.

'He had entered the Resistance during the first months. Everything that constituted his moral life, Christianity and respect for one's promise, had urged him to take his place silently in that battle of shadows. He had chosen the pseudonym that corresponded to everything purest in him; to all his comrades on *Combat* he was known as Clair.

'The only private passion he had kept—along with that of personal modesty—was poetry. He had written poems that only two or three of us knew. They had the quality he himself had—transparency. But in the daily struggle he had given up writing, indulging only in buying the most varied books of poetry, which he was saving for reading after the war. As for everything else, he shared our conviction that a certain language and insistence on honesty would restore to our country the noble countenance we cherished. For months his place was waiting for him on this newspaper, and with all the obstinacy of friendship and affection we refused to accept the news of his death. Today that is no longer possible.

'He will no longer speak that language it was essential to speak. The absurd tragedy of the Resistance is summed up in this frightful misfortune. For men like Leynaud entered the struggle with the conviction that no one had a right to speak until he had made a personal sacrifice. The trouble is that the unofficial war did not have the dreadful justice of the regular war. At the front, bullets strike at random, killing the best and the worst. But for four years behind the lines, it was the best who volunteered and fell, it was the best who earned the right to speak, and lost the ability to do so.

'In any case, the man we loved will never speak again. And yet France needed voices like his. That exceptionally proud heart, long silent in his faith and his honour, would have found the words we needed. But he is now forever silent. And others, who are not worthy, speak of the honour that was identified with him, while others, who are not trustworthy, speak in the name of the God he had chosen.

'It is possible today to criticize the men of the Resistance, to note their shortcomings, and to bring accusations against them. But this is perhaps because the best among them are dead. We say this because we are deeply convinced of it: if we are still here this is because we did not do enough. Leynaud did enough. And today, having been returned to the soil he enjoyed for so short a time, having been cut off from that passion to which he had sacrificed everything, he may find consolation, we hope, in not hearing the words of bitterness and denigration now being applied to that poor human adventure in which we took part.

'Never fear, we shall not make use of him, who never made use of anyone. He left the struggle unknown as he entered it unknown. We shall keep for him what he would have preferred—the silence of our hearts, an attentive memory, and the dreadful sorrow of the irreparable. But he will forgive us if we admit bitterness here where we have always tried to avoid it, and if we indulge in the thought that perhaps the death of such a man is too high a price to pay for granting others the right to forget in their behaviour and their writings what was achieved during four years by the courage and sacrifice of a few Frenchmen.'[18]

Finally, Camus tells us a story.

'Let me tell you this story. Before dawn, from a prison I know, somewhere in France, a truck driven by armed soldiers is taking eleven Frenchmen to the cemetery where you are to shoot them. Out of the eleven, five or six have really done something: a tract, a few meetings, anything that showed their refusal to submit. The five or six, sitting motionless inside the truck, are filled with fear, but, if I may say so, it is an ordinary fear, the kind that grips every man facing the unknown, a fear that is not incompatible with courage. The others have done nothing. This hour is harder for them because they are dying by mistake or as victims of a kind of indifference. Among them is a child of sixteen. You know the faces of our adolescents: I don't want to talk about them. The boy is dominated by fear; he gives in to it shamelessly. Don't smile scornfully; his teeth are chattering. But you have placed beside him a chaplain, whose task is to alleviate somewhat the agonizing hour of waiting. I believe I can say that for men about to be killed a conversation about a future life is of no avail. It is too hard to believe that the lime-pit is not the end of all. The prisoners in the truck are silent. The chaplain turns towards the child huddled in his corner. He will understand better. The child answers, clings to the chaplain's voice, and hope returns. In the mutest of horrors sometimes it is enough for a man to speak; perhaps he is going to fix everything. "I haven't done anything," says the child. "Yes," says the chaplain, "but that's not the question now. You must get ready to die properly." "It can't be possible that no one understands me." "I am your friend and perhaps I understand you. But it is late. I shall be with you and the Good Lord will be too. You'll see how easy it is." The child turns his head away. The chaplain speaks of God. Does the child believe in him? Yes, he believes. Hence he knows that nothing is as important as the peace awaiting him. But that very peace is what frightens the child. "I am your friend," the chaplain repeats.

'The others are silent. He must think of *them*. The chaplain leans towards the silent group, turning his back on the child for a moment. The truck is advancing slowly with a sucking sound over the road, which is damp with dew. Imagine the grey hour, the early morning smell of men, the invisible countryside suggested by sounds of teams being harnessed or the cry of a bird. The child leans against the canvas covering, which gives a little. He notices a narrow space between it and the body of the truck. He could jump if he wanted. The other has his back turned and, up in front, the soldiers are intent on finding their way in the dark. The boy doesn't stop to think; he tears the canvas loose, slips into the opening, and jumps. His fall is hardly heard, the sound of running on the road, then nothing more. He is in the fields where his steps can't be heard. But the flapping of the canvas, the sharp, damp morning air penetrating the truck makes the chaplain and the prisoners turn around. For a second the priest stares at those men looking at him in silence. A second in which the man of God must decide whether he is on the side of the executioners or on the side of the martyrs in keeping with his vocation. But he has already knocked on the partition separating him from his comrades. "Achtung!" The alarm is given. Two soldiers leap into the truck and point their guns at the prisoners. Two others leap to the ground and start running across the fields. The chaplain, a few paces from the truck, standing on the asphalt, tries to see them through the fog. In the truck the men can only listen to the sounds of the chase, the muffled exclamations, a shot, silence, then the sound of voices again coming nearer, finally a hollow stamping of feet. The child is brought back. He wasn't hit but he stopped, surrounded in that enemy fog, suddenly without courage, forsaken by himself. He is carried rather than led by his guards. He has been beaten, but not much. The most important lies ahead. He doesn't look at the chaplain or anyone else. The priest has climbed up beside the driver. An armed soldier has taken his place in the truck. Thrown into one of the corners, the child doesn't cry. Between the canvas and the floor he watches the road slip away again and sees in its surface a reflection of the dawn.

'I am sure you can very well imagine the rest. But it is important for you to know who told me this story. It was a French priest. He said to me: "I am ashamed for that man, and I am pleased to think that no French priest would have been willing to make his God abet murder." That was true. The chaplain simply felt as you do. It seemed natural to him to make even his faith serve his country. Even the gods are mobilized in your country. They are on your side, as you say, but only as a result of coercion. You no longer distinguish anything; you are nothing but a single impulse. And now you are fighting with the resources of blind anger, with your mind on weapons and feats of arms rather than on ideas, stubbornly confusing every issue and following your obsession. We, on the other hand, started from the intelligence and its hesitations. We were powerless against wrath. But now our detour is finished. It took only a dead child for us to add wrath to intelligence, and now we are two against one. I want to speak to you of wrath.'[19]

Yugoslavia is a comparatively young nation state, having emerged at the end of the First World War as an amalgamation of seven regions, Serbia, Croatia, Slovenia, Bosnia, Herzegovena, Monte Negro and Macedonia. Each of these possessed its own particular cultural traditions; valuable mineral resources in various parts of this large country gave special economic importance to some areas more than others; three brands of religion, Roman Catholic and Orthodox Christianity and Mohammedanism commanded three different kinds of spiritual allegiance.

'The outstanding problem of the new State was to find a form of government acceptable to all groups of South Slavs. This was never achieved during the inter-War period. The Serbs wanted a centralized state with its capital at Belgrade (in Serbia). Croats and other nationalities wanted autonomy in a federal state.'[20]

During the 1930's Yugoslavia became a dictatorship under Prince Paul, Regent for the young heir to the throne, Peter, and by 1939 it became 'a helpless economy and almost a political satellite of the Nazis'.[21] For the first year and a half of the Second World War (September, 1939 to April, 1941) Yugoslavia remained nominally neutral, but in October, 1940 Italy invaded Greece, Germany demanded passage for her troops through Yugoslavia to assist Mussolini, and the existing Yugoslav Government agreed. However, a certain General Simovic declared Peter King and seized power from Prince Paul; the new Government was unable to establish itself, German troops invaded the country on 6th April, 1941 and on 17th April, with the King and his Government already in exile, the Army capitulated.

Resistance had, however, already begun, and it was composed of two powerful elements, which were both complementary to but also, as we shall be seeing, tragically destructive of each other: these were the national opposition to foreign rule and the ideological opposition to the continuing domination of the former ruling classes. They both of them had to begin operating in a country the capital of which had been ruthlessly blitzed and the particularisms of which were unscrupulously exploited by the Occupying Powers, German and Italian. For example, Croatia, together with Bosnia and Herzegovena, was made into a so-called independent state ruled over by Pavelic, leader of the Croat Fascist Movement (the *Ustase*), while the northern part of Serbia was kept under German domination because of its *Volksdeutsche* inhabitants, and the southern part placed under a Serbian quisling, one General Nedic.

The first in the Resistance field was Drazha Mihailovich, a Serbian army officer who refused to accept his own army's capitulation and established himself in West Serbia with a number of followers called *Cetniks* or Members of a Company (after the original Resistance to Turkish rule). Mihailovich's allegiance was to the Yugoslav monarchy and Government-in-exile, He was a patriotic Serb, anti-Croat and anti-Communist in outlook, courageously determined to defeat the invaders of his country but definitely looking forward to the eventual restoration of the pre-War order of things. It was to Mihailovich and his supporters that Winston Churchill was referring when he told the House of Commons that Yugoslavs had 'saved the soul and future of their country'.[22] By October, 1941 a British liaison officer had reached his Headquarters, and his was the Resistance Movement which was to continue to receive such Allied support (British chiefly) as was available exclusively until well into 1943 and then in diminishing quantities until late 1944. We shall be returning to an analysis of his motives and methods later.

The second in the Resistance field was the Yugoslav Communist Party under the leadership of Yosip Broz, its Secretary-General since 1937. It naturally looked to Moscow for its inspiration, but as was the case with Resistance Movements in other countries, its activities were temporarily hamstrung by the Nazi-Soviet Pact of August 1939 which forced it into a position of neutrality. Nevertheless, its organization was sound and alert. Hitler's invasion of Russia in June, 1941 gave the signal for active Resistance. Broz, or Tito, as from now on he was to be known, organized his followers into an army called the Partisans, and by the late summer of that year he controlled a large part of the country outside the big towns.

Could these two Resistance leaders cooperate? The answer was to be 'no' for reasons which we shall consider, though a meeting between them took place and more than one attempt was made to achieve a united front. Through all the ups and downs of military fortune of Mihailovich and Tito it must never be forgotten that their affairs were always regarded by the Allies as subordinate to the supreme Allied purpose of fighting the Germans and Italians. So when eventually another British military mission under Fitzroy Maclean was sent to the Partisan Headquarters in the summer of 1943 and he reported that so far as military action was concerned, Tito and his men were the really dedicated, ruthless enemies of the Germans and Italians, Allied support was withdrawn from Mihailovich. The latter had in fact been created Minister of War in the exiled Yugoslav Government and also a General, but this was to avail him nothing in the end. For Tito and the Red Army entered Belgrade victoriously, the exiled King Peter and his Foreign Minister were forced to enter into an agreement with Tito for a provisional Government pending post-War elections, this itself gave place to the sole rule of Tito. Mihailovich, after being captured by Tito's men whilst still in hiding in the hills, was brought to Belgrade, given a Communist trial and shot as a traitor in June, 1946.

The triumph of Titoism in and through the Resistance Movement may be ascribed to a number of causes. First, as compared with Mihailovich, Tito was a much more ruthless as well as more gifted leader militarily and politically; the best evidence of this is the extremely skilful manner in which he organized the Anti-Fascist Council of People's Liberation of Yugoslavia and the adroit way in which he managed his personal relations with Churchill and Stalin. Secondly, from 1943 onwards Tito was the Allies' darling and Mihailovich their naughty and disappointing child, whom they felt they had backed wrongly in the first place. Thirdly, the geographical position of Yugoslavia meant that in the 1940 period until the break with the U.S.S.R., a Resistance Movement in Yugoslavia must reckon with the powerful influence of the Soviet, however slow in support Russia had been in the first place. Fourthly, Tito was borne up on a ideological surge of conviction and could convey a persuasive blend of national and ideological beliefs.

Mihailovich on the other hand, a gentler, weaker, more refined human being, was much more aware of the price in suffering for his own folk which Resistance demanded. Secondly, he believed that Communism was as great a menace to freedom as Nazism or Fascism. Thirdly, although some of his officers did undoubtedly collaborate with the Germans and Italians, his own form of collaboration, if such it could be called, was oblique—that is to say he helped them by often fighting against the Partisans and by refusing to undertake much military action in the expectation of a Western Allied invasion. Only after this did he feel it would be right for him to take the field. Reminding ourselves of the constant background of violence, sabotage, pitched battles, loyalties and bitterness, let us glance for a moment at some judgments passed on the Yugoslav Resistance Movement in general and Mihailovich's trial in particular, before attempting a comparison with the Resistance Movement in France.

'Many events in Yugoslavia during the War remain terribly obscure. The Yugoslavs will never settle among themselves just how the various national elements and leaders behaved under the pressure of competing national, sectional and class interests; and foreigners will certainly never settle it for them. At least three wars were in progress simultaneously, and they frequently overlapped. These were the patriotic war against the Nazi invaders, their Italian partners and their Hungarian and Bulgarian camp followers; there was the long-standing feud between Croats and Serbs, turned into what at times amounted to civil war by the anti-Serb excesses of the Croat (pro-Axis) militia (*Ustase*), and further complicated by special Slovene, Montenegran, Bosnian, Macedonian and other regional interests; thirdly, there was the social war between Communists and anti-Communists; tribal rivalry and social revolution thus superimposed separate and shifting patterns on the national struggle for freedom.'[23]

'There was a strong contrast between these *Cetnik* units and Partisan ones. The *Cetnik* units were usually made up of older men, married men, peasants from rich families. They remained in their villages, they slept at home and from time to time they were called to the Headquarters where they drilled. I had great difficulty in persuading the *Cetnik* commanders around Kragujevav to take part in the fighting against the Germans. They said they had no orders. On the other hand they criticized our Command because "we wasted mercilessly the blood of the Serbian people fighting against the Germans in an uneven struggle". They advised us that we should wait until the Germans were weaker before fighting against them. Partisan units were usually made up of younger people, who wanted to fight against the Germans. On the other hand there were some *Cetnik* units which did fight Germans in some other parts of Serbia. . . .'[24]

The next extract, from Fitzroy Maclean's *Eastern Approaches*, (Jonathan Cape, 1949), gives a vivid glimpse of his collaboration with Tito, its doubts as well as its splendours:

'We talked of politics in general. I said I was a Conservative; he that he was a Communist. We discussed the theory and practice of modern Communism. His theme in its broad lines was that the end justified the means. He developed it with great frankness. I asked him whether it was his ultimate aim to establish a Communist state in Yugoslavia. He said that it was, but that it might have to be a gradual process. For the moment, for instance (1943), the Movement was based politically on a popular front and not on a strictly one party system. At the same time, the Occupation and the War were rapidly undermining the foundation of the old political and economic institutions, so that when the dust cleared away very little would be left, and the way would be clear for a new system. In a sense the revolution was already in progress.'

The following longer extract from Maclean is particularly illuminating with regard to *Cetnik*-Partisan relations:

'The way in which the situation now developed was truly Balkan in its complexity. Mihailovich by all accounts continued to hate the Germans and to hope for an Allied victory and the eventual liberation of his country. But the *Cetniks* could not fight the Partisans and Germans simultaneously. From now onwards their attitude towards the Germans became increasingly passive, while they redoubled their efforts to crush the Partisans.

'The motives underlying this policy were not far to seek. In their early encounters with the Germans, the *Cetniks*, like the Partisans, had suffered heavy casualties; their operations had also led to savage enemy reprisals against the civilian population. They lacked the ruthless determination of the Communist-led Partisans, and this had discouraged them. They had also received over the wireless messages from the Royal Yugoslav Government in exile and from the Allied High Command telling them to hold their hand. Henceforward their aim became to preserve rather than to destroy; to keep alive the flame of Serb patriotism, as their ancestors had done under the Turkish occupation, in order that at some future period, after the Allied victory to which they looked forward, they might restore the old Serb-dominated Yugoslavia, which had meant so much to them.

'But to be able to do this, they must first eliminate the Communist-led Partisans whose revolutionary tendencies clearly constituted a dangerous obstacle to the restoration of the old order, while their presumed allegiance to Moscow represented a threat to Yugoslav independence. What had started as a war of resistance became in a very short time a civil war, in which, needless to say, the Partisans gave as good as they got.

'The Germans were well pleased. Nothing could suit them better than for the *Cetniks* to stop fighting them and turn all their energies against the Partisans, whose stubborn, savage resistance was already beginning to cause them serious embarrassment. A tacit agreement grew up by which Germans and *Cetniks* left each other alone and concentrated on putting down the Partisans.

'It was the start of the slippery slope which leads to collaboration; collaboration from motives which were understandable, patriotic even, but nevertheless collaboration. What was more natural than that units fighting against a common enemy should co-ordinate their operations? Some *Cetnik* Commanders went further still and attached liaison officers to German and Italian Headquarters, accepting German and Italian liaison officers in return. Some placed themselves and their troops

under German and Italian command, allowed themselves to be
supplied and equipped by them.

'Who was being fooled and who was getting the best of it?
The Germans, who had succeeded in neutralizing what had
started as a resistance movement? Or the *Cetniks*, who were
actually being armed by an enemy, against whom they hoped
one day to rise? It was all in the best Balkan tradition. Had not
Milos Obrenovic alternately fought the Turks and acted as
their Viceroy? Had he not sent to Constantinople the severed
head of his fellow-liberator, Kara Djordje?

'Mihailovich himself seems to have disapproved of factual
collaboration with the enemy though he himself had originated
the policy of abandoning active resistance and concentrating on
the elimination of the Partisans. But the control which he
exercised over his commanders was remote and spasmodic.
Soon, while some *Cetnik* commanders were still rather half-
heartedly fighting the Axis forces, and others doing nothing, a
number made no secret of their collaboration, and were living
openly at German and Italian Headquarters.

. . .

'Hitherto, Serbia had been regarded by us as being primarily
a *Cetnik* preserve. Such supplies as had gone there had been
dropped to Mihailovich. But the results had in the view of
G.H.Q. Middle East been disappointing. In particular there
had been little or no interruption of traffic on the Belgrade-
Salonika railway. It will be recalled that Mihailovich had been
given a limited period in which to carry out a certain specific
operation. This had now elapsed without his having complied
with this request, and the important decision was accordingly
taken to withdraw the Allied Mission from his Headquarters
and send him no further supplies. Supplies ceased at once; the
extrication of the British liaison officers took longer, and it was
not until the end of May that Brigadier Armstrong, my opposite number in the other camp, took leave of a reproachful
but still courteous Mihailovich. In the House of Commons
Mr. Churchill explained the Government's action. "The
reason," he said, "why we have ceased to supply Mihailovich
with arms and support is a simple one. He has not been fighting
the enemy, and, moreover, some of his subordinates have been
making accommodations with the enemy."

'Thus ended a connection which from the first had been based on a misapprehension. With the help of our own propaganda we had in our imagination built up Mihailovich into something that he never seriously claimed to be. Now we were dropping him because he had failed to fulfil our own expectations.'[25]

In turning now to consider the case of Mihailovich, one simple fact must not be overlooked, namely that whether or not his policy can be justified, the extent of his Resistance Movement in the early days of the German invasion of Russia—and at that time there was virtually no other, for the Partisans had not got into their stride—delayed the German offensive by taking off some of its troops for the Yugoslav front, to such an extent (four to seven weeks) that it did not reach the gates of Moscow before winter had got it in its grips. This may well have been a, if not the, decisive point in the whole of the Second World War, for German success in Russia then could have prevented or completely altered the nature of Western counter measures slowly being prepared during this breathing space.

In a 1948 speech Tito described Mihailovich and his supporters as 'the last remnants of the armed forces of the old, rotten, bourgeois order, who took up the patriotic fight so as to preserve the old social bourgeois order from the people who were fighting to build up their own authority parallel to their struggle against the invader.'[26] That, together with a picture of him as the arch-collaborationist with the enemy and traitor to his country, is the impression which his trial in 1946 and its one-sided report gave to the outside world.[27] There is an obverse side to this medal, however, which must be carefully examined if justice is to be done and the conflict of Yugoslav Resistance probed to its tragic depths.

'For military intervention supporting the Allied cause, especially at the most critical moment when Rommel's *Afrikakorps* stood before El-Alamein, General Mihailovich received congratulations and thanks from the Allied Commanders. General Eisenhower, General Auchinleck, Air-Marshal Tedder, Admiral Harwood and General de Gaulle emphasized the importance of his help. (The leader of the Free French even awarded the *Croix de Guerre* to this [his own words] "legendary

hero who has never ceased to fight against the common
enemy".)'[28]

In September, 1944 when, as a result of the Allies having
switched their support to Tito, Mihailovich's position was
becoming perilous, the Americans offered to get him out of
Yugoslavia but he refused the offer.

There were some protests from the West against the manner of
his trial, at which Allied witnesses for Mihailovich's defence were
not permitted. In a letter published in *Reynolds News* on May
18th, 1946 Churchill said among other things that he had 'no
sympathy with the Communists and crypto-Communists in this
country who are endeavouring to deny General Mihailovich a fair
trial. He it was who took the lead in making the revolution in
Yugoslavia which played a part in delaying the German attack
on Russia by several weeks.'[29]

At his trial Mihailovich pleaded completely not guilty but he
admitted responsibility for so many 'crimes' charged against him
that finally his plea of not guilty no longer had any meaning. He
was quoted as saying, 'I am very tired. Sometimes I am so tired
that I say Yes when I mean No.'[30] What, one wonders, had been
done to the prisoner before his appearance in court?

Yet, as our next extract makes clear, Mihailovich could not help
both by temperament and training being a man torn in his allegi-
ances; because he was not wholeheartedly behind the Allied military war effort he was bound to take on a collaborationist colouring.

'*Reprinted from the leading article in "The Western
Morning News and Daily Gazette" (Plymouth) of June
12th, 1946, by kind permission of the Editor.*

A BLUNDER

The opening stages of the trial of General Mihailovich have
confirmed the impression already formed that not only the
General but the Western democracies would be put on trial.
Tito has returned to Belgrade from Moscow, after discussions
which have resulted in the promise of substantial military aid.
We shall no doubt hear later—and perhaps disconcertingly—
what else he and his mission had secured.

Nothing has happened since Mr. Churchill in Brussels described his support of Tito as one of the greatest errors of the war to suggest any modification of that verdict, and it is more likely to be strengthened than weakened by future events. Few will now question that a political blunder was made. Those who were associated with it are now describing the military circumstances of the time in the endeavour to show that however unfortunate its consequences the decision was inevitable. On this point the evidence is not entirely conclusive.

The picture presented in some quarters of General Mihailovich ceasing to be interested in fighting the Germans and devoting all his attention to the Partisans, who for their part were anxious only to expel the invader, can not be reconciled with a good deal of first hand and apparently reliable evidence from British and American quarters. There is no doubt that General Mihailovich was very much concerned at the possibilities opened up by the evident Communist desire to seize possession of the country, and all that has happened since indicates that his fears were not groundless. It must be remembered, however, that he and his Chetniks were the first to take arms against the invader and that the Partisans showed no inclination to do so until Germany was the enemy not only of Yugoslavia but of Russia.

To say that General Mihailovich was more interested in his own country than in any other is to pay him tribute which patriots anywhere would wish to earn. It cannot be paid to Tito or to any other non-Russian Commissar in the Soviet service. Our primary concern, however, is not the personal virtue of either of the leading parties in this quarrel. It is with the effect of their activities on our interest. Even if we could accept entirely the military picture presented by those who seek to justify the change of policy when Mihailovich was abandoned, the historian would probably still have to record that a blunder was made in subordinating political consideration entirely to military. It is not the only occasion on which it was made, but it is the most flagrant.'[31]

'I wanted much, I started much. But the winds of the world carried me and my work away.' These last words of Mihailovich spoken at his trial hint at the human tragedy: 'the winds of the world' were the straightforward needs of the Allied military machine and the doctrinal pressures of Communist ideology. Whether or to what extent he collaborated with the Germans and Italians can be debated. What is beyond dispute is that he loved his country and was not given a fair trial. His end thus contemplated after twenty years still leaves an effect of conscience-stricken anxiety, which is also one of the more general legacies of the Resistance Movement everywhere.

'Reprinted from an article by Robert Speaight in 'Time and Tide' (London) of August 17th, 1946, by kind permission of the Editor and Author.

MEDITATION ON THE DEATH OF MIHAILOVICH

'As I sit writing these lines in the early dawn before a motionless sea, Mihailovich is facing the firing squad. I am not concerned with what the first of the *Maquisards* is supposed to have done or not to have done; what worries me is that nobody bothers about him . . . no, I am not going to pray for this world any longer, as it sits crouched on the atomic bomb, yellow with hatred, with its tongue babbling of social justice and its heart empty of love.'

Soon after reading this extract from Georges Bernanos' article in *La Bataille*, I came across a paragraph by Jean and Jerome Tharaud which told me that the last book Mihailovich was known to read was a volume of Maupassant. It is tantalizing not to know which story or novel he had chosen or found at hand, but it is not surprising that the tortured and betrayed patriot should have gone to his death bilious with the hatred of humanity. And then, as if in confirmation of his pessimism, I read that *The Times* gave its imprimatur to the verdict. The gentlemen of fortune who now direct the destinies of Serbia do not believe in an undue preparation for eternity. But there were still twenty-four precious hours during which the remnants of the Christian world could have conveyed its opinion to the man whom convention compels me to call Marshal Tito. The Professors of Printing House Square did not lose a minute—they told him to go ahead. And so the murder of Drazha Mihailovich becomes, like the murder of Jeanne d'Arc, a case for the English conscience.

It may be argued that after Miss Rebecca West's conclusive article in *Time and Tide*, there is nothing more to be said about Mihailovich. In a sense, that is true; no further argument is necessary. But it is of the essence of this particular judicial murder that men will go on discussing it for a very long time to come and those Englishmen who retain a memory of justice will ask themselves how far they or their fellow-countrymen were responsible. If they have lived through the last few years, it is not difficult to take the questions out of their mouths. Not for the first time, they will say, men have betrayed their friends to placate their enemies; but all the same it was an ironic accident that the Prime Minister who did more than any other single man to save the shreds of European freedom in 1940, should have consummated the most ignoble, the most fatuous, the most gratuitous and certainly one of the most fatal errors in the annals of British diplomacy. Having said this, they will admit that Mr. Churchill at least made the beginnings of an *amende honorable*—and for a great man that is already a great deal—but they will ask what happened to all those other voices that were so loud for liberty in 1940? Why were they so curiously silent, those *porte-paroles* of the national conscience, before the advance of an atheistic Communism, which, having no use for God, naturally has no use for man?

I am writing this far from home, and it is rueful to reflect that even here, where the Alps rise in their eternal poetry beyond the Lac de Bourget, one can still be asphyxiated by the fumes of English hypocrisy. Perhaps the old voices have spoken. I do not know. Perhaps Mr. Priestley has returned to the microphone. Perhaps Mr. Kingsley Martin has remembered that when Czechoslovakia was murdered at Munich he still considered murder a capital offence. Perhaps someone has even introduced the thin end of a principle into the foreign policy of *The Economist*. I am sorry to be so personal. But these were the people who once told us what was what, and their immense public will be curious to know what they think about the murder of Mihailovich. One is beginning to be able to count them on the fingers of two hands—the Just Men of the

Left. Mr. Gollancz, Lord Beveridge, Lord Pakenham, and a
few others. They have been alone for all too long. The Labour
Party, which has always derived its strength from English
idealism and the English instinct for natural law, has need of
some moral breakwaters. In the nature of things—or at least
in the nature of politics—Mr. Bevin cannot go on for ever.
And there is always Dr. Dalton.

These are speculations; but when we enter the realm of
certainty to find out what has happened to the English conscience, we discover that *The Times* has approved the verdict.
We know very little about the theology of Printing House
Square, but somewhere among those panelled rooms there
must be an altar dedicated to the *fait accompli*. The memory of
The Times, which is more or less the same thing as the memory
of mankind, is presumably immune from the pain of incon-
venient reminders; so I shall hardly flutter an editorial hair if
I recall the good advice given to the Czechs to sacrifice themselves to the Germans, or to the Poles to sacrifice themselves
to the Russians, or to the Greeks and Yugoslavs to hand themselves over to the same benefactors. They are quite simple—
the formulae of the new realism. Find out which of the Great
Powers, at any given moment, is most imminently hostile to the
basic principles of European freedom, then persuade all your
friends to commit hara-kiri in order that the Power in question
may become practically invincible; finally, "having exhausted
every reasonable compromise"—for that is the official meiosis
for the betrayal of an Ally—show a wide-eyed surprise and an
immense moral indignation when your own positions are
attacked. These are, in one respect of course, the politics of
Bedlam; but they are also, viewed at a more profound level, the
politics of a fundamental scepticism, and they illustrate very
vividly the relation between Truth and Action. Like Pontius
Pilate, *The Times* asks itself the question 'What is truth?' and
like Pilate it is careful to wash its hands. But somehow I doubt
whether Pilate himself would have welcomed a leading article
in approbation of his own sentence on the day when Roman
justice succumbed to a show of hands.

The death of Mihailovich will have served its mournful
purpose if it makes clear to the most confused intelligence that
there have been two wars in Europe and that our Allies of the

first are our enemies of the second. The professional revolutionary whom convention compels me to call Marshal Tito, has explained it to us. The sentence on Mihailovich was "a sentence on international reaction"; after all, this convinced Orthodox Serb had not scrupled to have "certain dealings with the Catholic Church". Very well, we know where we are; but if we are to be saved—for this is indeed a matter of salvation—we must recognize the enemy within the gates of our country, and, even more importantly, within the gates of our own conscience. There is an old formula which tells us the ways in which sin may be committed, *cogitatione, locutione, opere et omissione*; it is a formula from which there is no escape. Let everyone who has been occupied these last few years with politics or publicity ask himself whether he is wholly innocent of the blood of this just man.'[32]

Attempting now to compare the French with the Yugoslav Resistance, a useful and suggestive set of similarities and differences can be distinguished. First, with regard to the international context in which they occurred, we may note the following:

1. Both Resistance Movements were subordinated to the at any rate supposed interests of the Allied war effort, though the Yugoslav one probably contributed more to it than the French.
2. Both were a compound of patriotic and ideological motivation, but in Yugoslavia the ideological outweighed the patriotic.

Secondly, with regard to their ingredients:

1. Both inflicted considerable damage on the Axis occupying forces, but in France the Resistance contributed far more by Intelligence, while in Yugoslavia there were many more pitched battles between Resistance troops and the enemy.[33]
2. The Communist Party in both countries was ineffective and even in some cases hostile before June, 1941, when the Party line was settled after Germany's invasion of Russia. However, subsequently the Communists in Yugoslavia became the main instrument of the Resistance, while in France, though extremely active, they played only a minor role in the overall Resistance Movement.
3. The French Resistance Movement achieved and maintained

a sufficient degree of unity for the purposes of effective action, while the Yugoslav Resistance Movement was split between *Cetniks* and Partisans.

4. French Resistance under de Gaulle and Yugoslav Resistance under Tito both had outstanding leaders; however different their personalities they both rode out the storm of war and became the Heads of State of their liberated countries.

Thirdly, with regard to the end products of Resistance:

1. In Yugoslavia this resulted in radical social change—a revolution in fact with the emergence of a Communist State, but one which, perhaps because of Tito's Western contacts, was later to declare its independence of Moscow.

2. In France there was undoubtedly some social change but not a revolution.

3. Perhaps both in their different ways, the Yugoslav one totalitarian and the French one dictatorial/paternalistic, indicated the truth of the following critique: 'The Resistance, reacting against both Vichy and de Gaulle, pushed the triumph of representative government to the utmost degree of executive impotence at a time when the revolution and the scope of the State's functions made this a particularly serious mistake.'[34]

The leaders of the Resistance Movements in France and Yugoslavia, as elsewhere, represented more or less honestly the interests of those elements which were opposed to the Nazi and Fascist invaders of their countries—the patriotic motive: they also represented in obviously not nearly so cohesive a form the interests of those elements which wished to do away with the pre-war conditions of political life, and more especially with its domination by the forces of the Right—the ideological motive. Resistance leaders were inevitably caught in a dilemma by this dual inspiration: the very freedom it sought to achieve was hampered and liable to be perverted by the means it had to employ. The State's function, while hostilities lasted, could hardly be challenged: it was to defeat the enemy, but the Resistance element in that effort, just because of its aspiration to greater freedom and truer representation of all the people's interests, was unable, when hostilities ceased, to arrest the further increase in the scope of the State's functions. That is why so many of the 'Men of the Resistance' found that their Movement had been in some way betrayed: perhaps, however, it had only been postponed—a theme to which we shall return in Chapter Three.

Note.

A work which should be consulted is M. R. D. Foot: *S.O.E. in France. An Account of the Work of the British Special Operations Executive in France 1940–44.* H.M.S.O., 45/-, 1966. Fair comment from *The Times* review, April 28th, 1966: '. . . . let nobody pretend that this is official history. It is even worse—history with an official muzzle. That said, it has to be admitted that Mr. Foot has produced an absorbing book.'

REFERENCES

1. For a full treatment of this subject see *European Resistance Movements 1939–45. Proceedings of the Second International Conference on the History of the Resistance Movements held at Milan 26th–29th March, 1961,* Pergamon Press, 1964.
2. *E.R.M.* p. 102.
3. Stalin.
4. *E.R.M.,* p. 76.
5. *E.R.M.,* p. 94.
6. *E.R.M.,* p. 5.
7. Ronald Seth: *How the Resistance Worked,* pp. 61–3. Geoffrey Bles, 1961.
8. *E.R.M.,* p. 572.
9. Op. cit.
10. Liddell-Hart, p. 57.
11. See Philippe de Vomécourt *Who lived to See the Day. France in Arms 1940–45.* Hutchinson, 1961.
12. For a dramatic study of these 'hermits of the Resistance' see Charles Morgan's play and novel *The River Line.*
13. *Who Lived to See the Day.* pp. 81–2.
14. *E.R.M.,* p. 109.
15. Camus: *Letters to a German Friend.*
16. Op. cit. *Letters to a German Friend.* pp. 6–7.
17. Op. cit. *The Night of Truth.* p. 29.
18. Op. cit. *The Flesh.* pp. 31–32.
19. Op. cit. *Letters to a German Friend.* pp. 12–14.
20. Auty: *Yugoslavia.* p. 72.

21. Op. cit. p. 79.
22. *Hansard*, 3rd May, 1941.
23. H. F. Armstrong: *Tito and Goliath*. Gollancz, 1951.
24. Vladimir Dedijer: *Tito Speaks. His Self-portrait and Struggle with Stalin*. Weidenfeld & Nicolson, 1953.
25. Op. cit. pp. 335–7 & 437–8.
26. Op., cit. p. 31.
27. See *The World's Verdict: General Mihailovich*. John Bellows Ltd., 1947.
28. Op. cit. p. 12.
29. Op. cit. p. 14.
30. Op. cit. p. 44.
31. Op. cit. pp. 66 and 67.
32. Op. cit. pp. 87–9.
33. For fictional but eloquent comment on this, see Evelyn Waugh: *Sword of Honour*. Chap. X. *The Last Battle*.
34. *France: Change and Tradition*. Centre for International Affairs, Harvard University. p. 50. Gollancz, 1963.

CHAPTER TWO

Resistance in Germany: The Case of Adolf Reichwein

THE German Resistance Movement differed from other Resistance Movements against Nazism in two essentials: unlike them, it failed, but, also unlike them, it received virtually no support from the three great Allied Powers. Moreover, it had to operate within a firmly established and, until well into 1944, a victorious Reich. For these very reasons a study of it provides a special kind of interest, the significance of which extends far beyond Nazi Germany and far beyond the twelve-year period of Hitler's régime: it yields evidence regarding a persistent problem of our twentieth century, namely how to resist any kind of totalitarianism without becoming totalitarian in the process.

Already before 1939 there had been both an 'aussere' (outward) and 'innere' (inward) emigration—that is to say, attempts by those Germans opposed to Hitler to withdraw from his increasingly tight totalitarian net: refugees, especially Jews, had fled abroad: those who remained tried to contract out of the public life of Germany: it would be as wrong to ignore the latter's attitude or to regard it with contempt as it would be to underestimate the long-term resistance value of the exile of the former.

When war broke out, Germany had already experienced six years of totalitarian government: it had solved its unemployment problem and could look back on an unbroken line of successes in foreign policy: the majority of its people were well content with what Nazism had brought, a substantial minority was uneasy about but acquiescent to Hitler's treatment of the Jews and afraid lest his aggressive foreign policy might lead to war; a tiny minority was fundamentally opposed to the entire theory and practice of National Socialism. Some of the second and all of the third category may be reckoned as comprising the Resistance. The former had existed for many years, but their activities were veiled and, in the short run, without political significance; the latter met and conspired together and risked their lives for their convictions. Who were they?

> 'They consisted of a wide variety of men coming from all quarters: from industry and administration like Goerdeler, from agriculture like the big peasant Wenzel Teutschenthal, from the Christian trade unions like Nikolaus Gross, the miner and editor, from the Socialist trade unions like Theodor Haubach, Julius Leber and Hermann Maass, from the army like Generals Olbricht, Beck and many others, from the churches like Father Delp and the still surviving Father Rösch and Dr. Gerstenmeier, from diplomacy like Adam von Trott and Hanz von Haeften, from education like Adolf Reichwein, liberal middle-class men like the Minister Popitz and Socialist-Conservatives like Counts Yorck and Moltke.'[1]

The problem of the partnership between this varied group, not least in its swaying attitudes towards Communism and the U.S.S.R., their attempts to make contact with the Allies through Bishop Bell of Chichester, the climax of their activities in the abortive plot of July 20th, 1944, which so nearly succeeded and the failure of which had such dire consequences for the very flower of the German Resistance—these matters already form the corpus of an extensive literature.[2]

In what follows an attempt will be made to throw fresh light on it all by studying the German Resistance through the life of one man, who became one of its finest heroes and victims and who may fittingly be thought of as the conscience of Nazi Germany.[3]

The story of Adolf Reichwein is the story of an anti-totalitarian teacher, who has a place in the history of German education and politics between 1918 and 1945. His career is a particularly clear illustration of the relationship between teacher and society in general and between German teachers and the Germanies of Weimar and Hitler.

Born in 1898 of lower-bourgeois parents in the Rhineland, he attended primary and secondary schools and was an enthusiastic member of the Youth Movement (*Wandervögel*). A mere boy, he fought and was wounded in the First World War and on being invalided out of the army became a student first at Frankfurt and then at Marburg. From 1923 to 1926 he held an appointment as organizer of adult education in Thuringia with his headquarters at Jena. During the following year he made a trip to the U.S.A., Mexico and the Far East, partly as a curious traveller and partly as an academic investigator into the raw material resources of the world. On returning to Europe he worked for a time as press-secretary to Becker, the Minister of Education in Berlin (1927–30), and then went as Professor of Political Science to the *Pädagogische Akademie* (Teachers' Training College) at Halle.

When the Nazis came to power in 1933 he was dismissed from his post, but on his own insistence he was permitted to become headmaster of a small village primary school in the country east of Berlin. He stayed there until 1939, when he moved to Berlin as the person in charge of the school-work side of the *Deutsches Volksmuseum*—a position he held until his death in 1944. The last four years of his life were devoted on the one hand to his official pedagogical duties and on the other to taking part in the German Resistance Movement; the latter activity ended with his betrayal into the hands of the Gestapo and his brutal torture and execution at the hands of the Nazi authorities.

We take up the final thread of Reichwein's story in 1939 when he had come to see that educational anti-Nazi activity by itself could not prevent the inner and outer destruction of his own people: from then onwards he became an active resister. In his own words, 'There are no ways round a moment of decision.'

In the late spring of that year Reichwein had taken up his duties as Head of the Schools Section of the German Folklore Museum in Berlin; he obtained his appointment from the Education Ministry on the strength of his known and proved aptitude for relating school work to social environment. Most probably the motive on the part of the appointing Nazi authority was a two-fold one—to have him more closely under observation than had been possible when he was a village schoolmaster in the country but also in the hope of luring him indirectly into support for their own programme of *Blut und Boden*. Nevertheless, it is certain that Reichwein went into this new enterprise with both eyes open: 'However things turn out in the world at large,' he wrote at that time, 'prospects are bleak, and the more bleak they are the more essential education will become. However outward appearance may conceal the fact, the solidarity of the nation is dependent on the teacher.'

1940 was a year of ever-increasing professional activity and domestic preoccupation as well as one of constant enquiry among old friends, who might prove to be rallying points against the Nazi oppression. From his letters we learn of occasional skiing holidays and tentative plans for the partial evacuation of his family from Berlin, to which, in Reichwein's own words, 'Tommy was beginning to pay attention'. Many vivid pictures survive of his busy days and nights, but a half humorous remark in a letter to his father-in-law may be taken as revealing how even now he was groping his way into a more meaningful relationship with the grim political reality surrounding him: 'You see—there's a lot happening but precious little getting done!' A friend of his wrote: 'His office in Prinzessinen-Palais, Unter den Linden became a meeting place for many illegal anti-Fascists from the year 1940 onwards. Together with his compatriot and friend Carlo Mierendorff, he belonged to Leuschner's group of workers, whom he knew from his Darmstadt days, and at the same time to the Kreisau Circle of Graf von Moltke, between which two groups he was in many respects the link.'

Reichwein's attitude towards politics has been described as follows:

'Reichwein was powerfully attracted by political life. Like all forms of conflict, he enjoyed political conflict. He knew how important politics were for communal life. On his lips the word politics had the sound and meaning which the word *polis* has carried ever since the beginning of Western history, thanks to the thoughts of countless noble minds. And yet Reichwein could not be described quite simply as a political type. A born politician, even in the good sense of that word, is aware of the possibilities of meanness, cunning, fraud, intrigue and treachery and is always reckoning with them. Although Reichwein had no illusions about the characteristics and methods of his opponents, he was not, because of his own nature, really able to treat them seriously. Although he knew that gentlemanly behaviour was not suitable for this kind of opposition, that was in fact the only form of political struggle which he understood and was prepared to engage in. Just

because honesty, plain dealing and sincerity were the hallmarks
of his own character, he always assumed, in spite of every conscious precaution, that these were the motives that inspired his
opponents. Reichwein was not a woolly dreamer; he never
tried to disguise or to hide the sinister signs of the times for a
moment, but on the contrary took up the fight against them.
Yet his deeply-rooted belief in the humanity of man prevented
him from reckoning with the depravity which he acknowledged
and opposed in the mass; he could not believe it possible of the
individual enemy.'

Referring to Reichwein's work both as village schoolmaster and
museum curator his friend Professor Bohnenkamp wrote:

'It was a cloak, daily becoming thinner, for his own passionate activity. His professional demotion had not injured him as a
person; he had disciplined himself to take hard knocks. In
addition he retained at first the admiration of his Nazi opponents, and so managed to gain from them a sphere of activity
and their grudging respect. But the Socialist in him was deeply
outraged by the pseudo-Socialism of Hitler, the German by the
distortion and disfigurement of German art, the lover of truth
by the deceitful and perverted misuse of true values, the free
man by the suppression of free speech, the humanitarian by
brute power. At first he hoped that the thunder clouds would
soon pass, that in the meantime he could take shelter in the
kind of educational work he was doing and then start again
when the air was clear: for a long time he underestimated the
cold consequence of pure will-to-power and the dynamism of
imprisoned forces which were at work in it. But the more
Germany was dazzled by it, the more disorder broke loose and
the more threatening the evil became, the more determined
grew his resistance every day. He began by making thorough
enquiries as to the whereabouts, outlook, occupation and
'cover' of old acquaintances. Of these only a few had to be let
go, while new ones were added to them, so that the net of his
contacts became finer rather than coarser.'

At the beginning of 1941 Reichwein was refreshing himself
with a skiing holiday away from the wear and tear of city life in
Berlin in order that he might become, as he put it, 'a normal man

again'. One of his letters portrays his grief over the loss of acquaintances:

'With each person we lose, the burden on our own shoulders becomes heavier—it can only become lighter if we actually realize this and feel ourselves committed. In the last resort, all of us, the dead as well as the living, serve the same eternal cause, namely to roll aside from mankind the fantastically heavy tombstone which presses on it, so that men really can be men, and so draw closer to one another—in death as well as in life.'

In another letter he writes:

'It is really the most profound subjects for the sake of which we act at the surface level, and we must always remain conscious of this relationship between the two. Then there are no superficialities left, and everything we do is important in so far as it is related to fundamentals. Surely the Germans, taken as a whole, are the most fundamental of all Western peoples. If only this creative thoroughness could be brought into vital relationship with political endeavour.'

In that last sentence Reichwein was touching one of the nuclei of the German problem, and during that year 1941 he was actively trying to solve it for himself and others by the increasing part he played in political consultation and planning. As a friend reported, 'His preparations for revolutionary action can to the best of my knowledge be traced back to the year 1941. He was convinced that such a revolutionary movement could only succeed with the support of the left wing workers' groups.'

Before dealing with the events of 1942 a word must be said about the particular role played by the Kreisau Circle in the German Resistance Movement.[4] This information is of great importance as throwing light on the motives and mechanisms of Reichwein's life during its last and crucial phase and as explaining his own approach and relationship to the anti-Hitler forces. The Kreisau Circle came into existence and started systematic discussions among its members in the summer of 1940. It consisted of Conservatives and Socialists, propertied gentry and trade unionists, Protestants and Catholics: they were united by a common desire to see the end of the Nazis, but some, probably the majority, at least until quite near to July, 1944, were primarily concerned with plans for the creation of democratic government and post-war reconstruction in Germany after the anticipated Allied defeat of Nazism; the attitude towards the army generals of these elements and of the minority within the group who favoured active conspiracy to assassinate the tyrant always remained ill-defined. The three premises from which the group set out were that National-Socialism was an absolute departure from the German and European tradition and a denial of the Christian and Humanist conception of man, that Germany's military position was hopeless but that the onset of military defeat constituted grave dangers to Germany and Central Europe, which it was the duty of every responsible person to guard against; lastly, the recognition that any large organized political opposition in Germany being in the circumstances of 1940 out of the question, new forms of activity must be discovered. The group sought to devise a positive programme uniting all shades of political and religious opinion and was emphatic, especially in its early phases, as to the impossibility of any active revolutionary coup. The agreed policy decisions of the group were listed under the headings of reconstruction of the State, industry, Church and educational institutions, the judicial treatment of war criminals and offenders against the laws of the State. The group felt that attempts made by ecumenical circles to establish contact with the Allies had done more harm than good, that it was non-realistic of the Allies to expect any active military movement in Germany, especially as before 1942 there did not exist even the framework of political cooperation within the ranks of the Resistance.

'Untroubled by the fact that officers too belong to our Circle, wrote one member of it, 'we are a political group, which because of its fundamental viewpoints feels responsible and which because of its accurate knowledge of the situation and its far-reaching opportunities for influence in Germany, wishes to help in averting the threatened spread of catastrophe into chaos. . . . The situation is such that the only possible thing for us to do, unless quite unforeseen circumstances arise, is to await military defeat before trying an initiative regionally or centrally.'

Within the Kreisau Circle there were undoubtedly certain unresolved conflicts, such as whether violence was justified in the

removal of a tyrant; there was also conflict as between those who
inclined to the East and those who inclined to the West as the
most likely source of Allied understanding; there was conflict
between the older and the younger generation and between the
right wing and left wing elements. It is hard to estimate fairly
the significance of the Kreisau Circle. A large number of its
members were destroyed by Hitler after the failure of the July
20th plot; it was a part of the overall failure of the German
Resistance Movement; it never really made up its mind whether
it was a conspiracy or a preparatory commission discussing post-
war reconstruction; it seemed to be concerned with what Moltke
called a 'directed defeat'. In his book *The Nemesis of Power*
Wheeler-Bennett described the Kreisau Circle as 'the conscientious objectors of the Resistance' and of Moltke and Yorck he
remarked 'their remedy was little more than an amalgam of
Prussian mysticism and Prussian Christian-Socialism.'

Yet, from a study of the dedicated lives and courageous actions
of many members of the Kreisau Circle, Reichwein not least,
there emerges quite unmistakeably a sense of heroism and self-
sacrifice and a quality of nobility which gives to the whole
Kreisau enterprise a touch of tragic splendour. As a contemporary
wrote of them, 'Right from the start they were conscious that their
endeavour demanded of them that they risk their lives; out of
this there arose a certain spiritual exaltation, which radiated out
among other men and led on to its final climax. When their lives
were demanded of them they surrendered them without knowing
whether their deaths would bear any visible fruit, but each one
of them offered his life as penance for a commonly shared and
acknowledged guilt.'

It is into a climate of opinion such as this that we must think of
Reichwein entering with his established reputation as a peda-
gogue. His correspondence gives glimpses of him, during the
spring and early summer of 1942, busy with his triple task of
looking after his family in their, and his, increasingly frequent
absences from Berlin, pursuing his contacts with individuals
pledged to resist the Nazi régime, and carrying out his official
educational duties.

'You ask me,' he writes to a friend, 'whether I still take such a
grave view of things. I do not think that is the right way to
formulate it. I have always tried to look at realities and to base my

judgment on them. I have always claimed the right to express such a judgment, and it has always stood beyond optimism or pessimism. All around me I experience today, as I have always experienced, a kind of illusion which rigs itself up as optimism— or rather, which is even worse—cynicism, which mistakes itself for pessimism.'

Another friend wrote of Reichwein whom he did not personally encounter until near the very end: 'I knew of Adolf Reichwein and of his glowing idealism, which, contrary really to his own original intentions, drove him into political activity. This activity on his part arose from a holy passion sustained by an inextinguishable consciousness and faith that freedom was the spirit's natural element. He was concerned for the freedom of that spirit and all human personality. That was why he was a Socialist. That was why he became an active worker against Hitler.'

At the beginning of 1943 Reichwein let fall a remark which shows that he was under no illusion as to the reputation which Germany had acquired for herself, even among the neutral nations: 'One notices that we have no friends in the world, whose hearts might be moved by our fate.' In August, 1943 he was on a tour in the north of the U.S.S.R. lecturing to the German armed forces and, characteristically, thoroughly enjoying the sumptuous rations he was getting in the officers' mess, whilst at the same time encountering the grim facts of war by sharing in some part of a local Russian counter-attack on German positions. At the end of September he was in Paris on a similar mission and wrote: 'Parisians still know how to live in spite of misery and shortages: at weekends they travel into Normandy to fetch butter and eggs, and they have not surrendered their basic optimism, but as a German in this half-dead city one has one's own secret thoughts.'

Reichwein's Berlin home had been blitzed in August in the absence of the family with the loss of much of his personal property, and he was already writing to his wife that perhaps the time had arrived for her and the children to move out to Kreisau in East Germany where the von Moltke family had offered them asylum from the cold and bombing in Berlin and the West. He arranged to spend Christmas with his family there, but it is clear that by the end of this year Reichwein was not a little exhausted by the domestic plight of his bombed-out family, by his uneasy educational work and, most of all, by the ever closer contact he was keeping with the network of the anti-Hitler conspiracy.

January, 1944 found Reichwein on yet another tour in Denmark lecturing to the forces and hearing appalled of the ever-increasing destruction of Berlin from the air: he realized too how hated was the presence of his countrymen among the Danes. In March and April he was lecturing again in Germany and in the so-called 'Protectorate' of Czechoslovakia, and at Easter he managed to visit his family in Kreisau. In a letter at that time he mentioned that he had been reading Christopher Dawson's *The Making of Europe*, but 'I am further than ever away from cultural leisure. Sometimes I envy those who withdraw into their books and leave it to others to maintain the struggle for the future. But I am strengthened in my self-denial by the conviction that epochs can only be fulfilled if their thresholds are first fought for and won. And the fewer the fighters, the more responsibility there rests with those few. I have learned very thoroughly in my own life what missed opportunities this lack of determination has caused. A dreadful, half-finished torso of abortive attempts lies in our wake. . . . How difficult it is to combine action and contemplation in a living way.'

These springtime months were charged with all the intense activity of his political work and culminated in his arrest by the Gestapo at the beginning of July. From then until his brutal execution on October 20th, 1944, he was in the hands of the Nazis, imprisoned and tortured in Berlin. His letters of farewell to wife and children were grave, tender and courageous; two extracts speak for themselves:

'I need hardly say that my thoughts are constantly taken up with my own past life. But I cannot really write about that now however beneficial it might be. One thing stands out clearly from contemplating those past decades—how rich and beautiful the time has been for me. The pain of the First World War fades into insignificance and the healthy country life of unfettered youth shines out all the more brightly—the ten years with the *Wandervögel* and the excursions near and far —the friendships of youth—happy student days in Frankfurt, Marburg, with yet other indissoluble friendships—then my enthusiastically lived professional existence in adult education, the exceptional privileges of my travel in Europe, Asia and America, four years of flying and looking down on the earth from an eagle's perspective—in between, academic work, which cost nights as well as days of labour, and finally, the loveliest and richest of all—twelve years with you and the children. How much cause I have to be grateful.'

And then his last letter:

'My dear Romai, Judgment has been passed. For the last time I am writing your name, which has become so precious to me. In this last hour of mine on earth my thoughts are turning ever again with special intimacy to you and the four children who you gave me and who for years, which to me seem many, were such a joy, comfort and edification.

These three months have been a time of great inner significance to me in spite of the pain: they have helped to clarify and, I hope, also to purify a great deal. I depart with calm because I know that the children are in your care.

Since July 5th my daily prayer has been the Our Father and, attached to it, a petition for you, the children and our parents. It is to this prayer that I owe my strength from day to day.

May God give you the strength to overcome difficulties and to continue your life steadfastly. Let the children, as they grow into the future, be your consolation and then your joy. Thank your parents, relations and friends for all their goodness. For you, my whole heart, Your own Adolf.'

On July 20th, 1952 a special number of the German newspaper *Das Parliament* was devoted to an account of the attempted anti-Hitler coup of July 20th, 1944 and gave character sketches of many of those concerned in it. Here is what it said about Reichwein:

'Adolf Reichwein, until 1933 professor in Halle, emerged from the Socialist Youth Movement and was one of its best representatives. Both as man and teacher he was an idealist of an exceptional kind. The teacher in him, who felt responsible for the spiritual growth of the young, who tried by his own example to lead young people towards true goals, was drawn into a politically decisive action. "In the hour of decision there can be no evasion; the fewer the fighters—so much

greater the responsibility that rests on the few." His understanding of life expresses itself in these words of his. In his
struggle for freedom—he once called freedom "the true and
natural element of the spirit"—and in his desire to achieve
something new and great, it often seemed as though the extent
of the danger he was running hardly penetrated his imagination. He joined forces with Leber in the idea of an all-em-
bracing People's Movement.'

As a matter of fact, Reichwein and Leber were both concerned
in the holding of secret consultations with representatives of the
Communist section of the Resistance Movement, and at one of
these meetings a spy was present. It is a supreme irony that this
should have occurred, as Reichwein himself had been the main
promoter in the Kreisau Circle of contacts with the Communist
elements and had acted as chief liaison officer in this matter.

Let us marshal yet more testimony on behalf of this remarkable man. The following extract comes from the *Telegraf* of
October 20th, 1946:

'The hearing against the Social-Democrats, in which three,
Adolf Reichwein, Julius Leber and Hermann Maass were
condemned to death, took place on October 20th, 1944. On the
very same day Reichwein and Maass were executed. Reichwein
had been committed to Socialism and the idea of freedom, and
the last years of his life were entirely devoted to his own work
and the overthrowing of National-Socialism. He was one of
those men who are so obviously being missed today in our
work for reconstruction—in the sphere of popular education
especially his place has not been filled.

The general public hardly knows of Adolf Reichwein, who
was not an orator for big meetings, but he was the centre of a
large circle of friends extending beyond Germany all over
Europe and exerting a sterling influence. What was especially
distinguishable about Reichwein derived from the middle-class
Youth Movement and from his way of looking at people—
particularly young people—in such a way as to fascinate them.
So far as I can remember his preoccupation with a coup dated
back to 1941. He was sure that such a coup could only succeed
with the help of the Left-Wing Workers Movement. I talked
with him for the last time two days before his arrest on the

occasion of the preliminary contacts with the Communists. His eyes were shining with the hope that the decisive event would occur within a few weeks—the event for which he had risked his life.'

The second piece of testimony comes from a Latvian exile who first met Reichwein in Berlin in 1943:

'It is rare to come across men in whom idealism and patriotism shine forth so clearly, whose devotion to their countrymen and their belief in equal rights for all enable them to meet the greatest dangers intrepidly. His warm sympathy for my own fate soon led to a close friendship between us. Professor Reichwein was a convinced German patriot. He believed that God had set the German people, as any other, to fulfil a mission, which it must complete, not however by repressing other peoples but by cooperating with them. I met Professor Reichwein for the last time at the end of June, 1944, when he said: "Decisive steps must be taken to rescue the German people and European culture. It is tragic that we have to have recourse to means which the whole of my inner conviction rejects. At best we shall no longer have any private life—that we must sacrifice for the sake of our children and the future of the German people. For the very sake of that future, so it must be. Already it is late, very late, but still not too late. Very soon now you will see another Germany, and this new Germany will have quite a different attitude towards your own country than the present one has." It was only after the attempted coup on July 20th, 1944 became known that I fully understood those words. And when, later, I received a short message saying Professor Reichwein is no longer alive, I knew that there was one less noble spirit in the world.'

The third testimony is taken from Becker's memorial address on Reichwein of 1946:

'When we consider the events connected with July 20th, 1944 we are treading on sacred ground. We will say nothing about its political success or failure, nor consider what would have been the political results had the conspirators achieved their end—the removal of Hitler. We will only consider the plot from his point of view. The beginning of war had not

aroused any enthusiasm in the German people. It was too connected with evil and guilt, even though the mass of the people
were not yet aware of the utter evil of Nazi methods.

With the first military successes, the 'blitzkriegs' and their
concrete advantages, the mood of the nation relaxed for a time,
but subconsciously the anxiety remained: "What will be the end
of it all?" When Hitler attacked the Soviet Union temporary
success could no longer hide from thinking people that the
War could only end in indescribable disaster for Germany.
The enemy had not yet developed their armament potential,
but well-informed people in political and military circles did
not doubt that by 1943 at the latest the output of enemy
armaments would be such that Germany would be helpless.
As people also realized that Hitler and his fellow criminals
were gambling with their lives, and as their unlimited brutality
and egoism were well known, it became evident that Hitler
would be the gravedigger of the German people, if he and his
closest associates could not first be destroyed.

These thoughts were familiar to thousands of Germans and
discussed by them with their intimate friends. But only in a
few did thought become decision to protect the German people
by destroying the man who was steering headlong to the abyss.
Such ideas arose in many different circles, and those circles
which turned the ideas into decisions were structurally very
varied. Long negotiations were needed before the threads were
drawn together. The groups which finally took part in the
attempt of July 20th embraced practically all sections of the
German Resistance Movement. Trades unionists, high-ranking
serving officers, Socialists, Roman Catholic priests and Protes-
tant theologians, agriculturists, active diplomats, high officials
in the Home Office were all united in one aim: to save the
German people from the last and most terrible mile of its road
to death by destroying the Nazi leader and his closest colleagues.

We cannot here describe the tedious detailed work of years
which had to be carried through, under the constant threat of
the Gestapo, by the chief participants before these groups,
whose political and philosophical points of view were so
different, could so far agree that united action was a possibility
after Hitler's removal. We will only indicate the parts played

by Adolf Reichwein and his friends in these negotiations. True to his principles, Reichwein, along with his friends, directed his efforts to a Socialist programme for re-building the German state and reorganizing its economy after Hitler's fall.

Reichwein fell into the hands of the Gestapo owing to his efforts, shortly before the frequently postponed attempt on Hitler's life, to include the Communist Resistance Groups. He was arrested on the night of July 4th, 1944. When the plot failed, Reichwein was doomed. Before his death on October 20th he had to endure all the cruelty which the Nazi system used against its mortal enemies. Many hundreds of prominent men and women of the German Resistance Movement died with him in the months between July, 1944 and the collapse of the Nazi system. They bear unforgettable witness that, in spite of the Nazi terror, the opposition of the German people to Hitler had not been broken. The Blood of the Martyrs is indeed the seed of the Church and the death of the men and women of July 20th, together with the many hundreds and thousands of upright witnesses against Nazism who laid down their lives in the concentration camps, the prisons and trials of the Third Reich, is the sacred seed from which a new and better Germany will arise. That all political, philosophical and social circles of our nation found themselves united in death, gives us hope that in the life that lies ahead there will be no unsur- mountable barriers between those who seriously honestly and unselfishly have a new and better Germany at heart. Each individual sharing in this highest sacrifice is unforgettable in the circle of his friends. Adolf Reichwein belongs to the noble and outstanding men who are a reminder, an inspiration and an assurance for many Germans of what is best in humanity. We salute him in deep gratitude and reverence and salute also those eternal powers which permitted his life to become a lifelong example for us, a victor over death and the devil, a sample of human purity, bravery and kindliness.'

A fourth testimony comes from another intimate friend of Reichwein, Professor Bohnenkamp:

'The Kreisau Circle was not a conspiracy to use violence against Hitler but rather a conspiratorial preparation for what would have to happen after the rapidly approaching end of his power. After frequently renewed hesitations Adolf had rejected the idea of hastening this end by assassination. "The cure is appalling but it must be complete: in no other way will Germany learn." he said to me in conversation, but he let it be known how difficult it would be for him to stick to that point of view if fresh news reminded him too sharply of the seemingly never-ending death roll. When I visited him for the last time in January, 1944 he was full of grief at Mierendorff's death and very anxious about the approaches being made by some of the Kreisau Circle to Gordeler. This anxiety proceeded from the not unfounded suspicion that the Gordeler Group was not careful enough to screen its activities and also no doubt from his fear that it was not sufficiently in sympathy with left wing elements. A short while after Moltke was arrested, Adolf wrote that lightning had now struck his own roof. At the end of May when I was in Germany for a brief space, we missed each other because our telegrams miscarried and I did not meet Adolf. At the beginning of July, when I might have had half a day to look him up, he had disappeared, and I departed, fearing the worst, back across the frontier to rejoin my unit.

It can have been no light decision—if in fact it ever happened—for Adolf and his friends to agree to a coup by violence and to take part in it. Adolf's own courage, work, human trust in people and the breadth of his personality fitted him for the last step he took; he and Leber negotiated with the Communist Resistance Groups and were thereby betrayed by a spy and arrested, even before his friends were shipwrecked on July 20th.

Chained, tortured, not losing hope and unbowed, Reichwein spent three and a half months in the dungeons of the Gestapo until the sneering presiding Nazi judge passed judgment on him within the precincts of the "People's Court". What we were able to do by way of playing down his activities in the eyes of the régime and by working at least for a pardon was little and futile. On the afternoon of October 20th, 1944 his wife, Countess Moltke and I sat together in hushed and stricken conversation while his life was taken. The way in which it was taken, the cowardly manner in which the most tender, frail and tolerant of men was brutally and secretly done to death remains a strident contradiction.'

The fifth testimony comes from Gustave Dahrendorf, himself a prisoner of the Gestapo with Reichwein in Berlin:

'Adolf Reichwein was arrested on July 4th, 1944. I saw him for the first time in the Gestapo prison in the Lehrterstrasse in Berlin when Dr. Julius Leber, Herman Maass and I had been brought there from Ravensbruck, where we had spent seven weeks in the arrest house of the women's concentration camp for interrogation. My cell was on the first floor of that wing of the prison building which the Gestapo had cleared out in preparation for those arrested in connection with July 20th. During the daily putting out of the bucket and water jug I occasionally had the chance for a few seconds of seeing the cells on the opposite side of the ground floor. I shall never forget what I saw: it was early in the morning: Reichwein's bed was a mattress which had been laid down exactly behind the cell door. S.S. security men were there taking off Adolf Reichwein's chains. Every evening he was fettered. One arm was tied by chains to both legs and in this unhappy state Reichwein had to sleep through the night. In the morning the chains were removed. It was during this procedure that I first caught sight of him. There was no doubt that it was he. His face was pale and lacerated, marked by the spiritual and physical tortures of arrest. It is not important, and yet I must mention that it was exactly at the same moment that I spotted Reichwein, the men who were unchaining him, the hard sleeping place and a corner of the folding table up against the wall of the cell on which was lying a packet of crisps. It was the same at night when his chains were put on. I could often see his cell through the opened spy-hole of my own.

'It must have been on October 14th, 1944 that at about noon my cell door was suddenly unlocked. I was just swallowing the watery soup. "Hurry up—quick. You are being sent out. Hurry." I guessed that I was only being sent out from the Lehrterstrasse to be transferred to the Gestapo Headquarters, certainly not to be set free. And yet I trembled as I hurriedly collected my pathetic little pile of belongings, walked out of the cell and obeying a loud command, descended the iron stairs to the ground floor, to remain standing near an office opposite the exit. Standing there already were Dr. Julius Leber, Adolf

Reichwein, Herman Maass and Dr. Loeser. We had to go one
after another into the office to receive back the various articles
which had been taken off us on arrival. While waiting we had
to stand upright with our faces to the wall. For about ten
minutes I stood like that a yard or two away from Adolf Reichwein. In an unobserved moment I whispered to him: "How are
you feeling Reichwein? What are the prospects?" He answered
softly that he had hopes of surviving. I no longer remember
the exact words, but they were words of hope. His speech and
manner at this time, as later, when on trial before the "People's
Court", cannot be better described than they have been by
Annedore Leber in her memorial article: "It often seemed as
though the extent of his danger could not have penetrated the
realm of his imagination. . . ." On the evening of October 19th,
1944 about 6.0 p.m. the charge sheet against Julius Leber and
four others was presented to him. "Betrayal of the Fatherland,
aiding the enemy, high treason, failure to report a high treason
plot" were the charges. Fourteen hours after the serving of the
charges the case before the "People's Court" began at 8.0 a.m.
on October 20th. Early that morning we five accused were
transported (handcuffed) to the Elsholtzstrasse in Schöneberg.
I saw Reichwein again. Surrounded by a thick force of uni-
formed police officers we were led into the court. The proceedings bore all the signs of a stage performance. Freisler, the
prototype of the Nazi agitator, of Nazi bestiality, the most
well known tool of Nazi law, presided. Next to him were
"People's Judges", nameless nonentities, on one side the representative of the Chief Justice and representatives of an
attentive and obedient press, official counsel for the defence who
was deserving of either pity or contempt, a few spectators,
representatives of the Wehrmacht, the Gestapo, wounded
soldiers and a few civilians.

'Freisler shouted and gesticulated. Not a sentence without
some frightful wickedness or brutality, not a spark of humanity, not even a sign of formal propriety. Interrogation? None of
the accused was interrogated: so it was with Reichwein. He was
scarcely permitted a yes or no. Freisler shouted himself hoarse
as he read out the accusation against Reichwein: the important
work of popular education which Adolf Hitler had entrusted
to him, had been shamefully abused by treason to the Father-

land and high treason. There was not a hope of risking a single sentence against distortion of the facts, against lies and abuse. It was even impossible to utter an affirmation of belief.

'In the course of the case against Adolf Reichwein a big and shattering indictment was heard. His official defence, when every attempt to object against the presentation of the facts had been cut short, finally requested that the court should take into consideration the unusual human qualities of his client. It looked as though Freisler was going to let Adolf Reichwein speak. Reichwein began quite quietly. He could not speak any louder. Detention, with its spiritual trials and bodily mis-handlings, had deprived him of his voice. I could hardly catch the sound of it. For a few seconds all eyes were fastened on him. I was filled with an immense pity for the man. As he stood there, he was the symbol of all things human, from whom at that moment all the torture of suffering fell away. He began to speak of his work. He began . . . and then all murder broke loose from Freisler. Humanity?—Values? Whoever had, like Reichwein, betrayed so great a trust had forfeited the right to be assessed in human terms. Shut up! Not another word! Crimes! Criminals! A storm of brutalized declamations broke the silence which just for a moment—no longer—had sur-rounded those men. Reichwein did not later make any formal statement. He listened to the verdict: "In spite of his one time Social-Democratic leanings the Reich had most generously granted Adolf Reichwein the possibility of responsible work. He knew of the traitor Gordeler's plans for a coup but did not do anything against them. In addition, he was certainly con-nected with negotiations with the Communists. All three had shared in the treason which, if it had succeeded, would have surrendered our people defenceless into the hands of the enemy. They have dishonoured themselves for ever. They will be punished by death. Their property is forfeit to the Reich."

'On the afternoon of October 20th, 1944 Julius Leber, Adolf Reichwein, Maass and I, escorted by Gestapo officials, were brought back to the Prinz Albrechtstrasse in a small lorry. We sat in the body of the vehicle, myself directly opposite Julius Leber, obliquely opposite Adolf Reichwein. We could not speak. Our eyes met and sank into each others. Reichwein's

eyes sought mine. I had been sentenced to seven years' imprisonment. I would be alive when Hitler and Hitler's Germany
had long vanished. Reichwein's eyes spoke: they gave messages
to his wife, children, his many friends. They betrayed behind
his mortally weary spirit the eternity of all that is human, which
by reason of his actions and his death would again be resurrected. That evening I was visited in my cell by men from the
Gestapo. They wanted to see the first man who in the case of
July 20th had got away with a time sentence. One of the visitors
entered saying, "Well, your friends Reichwein and Maass
aren't alive any longer." They are alive—in us and through us.'

We cannot fail to be impressed by the simple dignity with
which Reichwein in his last hours looked back on his career and
to respect the manner of this human being's tragic catharsis in the
midst of collective social chaos. We should ask ourselves how far
Reichwein was justified in making the degree of compromise
with Nazism, which in fact he had to make in order to work
publicly at all between 1943 and 1944. It could be argued that by
accepting a Nazi salary and by appearing on behalf of Nazi
educational authorities at Nazi-sponsored conferences and by
lecturing to the German armed forces he was identifying himself
with the régime—at any rate in appearance—and so betraying the
very cause he was trying to serve. This is one of those profound
problems of human motivation, the resolution of which can lie
only in the character of each single individual; it raises the
question of how far the good man may go even in the sacrifice and
soiling of a bit of his own personal integrity for the sake of remaining by the side of his fellows. As Berdyaev remarks in *The
Destiny of Man* (London, 1937): 'The moral problem is to share
the burden in the name of love and yet to have no share in the
world's falsity.'

Reichwein, through his acute experience of general socio-
political tensions realized that the mere overthrow of Hitler was
not enough to redeem German society; hence his vacillation about
the rightness of the conspirators using violence to overthrow
Hitler, although it should be noted that he and they were prepared to approve the violence of the Allies in doing it for them.
How far was he correct in his idea that Germany needed to under-
go the cure of complete military annihilation as a pre-condition of

healthy post-war reconstruction? At any rate he realized the need for a constructive programme, especially in education, to provide the dynamic for that social and moral revolution which he believed to be necessary in Germany and for which he sacrificed his life.

The impossibility of the German Resistance showed itself nowhere more clearly than in its diffuse nature: it could be described as consisting of Resistance by intention and Resistance by deed, if we leave aside the absurdity of those many thousands of Germans who after the event claimed to have been resisters all the time! Reichwein started by belonging to the former category and passed over into the second—in either case equally under the doom of ultimate defeat.

The necessity, utterly hateful to Reichwein himself, of making some degree of compromise with the Nazi authorities during his public work, is yet another illustration of the impossibility of uncompromising resistance to totalitarianism: either the compromise does not last, as in Reichwein's case, or else it becomes acquiescent collusion. Education might be the long term answer to the causes of totalitarianism, but totalitarianism itself was destructive of any such long term project. So Reichwein took up his double life of museum curator and conspirator and found himself, however reluctantly, like others in the Kreisau Circle, compelled to transmute his impatience and agony over the last days of the Nazi régime into that active conspiracy which was to cost him his life. This was because he must have realized the basic lack of realism in all the blueprints for the remaking of Germany after Hitler's overthrow, at a time when that overthrow was not really desired by the bulk of the nation for the right reasons.

Reichwein, then, was a minority figure involved in the impossibility of internal Resistance to Nazism, politically a failure, educationally of some consequence, personally of fine human quality, whose most obvious and immediate legacy is to be seen in the small but not uninfluential group of educators in Germany today whose affection for him remains as a continuing source of inspiration to their own educational endeavour.

REFERENCES

1. This quotation comes from an address delivered by Harold Poelchau on the Berlin Radio at a dedication service in memory of the plot against Hitler, July 20th, 1944, on July 20th, 1946; he had been the prison chaplain in Berlin who had been pastor to some eighty of the anti-Hitler conspirators during their imprisonment.

2. See Meinecke: *The German Catastrophe*. Cambridge, Massachusetts, 1950; Schlabrendorff: *The Secret War against Hitler*, London, 1966; Kirst: *The Twentieth of July*, Collins, 1966. (A Novel.)

3. Much of the material used here has appeared in *British Journal of Educational Studies*, Vol. IV, No. 1, November 1955; *The Conscience of Nazi Germany: Adolf Reichwein* by James L. Henderson, Lecturer in History, University of London Institute of Education, pp. 57 et seq.; and, by kind permission of Deutsche Verlags Anstalt, Stuttgart, in *Adolf Reichwein, Eine Politisch-Pädagogische Biographie* by James L. Henderson.

4. See Helmut von Moltke: *A German of the Resistance*, Oxford University Press, 1946.

CHAPTER THREE

Resistance since 1945: Three Different Strands

BEFORE reaching the panoramic sweep of those National Liberation Movements which form the subject of the second half of this book there may still be discerned a number of events which, by reason of their peculiar characteristics, can be reckoned in the category of Resistance. These include such diverse phenomena as the East German Rising of 1953, the Hungarian Uprising of 1956, the Vorkuta Camp Demonstration of 1953, the crusade of Danilo Dolci, the Campaign for Nuclear Disarmament, Resistance in Central and South Africa, the Civil Rights struggle in the U.S.A. and the general issue of Conscientious Objection to War. The three strands of recent Resistance, which will be selected for treatment here are first, the East German and Hungarian Risings because they illustrate attempts to resist the Communist form of totalitarianism, secondly, the Civil Rights struggle with a glance at its African reverberations because it exhibits the racialist element in Resistance, and thirdly, Conscientious Objection because it bears witness to the most extreme form of Resistance to War.

Our first strand prompts a comment on the paradox that, whereas during the Second World War Communists were both theoretically and to a considerable extent practically, part of the Resistance to totalitarian rule, since 1945 they have in these two cases, as well as in some others, constituted the totalitarianism against which others have resisted. Perhaps we have here in our grasp a fundamental principle, namely that an essential quality in Resistance that will give it its peculiar nature, is passionate protest against the violation of the sanctity of individual conscience.

81

After the Allied victory in 1945 Germany was divided into four Zones of Occupation which soon became the Western Zone (British, American, French) and the Eastern Zone (Soviet). Then came further dissension between the former Allies, the creation of the independent German Federal Republic in the West and of the German Democratic Republic in the East—also independent in theory but in practice the subservient satellite of the U.S.S.R. After various incidents, culminating in the creation of the notorious Berlin Wall in 1961, the present state of affairs was reached, namely a divided city of Berlin, in a divided Germany, itself part of a divided Europe, divided in its allegiance to Communism and Western democracy. Within the context of this series of events occurred the East German Rising of June 17th, 1953, this 'remarkable and quite unprecedented rising of the working people and peasants of a totalitarian country against their oppressors, astounding in its spontaneity and significant in the universal pattern it followed in each sector, however remote, although no plan of coordination was possible.'[1]

Two factors are important in understanding how the Communized East German State came to have rebellion within its gate: one was the steady flow of refugees from East to West—in January, 1953 for example over 22,000 arrived in West Berlin; the other was an agricultural crisis due to mishandling of and resistance to Soviet-type management of farming, for example the fact that by April, 1953 the Soviet Zone had exhausted its potato reserves. Nevertheless the Socialist Unity Party, under the command of Herr Ulbricht, went relentlessly ahead in its policy of total Communization of the country. However, on March 6th, 1953 Joseph Stalin died, and this was the signal for an easing by the Ulbricht Government, on instructions from Moscow, of their repressive measures. On May 28th the Red Army was relieved of its political functions in Germany, and Semyonov, exponent of relative moderation, returned there as Soviet High Commissioner. On June 10th the Prime Minister, Grotewohl, invited the Evangelist Church leaders to a discussion with the Government, and a communiqué was issued announcing 'wide agreement on the restoration of normal relations between State and Church—a guarantee of the Church's independence.'[2] Then the Politbureau of the Socialist Unity Party (S.E.D.) issued the text of a resolution calling a halt to Socialism 'designed to bring about a decisive improvement in the standard of all sections of the population and to strengthen the legal rights of individuals'.[3] A kind of 'thaw' had very definitely set in, but it was to the farmers and to the middle-class that this and other concessions were made; the industrial proletariat was hardly affected by them, and members of it were in fact being put under still greater pressure to increase production by, as the saying went, their 'voluntary raising of norms'.

On June 5th the building workers of East Berlin discovered that their pay packets had been reduced—the building operatives of Block 40, Stalinallée, the Government's show housing project, became mutinous and protested against the new rates, which would have become operative on June 30th, being introduced three weeks earlier. On June 16th at 10.0 a.m. 300 men from Block 40 started marching toward the Government building in the middle of the city carrying a notice: 'We demand a reduction in the norms.' An hour or so later a deeper note was struck: 'It's not only a question of norms and prices. We're not just from the Stalinallée; we are from all over Berlin. This is a rising. The Government have made mistakes and must take the consequences. We demand free elections and a secret ballot.'[4] The news of these actions and the pending strike was spread through the country by R.I.A.S., the West Berlin Radio Station: at 6.30 p.m. it sent out a message congratulating the East Berlin workers on their initiative and advising them to 'demand what is reasonable'.

Sunday, June 17th was the decisive day: thousands of workers from all industries converged on the Potsdammerplatz, but then units of the Red Army appeared with tanks.

'The strikers were without leaders; there was no strategy. Could they have thought that the Russian and German dictators would give way before a rising of unarmed men? They did believe just this . . . this was a revolution.'[5] Part of the pathos in this attitude lay in their attempt, quite hopeless under the circumstances, to keep the matter purely German, a protest against the Ulbricht Government, nothing to do with the Russians or the Western Allies! Inevitably, shooting and violence began, and inevitably by late afternoon the Berlin Rising had been crushed. However, it is important to record that there had been a general reaction to these events—in Brandenburg, Magdeburg, Leipzig, at the Zeiss works in Jena, in Dresden and in the North German coastal belt—all of no avail.

What then, if anything, had been accomplished by this resistance? Perhaps the single most important thing was the demonstration that power without authority (the position of Ulbricht's Government) was rotten and vulnerable unless that power was overwhelmingly backed by strength from without (the Red Army). Secondly, that if totalitarian pressure is relaxed on one sector of society, while at the same time it is increased on another, especially the industrial part, then the time is ripe for explosion. But thirdly, that the explosion will be without serious consequence unless its agents are well organized and can look for other outside power to balance the power of the already existing controlling power.

'Attempts have been made to draw a distinction between the two great and tragic days of German revolt against the modern totalitarian state—July 20th, 1944 and June 17th, 1953—by describing the first as Resistance and the second as a rising. June 17th, it has been said, was one of those simple eruptions which occur at intervals in history and which may or may not be of consequence . . . a rising takes place within the rudimentary sphere of politics; Resistance, on the other hand, is a matter of ethics. . . . A rising is concerned exclusively with unbearable aspects of the existing situation; Resistance is determination to replace them with something better. It is right to interpret Resistance as an ethical achievement. Certainly there can be no such thing as ethical achievement by the masses, only of individuals. But the argument ignores the fact that a rising requires the sum of the will to resist of the individuals taking part. The revolt against Hitler of July 20th, 1944 was the act of an elite, of a few who were compelled to work in tragic isolation from the people. The anonymous elite of the revolt against the Communist State always knew itself to be in complete accord with the bulk of the population. But the objective in each case was the re-establishment of law, order and justice. The events of July, 1944 and June, 1953 have this in common: each called upon individual men and women who had been prepared for action by years of personal opposition and open or secret resistance.'[6]

Resistance in Hungary three years later needs to be seen against a historical background, the Hungarian Liberal Revolution of 1848, the Industrial Working-class Revolution of 1918 (both with strong nationalist overtones), the régime of Admiral Horthy between the two Wars and the defeat and occupation of Hungary by Soviet troops in 1945. Returning with them to Hungary were Mutzai Rakosi and Erno Gerö who proceeded to re-organize the Hungarian Communist Party. For a while, however, they worked as part of a Popular Front Government, set up according to Russian instructions and consisting of the Smallholders Party and the Social-Democratic Party and the National Peasant Party. This Coalition carried through an extensive land reform, largely under the guidance of the Minister of Agriculture, Imry Nagy. By 1948 this form of government had given way to a Communist Dictatorship under Rakosi, and as he himself remarked: 'Our force was multiplied by the fact that the Soviet Union and the Soviet Army were always there to support us with their assistance.'[7]

The Hungarian peasants were treated on the Soviet model, being regarded simply as a rural labour force, paying for the process of industrialization, into which went most of the régime's energies. Although intellectual and religious freedom were crushed, the number of university and technological students greatly increased, and this extension of opportunity was a real achievement. Christian resistance to the pressures of Communism came from Cardinal Mindzenty, who in December, 1948 was arrested and condemned to life imprisonment.

Then, again soon after Stalin's death, a modification of Communist measures in Hungary began. Rakosi, although still remaining First Secretary of the Party, was replaced by Nagy as Prime Minister: the latter initiated a 'new course', which went further than any other East European country. However, in April, 1953 this tendency was reversed with the removal of Nagy from the Central Committee of the Party and from the premiership, but Rakosi's counter-attack did not last long. In July he had to give way, on orders from Moscow, to Gerö, partly in deference to pressure from Tito in Yugoslavia, who had always opposed Rakosi, and partly to a new rally of strength inside Hungary. This was the core of the Resistance and it stemmed from the Writers' Association and the Petöfi Club (so called after a revolutionary party of that name in 1848). It demanded the restoration of Nagy, and tat he end of September it played a considerable part in stimulating a large demonstration and the re-interment of Rajk, the former Minister of the Interior who had been a victim of the Rakosi purge.

On October 23rd, 1956 street fighting broke out in Budapest.

'A special feature of the 1956 Revolution is the part played by the working-class. The workers were slower to move than the intellectuals, but once they were fully engaged they showed themselves very stubborn. It was the workers who provided the main fighting force in Budapest—stiffened of course by army units. The last centres of organized fighting were the great industrial centres. . . . After military resistance had ended the workers in factories and mines continued strikes and passive resistance. Throughout the winter of 1956/57 resistance continued. If the disparity between the strength of the combatants is taken into account, one may say that the effort of the Hungarian workers is the greatest single effort of resistance ever made by an industrial working-class against an oppressor.'[8]

Yet, because the Western democracies could not or would not intervene, Red Army forces crushed the Hungarian Resistance. Although the tragic episode may have shown that a totalitarian régime can be resisted and even overthrown from within, nevertheless, when that régime is part of a large and more powerful ideological structure (in this case the Soviet controlled sectors) then it is impotent to effect lasting change. Yet, as Mr. Seton Watson does well to remind us, the shooting on workers in Budapest was done by Soviet soldiers, who cannot fail to have been impressed and possibly shaken by the contradiction between their deed and Marxist theory, as they shot at working-class women in food queues, arrested leaders of workers' councils and suppressed strikes. As that author remarks: 'The Hungarian Revolution may prove to have been Bolshevism's 1905'.[9] In any case, it was certainly a fine example of that heroic protest which is integral to the definition of Resistance adopted in this book.

Taking up now our second strand, the Civil Rights Movement in the U.S.A., we need first to remind ourselves that this is a recent happening. Against the background of more than three hundred years slavery, the negro renaissance began about 1920 and received enormous impetus from the Second World War, the direct outcome of which was President Truman's 1946 Commission on Civil Rights. In May, 1954 the National Association for the Advancement of Coloured People achieved its greatest triumph when the U.S. Supreme Court issued its famous judgement:

'To separate them (negro children) from others of similar age and qualification solely because of their race generates a feeling of inferiority as to their status in the community that may affect their hearts and minds in a way unlikely ever to be undone. . . . We conclude that in the field of public education the doctrine of "separate but equal" has no place. Separate educational facilities are inherently unequal.'

From that moment in the fields of education, employment, housing and politics there has been a tale of swelling negro Resistance to all attempts on the part of white reactionaries to frustrate the full implications of this piece of legislation. In 1956, as a result of a negro bus boycott in Montgomery, Alabama, segregated seating in the buses was abolished. At the beginning of 1957 the Little Rock School Board, in compliance with the 1954 decision, decided to admit seventeen specially chosen negro students to the hitherto all white Central High School. The Governor, defying Federal law, stationed the Arkansas National Guard outside the school, theoretically to prevent racial violence, actually to prevent the negro students from entering the school. A trial of strength ensued between the negroes and the State of Arkansas, but also, and far more fatefully and decisively, between that State and the Federal Government, intervening to uphold a Federal Court decision, an ultimate step taken towards negro emancipation. In 1960 there were 'sit-ins', the Congress for Racial Equality organized 'Freedom' riots. In 1962 there was the famous case of James Meredith and 'Ole Miss', the negro student and the University of Mississippi. This incident has been brilliantly described by Professor Silver in his book *Mississippi: The Closed Society* (Gollancz, 1965). In August, 1963 came the great Washington Civil Rights Rally and in 1964 the passing into law at last of the Civil Rights Act, guaranteeing the negro equal rights to register and to use his vote.

In spite of this tremendous achievement, however, the battle for negro emancipation has not yet been won, neither in the South where intimidation and ignorance remain as serious barriers to exercising his political function, nor in the crowded industrial cities of the North where racial misery is an ingredient of class poverty. To understand why this is so it is wise to meditate on the following passage from Martin Luther King's *Letter from Birmingham Jail*, April 16th, 1963:

'For years now I have heard the word "Wait!" It rings in the ear of every Negro with piercing familiarity. This "Wait" has almost always meant "Never". We must come to see, with one of our distinguished jurists, that "justice too long delayed is justice denied".

'We have waited for more than 340 years for our constitutional and God-given rights. The nations of Asia and Africa are moving with jetlike speed toward gaining political independence, but we still creep at horse-and-buggy pace toward gaining a cup of coffee at a lunch counter. Perhaps it is easy for those who have never felt the stinging darts of segregation to say, "Wait". But when you have seen vicious mobs lynch your mothers and fathers at will and drown your sisters and brothers at whim; when you have seen hate-filled policemen curse, kick and even kill your black brothers and sisters; when you see the vast majority of your twenty million Negro brothers smothering in an airtight cage of poverty in the midst of an affluent society; when you suddenly find your tongue twisted and your speech stammering as you seek to explain to your six-year-old daughter why she can't go to the public amusement park that has just been advertised on television, and see tears welling up in her eyes when she is told that Funtown is closed to colored children, and see ominous clouds of inferiority beginning to form in her little mental sky, and see her beginning to distort her personality by developing an unconscious bitterness toward white people; when you have to concoct an answer for a five-year-old son who is asking: "Daddy, why do white people treat colored people so mean?"; when you take a cross-country drive and find it necessary to sleep night after night in the uncomfortable corners of your automobile because no motel will accept you; when you are humiliated day in and day out by nagging signs reading "white" and "coloured"; when your first name becomes "nigger", your middle name becomes "boy" (however old you are) and your last name becomes "John", and your wife and mother are never given the respected title "Mrs."; when you are hurried by day and haunted by night by the fact that you are a Negro, living constantly at tiptoe stance, never quite knowing what to expect next, and are plagued with inner fears and outer resentments; when you are forever fighting a degenerating sense of "nobodiness"—then you will understand why we find it difficult to wait. There comes a time when the cup of endurance runs over, and men are no longer willing to be plunged into the abyss of despair. I hope, sirs, you can understand our legitimate and unavoidable impatience.'[10]

Another thing which makes the issue still a sore one is that with the taste of freedom at last on his lips the black man is tempted into arrogance and even anti-white sentiments, which again in turn fan the flames of anti-black racialism. Yet the outcome is not now in doubt and has to be seen in its global setting—on a small scale for instance against the manner in which Great Britain succeeds or fails in adapting herself to a non-racial society.

'. . . our responses to our fellow-Britons with black faces are going to be very different from what they were to their parents or grandparents. What is more—much more—we have an opportunity not given to any nation since the colour question was first asked, an opportunity which sets us off very sharply from the U.S., who never had the opportunity at all. We will, if we are sufficiently farsighted and intelligent, be able to look on our coloured compatriots with eyes unclouded by guilt. For they will be, as the American negroes are not, the descendents of men and women who came to Britain voluntarily and who arrived with full equality under the law.'[11]

On a much larger scale the resistance to oppression by the American negro must be seen against the global awakening of the non-white masses of Asia and Africa with all their legitimate aspirations to the Four Freedoms of the Declaration of Human Rights. Far and away the most important aspect of the Civil

Rights Movement—potentially at least—has been its reliance on non-violence.

'In any non-violent campaign there are four basic steps: collection of the facts to determine whether injustices exist; negotiation; self-purification; and direct action....'[12]

'In measuring the full implications of the civil rights revolution, the greatest contribution may be in the area of world peace. The concept of non-violence has spread on a mass scale in the United States as an instrument of change in the field of race relations. To date, only a relatively few practitioners of non-violent direct action have been committed to its philosophy. The great mass have used it pragmatically as a tactical weapon, without being ready to live it.

'More and more people, however, have begun to conceive of this powerful ethic as a necessary way of life in a world where the wildly accelerated development of nuclear power has brought into being weapons that can annihilate all humanity. Political agreements are no longer secure enough to safeguard life against a peril of such devastating finality. There must also be a philosophy, acceptable to the people, and stronger than resignation toward sudden death.

'It is no longer merely the idealist or the doom-ridden who seek for some controlling force capable of challenging the instrumentalities of destruction. Many are searching. Sooner or later all the peoples of the world, without regard to the political systems under which they live, will have to discover a way to live together in peace.

'Man was born into barbarism when killing his fellow man was a normal condition of existence. He became endowed with a conscience. And he has now reached the day when violence toward another human being must become as abhorrent as eating another's flesh.

'Nonviolence, the answer to the Negroes' need, may become the answer to the most desperate need of all humanity.'[13]

The connection between our second and third strands of Resistance is evident. The question we must now consider is, what of war resisters and conscientious objectors? How do these fit into the picture of twentieth century Resistance Movements? Resistance to war is resistance to a symptom, namely the phenomenon of fighting as a means of settling disputes. That is why in the first place it tends to take the form of individual protest against an evil which is itself the effect of a number of complex causes: it is the expression of a kind of sincere moral outrage against man's inhumanity to man. So much is clear when we consider the matter historically, first in the period before 1914 where there is impressive evidence from Confucianism, Taoism, Buddhism, Hinduism and parts of Christianity that religious motivation based on divine sanction is a strong element in the tradition of non-violent resistance, whether to all kinds of oppression or specifically as conscientious objection to war. The First World War in Europe and Gandhi's campaigns in South Africa and India produce further developments in both these spheres. During the inter-war years 1918–1939 in Britain, but also in the U.S.A., the Scandinavian countries, Germany and Switzerland, the movement took on a new depth and complexity. It was made up of religious, political, economic and aesthetic components; it drew to itself men like the Reverend Sheppard, Lansbury, Max Plowman, Carl Ossietsky. Against the menacing totalitarianisms of the 1930's its voice though persistent was tiny and quite powerless to affect public policy.

The Second World War saw two further tendencies grow, particularly in Britain where the first generation of conscientious objectors in the 1914–18 War had won a great part of the battle for the freedom of individual conscience. On the one hand there was not nearly so much victimization of C.O.'s and on the other the C.O.'s themselves were prepared in considerable numbers to witness to their convictions by undertaking alternative services to military duties: even so, their number was a mere 60,000 out of eight million involved in the war effort. Certainly the conviction grew mightily that resistance to war by itself was an inadequate policy; it was merely trying to treat the symptom—necessary and helpful perhaps as example but futile unless it included also attention to the causes. After the War began conscientious objection increasingly began to merge with the more general movement towards the use of non-violence as the only realistic method of resisting such social evils as racial prejudice, poverty and malnutrition, frustration in work—all of them roots of war— and indeed of changing society as a whole.

Sir Michael Tippett, the distinguished English composer,

after serving a prison sentence for his own conscientious objection, remarked: 'Much more has been accomplished by our witness this time than we know or perhaps than we deserve.' What
he was getting at was that war resistance, though numerically
insignificant and politically ineffective, was slowly altering the
climate of public opinion. Moreover, as the nature of war itself
changed—from what over the ages it had been—to genocide,
so the whole scope and significance of Resistance had begun to
change drastically. There are far more men and women able
and willing to see sense in resisting genocide than there were
when this was still war. It may be that the battles of the future,
especially those of national liberation, whose genesis and fortunes
will be traced in the succeeding chapters of this book, can only be
won, in any sense in which victory has a meaning, by non-violent
means. In the relationship between the individual and the State
the stand of such non-violent resisters can be truly prophetic.
For, as Fenner Brockway remarks in his introduction to Dennis
Hayes' book *Challenge of Conscious* when referring to the pre-
cedents established by the legal rights won for C.O.'s in
Britain:

> 'The implications of these decisions are immense. They
> mean literally that it is recognized that the final judgment on
> participation in any war should be made not by the State but
> by the individual. This is a revolutionary invasion of the sphere
> of the State. It is a revolutionary acceptance of the right of
> the individual within the most totalitarian form which a State
> can assume, the State mobilized for war. The significance of
> this is the greater because we are living in a period when
> generally speaking the power of the State is growing—when we
> see the struggle of the Conscientious Objector as part of the
> wider struggle to retain the liberties of the individual from the
> encroachment of the State, still another significance becomes
> attached to it, a significance of peculiar interest to us because
> it is related to the issue of peace and war.'

This third strand of Resistance seems to have a special reference to the use of the nuclear deterrent as a means of deterring
politicians from going to war. It brings to an almost eschatological
climax the age old dispute of ends and means, so this Chapter
may fittingly conclude with four lines of poetry, the logic of which

is gravely and memorably illustrated in Peter Watkins' documentary film *The War Game*—

> Point not the goal until you plot the course
> For ends and means to man are tangled so
> That different means quite different aims enforce
> Conceive the means as ends in embryo.[14]

REFERENCES

1. Stefan Brant: *The East German Rising*. Thames & Hudson, 1955.
2. Brant, op. cit.
3. Op. cit., p. 48.
4. Op. cit. p. 64.
5. Op. cit. p. 71.
6. Op. cit. pp. 193–4.
7. H. Seton Watson: *Nationalism and Communism: Essays 1946–63*, p. 152. Methuen 1964.
8. Seton Watson, op. cit. p. 160.
9. Op. cit. p. 162.
10. *Why We Can't Wait*. Signet Books, 1963, pp. 80–2.
11. Bernard Levin: *Black Englishmen: New Statesman*, April 29th, 1966.
12. *Why We Can't Wait*. p. 78.
13. Op. cit. p. 152.
14. Ferdinand Lassalle's *Franz von Sickingen*.

PART TWO

LIBERATION

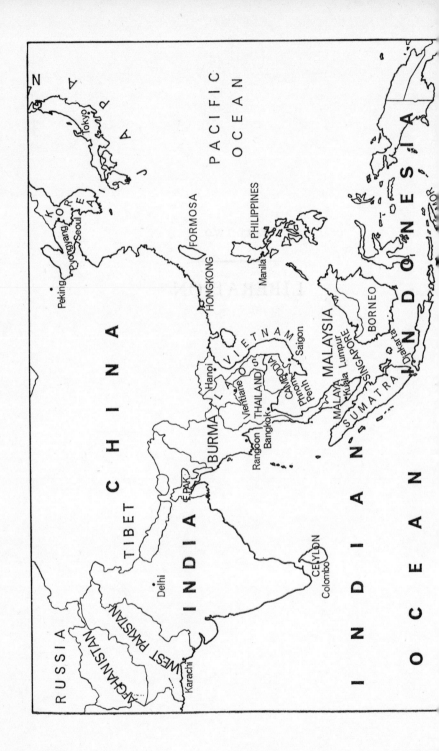

CHAPTER FOUR

Colonialism

THE handful of men in frail craft who ventured boldly into un-
charted waters from the harbours of Europe in the fifteenth and
sixteenth centuries would surely have been astonished had they
been able to foresee the extent of empire for which their explor-
ations paved the way. The tiny ships inching down the coasts of
Africa and America and across the Atlantic, Pacific and Indian
Oceans certainly did not look like the outrunners of invincible
conquering armies. Indeed the numbers of Europeans involved
at this stage are to be tallied in their dozens and hundreds rather
than in their thousands. Yet all the millions of Asia, Africa and
Latin America were powerless to halt the expansion of Western
power and influence until the whole southern hemisphere as well
as the north had been effectively subjugated.

At their first contact with the non-white world, the Europeans'
advantage was not so apparent as it was subsequently to become.
But social and economic developments in Europe, coupled, and
indeed connected, with the proliferation of trade contacts throughout the world, steadily, if imperceptibly at first, enabled the West
to open up a significant organisational and technological—and
not least military—gap, which, once established, rapidly widened
in a cumulative way. From traders competing on more or less
equal terms in Africa and Asia with Arabs, Indians, Chinese
and others, the Westerners were led step by step by the logic of
their situation to establish permanent garrisons and colonies.
Where the original inhabitants of desirable territories were weak
(as in Tasmania, Australia and North and South America) they
were exterminated or rounded up into pitiful reserves with a
callousness that was the dark side of the West's exuberant self-
confidence in its world mission. Where they were too numerous

97

to eliminate or corral, they were beaten unmercifully and, if possible, put to useful work for the profit of the white master and the greater glory of his God. Through the hills and jungles of Latin America, across the plains of India, into the interior of North America, among the islands of South-East Asia, up the rivers of black Africa and down the China coast rampaged the conquering armies and reckless adventurers of Europe, until, by the end of the nineteenth century, it seemed there were no more worlds left to subdue and exploit: by fire and sword, the best part of Asia, Africa and South America had been made over into an agricultural hinterland for the industrialising countries of the northern hemisphere and their off-shoots in Oceania, and into a huge market for their goods and a profitable outlet for their investments. Millions of square miles of land and hundreds of millions of subject peoples felt the impress of the white man at the high-tide of Caucasian empire.

But in victory lay the seeds of eventual defeat. The ruthlessness of the colonialists and their growing arrogance, as the course of world history seemed to 'prove' white superiority, could not but stir bitterness and hatred among the 'lesser breeds', whose allotted role in the scheme of things was as drawers of water and hewers of wood. If at first these hostile and vengeful reactions did not generally ignite into rebellion, it was partly through fear of the white man's terrible reprisals when his power was challenged or defied, and partly through a reluctant acquiescence in, an almost fatalistic acceptance of, the myth of white superiority and invincibility. Nevertheless, oppression went beyond certain limits only at great peril to the oppressors themselves. Terror may seem to engender only numb despair; but the sullen acceptance of blows and humiliations—to all outward appearances—can conceal truly explosive tensions and resentments liable suddenly to erupt at a moment's notice on application of the appropriate spark. It was thus that there was never total peace in the white man's coloured empire, even at its serenest pinnacles of apparent security and achievement. Always somewhere in the non-white world there was trouble; some tribe or people or group driven beyond the limits of endurance, goaded into the kind of irrational, hopeless up-risings, those with no prospect of success, only of temporary reprisal and revenge against the oppressor, known as primitive revolts.

Lest it be thought that the preceding paragraphs give altogether too black an impression of Western imperialism, it might
be advisable at this point to consider briefly what subjection
meant for the colonial peoples. This does not necessarily mean
the spectacular and rather familiar abuses and atrocities such as
the infamous barbarity of the slave trade, the intolerable greed
and inhumanity of the Dutch in Indonesia during the Culture
System, or the unscrupulous rapacity of the early British Sahibs
in India. These things, and other equivalent episodes, stand out.
But one should think too of the day to day wrongs heaped on the
average colonial subject in the ordinary way of things. Unless
this reality is understood, primitive revolts must appear as
baffling and inexplicable side-tracks along the path of fulfilment
of the white man's mission in bringing economic development
and modernisation to the colonial countries and in guiding their
peoples step by careful step to viable independence.

Think, for example, of the contract workers of Sumatra during
the spectacular development of the island under the Dutch after
the opening of the Suez Canal (1869):

'They may not run away from their work, for that is for-
bidden by their contract which the ignorant, misled coolies
signed somewhere in Java or China. They are doing forced
labour, or, if you like, they are slaves. The coolie slogs from
morning till night, toiling and stooping; he has to stand up to
the neck in stinking marshland, while greedy leeches suck his
thin blood and malaria mosquitoes poison his sickly body. But
he cannot run away; for the contract binds him. The *tjentengs*,
the watchmen and constables of the firm, who have the strength
of giants and are bestially cruel, track down the fugitive. When
they catch him, they give him a terrible hiding and lock him
up, for the contract binds him.'[1]

The recaptured coolie was commonly slung on a pole, like
an animal trophy, and his captors received a few coins for
each successful tracking. As for the coolie's wife, she could be
purchased by the white master as his *nyay* (woman) for ten
guilders.[2]

Or consider the plight of the Filipino peasant. Progressively
impoverished and dispossessed by centuries of Spanish rule,
his condition under the Americans this century remained that

of a virtual slave because, despite the somewhat enlightened complexion of US colonial policy in certain directions, no effort was made to undo the grossly inequitable distribution of land-holding (in parts of Luzon Island 2 per cent of the population owned 90 per cent of the land) and to give the peasant back his land. The following, though relating specifically to the Philippines, might be taken as, in general, typical of colonialism-feudalism throughout a large part of the non-white world, which is why it is quoted at length.

'The Nueva Ecija peasant lives with his family of five or six in a small house on the corner of the piece of land he cultivates —big or small as it pleased the *Hacendero* (landlord) to apportion him. No matter how industrious and thrifty he may be, he cannot hope ever to own the land he labours on, nor any other piece of land in the province, for in Nueva Ecija and other Central Luzon provinces, the agricultural lands are owned by a few rich Hacenderos, and no tenants' money can buy such land. Nor can he shift, for he has no money to take him to kinder lands. He usually hires his work animals from the Hacendero. He keeps them in a small enclosure at night, and gets up at four or five in the morning to let them graze under his own watchful eye. If a tenant's carabao is even found in the rice field of another tenant, whether or not the animal has done any damage, the tenant pays a fine of ten cavans (a cavan is equivalent to somewhat over two bushels) of palay (rice-on-the-stalk) to the Hacendero—according to the so-called "Laws of the Hacienda"—made by the Hacendero himself.

'The Hacendero furnishes half of the seed; the other half comes from the tenant. It is sown in the seed-beds in June. When the seedlings are large enough, and the paddies . . . are ready, the transplanting begins. The tenant does not do this alone, but invites his neighbours to help him. He pays them . . . (a traditional amount) half of which comes from him and half from the landowner.

'For whatever amount the tenant borrows for other purposes, the Hacendero charges him 50 per cent interest. The Hacendero will deny this, because it is against the law, but it is true nevertheless. If a tenant borrows a sum of money equivalent in value at the time to 20 cavans of palay, the Hacendero

makes it appear in his book, the item signed or thumb-marked
by the tenant, that the latter owes him 30 cavans. Such is the
easy escape from the so-called usury laws of the Philippines!
And on his part, the tenant takes the money at any cost and
keeps mum about it. He has no other source of income than
farming, and no one but the Hacendero would lend him the
money he needs.

'When the grain has matured, he makes another trip to the
Hacendero's office for money to pay those who will help him
cut the palay and gather it in bundles for the threshing. The
trilladora (threshing machine) hums in field after field. Sometimes when the farmer has no more rice to eat, he will himself
thresh a small part of the still undivided harvest to save his
family from starvation. But if he is caught, he either forfeits
the whole harvest to the landowner, or is hauled into court,
whence he goes straight to jail for theft.

'The Hacendero's huge trilladora must do the job, and for
every 100 cavans of palay threshed, the tenant pays the landlord 10 cavans. The palay pouring out of the threshing machine
is put in sacks. After it has been weighed, the farmer hauls it
to the provincial road, alongside of which it is piled up and
watched day and night, until the Hacendero's truck comes
along. Then the tenant goes to the landlord once more for
his clearance.

'Generally, the farmer has had no schooling, and even if he
has learned a little reading . . . he is weak at figures. So before
he goes to the office he fills his pocket with small pebbles or
grains of corn with which to count. Each grain represents a
cavan of palay. One half of the harvest goes to the Hacendero.
Then from his share the tenant pays the landlord his part of
the expenses. Then he pays his personal account with interest,
these often amounting to 30 or 40 cavans. Hence it often
happens that even if the harvest comes to a 100 or more cavans
only 1 or 2 cavans remains for him and his family in payment
for a year of labour.

'What about the 12 months until the next harvest? There
is no other way: he borrows from the Hacendero at the same
usurious rates of interest. And so it comes about that the
tenant's life on the haciendas of Nueva Ecija is reduced to a
state of perpetual dependence and indebtedness. The tenant

feels that something should be done about it; he thinks the Government should do something about it, but since it does not he sometimes considers making the effort to take the matter into his own hands.

'He goes to other tenants and they discuss the possibility of forming some sort of peaceful union with the aim of securing better conditions. But he is told that before the first meeting is over they would all be arrested as "Reds". And if they escaped the ever-watchful Constabulary agents, there is still the Hacendero. The moment he learns that a tenant is a capisanan (member of an organization), he would expel him from the hacienda. And where could the poor tenant go? Where could he get the money to move to another part of the country and establish himself there? So, generally, he decides to slave on. As long as his wife and his little ones, whom he loves so well, live, he will continue to bow to oppression.'[3]

The forms and the intensity of colonial expropriation and exploitation varied, but everywhere the rural people were rudely and callously shaken out from their traditional patterns of life by the combined forces of money economy, Western land law and the needs of the plantations and mines for cheap labour. Untold miseries and wrongs were thereby inflicted, provoking the revolt of the desperate and the resistance of the defiant.

'The Africans did not take easily to enslavement. They rose in desperate rejection at the African ports, flung themselves from the side of the slave ships, starved themselves to death, or plotted on the American plantations. In Brazil they gathered themselves into well-organized rebel groups called *quilombos*, and in the seventeenth century several of these joined to form in the north-east the Republic of Palmares, which survived for nearly seventy years.'[4]

The Atchinese never really succumbed to Dutch rule in Sumatra, while the prickly and aggressive Vietnamese would bow to no foreign yoke. In India, the

'. . . violent *Wahhabi* peasant revolts, culminating in the Indian Mutiny were to a certain extent reactions against the disturbance which Western imports had caused in India's agrarian economy. In their traditional way the uprisings aimed

at an overthrow of those in authority who had failed to protect
the peasantry from distress. But this time they did not succeed,
as a basic change in the structure of society had occurred, and
the influence of Western economy could not be eliminated.
The Western powers usually chose the policy of backing the
Oriental rulers and so propped up the collapsing feudal
structures.'[5]

The Philippines erupted periodically in peasant revolt throughout the four hundred years of Spanish rule. Such risings were
ferociously punished: during the 1896 rising of the *Katipunan*
('patriots' league'),

> '. . . the monastic and civil officials lost their heads. Other
> than those natives strangled by the garrote or shot, hundreds
> were tortured to elicit information by crushing their bones or
> by hanging them up by their thumbs. Five hundred other
> Filipinos were imprisoned. Seventy of them died of suffoca-
> ation in Fort Santiago when a jailer threw a rug over the venti-
> lating shaft. . . . Filipinos arrested in Vigan Province were
> shipped to Manila tied up like bundles of freight, and then
> swung out onto the quay by derricks.'[6]

Even comparatively favoured Malaya witnessed the murder of a
British Resident in 1875 and an uprising in Pahang (1891-95).
(British policy at this time was founded on the principle that '. . .
the Malays like every other rude Eastern nation, require to be
treated much more like children, and to be taught,'—General Sir
Andrew Clarke, Governor of the Straits Settlements 1873-75;
he might have added 'and to be punished'.)

But already with the Katipunan, we are moving from the era
of primitive revolts to the era of modern nationalism, with its
more comprehensive and better articulated demands, and more
broadly based and better organized leadership. The fore-runners
of the Philippine Revolution, the 'Propagandists', were, typically
drawn from the Western-educated indigenous middle-class.
One, Jose Rizal, novelist, poet, philosopher, surgeon, painter and
sculptor, became the embodiment of Filipino protest; his execution in 1896 helped spark the revolution. But the revolution
was premature. Although it had among its aims the nationalization of Church lands, which constituted the better part of the

Philippines' agricultural endowment, there were enough land-owners and nervous bourgeoisie in the leadership to damp the revolutionary ardour of the peasant supporters. Moreover, American intervention, culminating in the defeat of the Spaniards in 1898, confronted the revolutionaries with much more efficient forces of suppression, and by 1902 the Philippine Revolution was over. 'It is nevertheless significant,' comments an American scholar,

'. . . that the proclamation of a Republic (in 1899) marked the Filipinos as the first Asian people to try to throw off established European colonialism. In addition to nationalist fervour, they had certain political skills. They had drawn up a constitution, which evidenced familiarity with the constitutions of Europe and America, established a government in accordance with constitutional provisions, and set up administrations in several provinces.'[7]

Two points are of interest. First, here we have an early example of what was to become a characteristic feature of national liberation struggles, namely the creation of 'parallel hierarchies' —that is, alternative government to the discredited régime against which the revolt has taken place. Second, the crushing of the Philippine Revolution advanced American experience of what was later to become known as 'counter-insurgency':

'. . . after the occupation of the Philippines, this repressive policy made its appearance again in Mexico in 1914, when General John Pershing (who won his spurs repressing Indians, and then Filipino Mohammedans in Mindanao) invaded that country to suppress the Mexican revolutionary guerrilla leader, Pancho Villa. The same policy was put into operation in Haiti in 1917, and was repeated in Nicaragua in the later 1920's and early 1930's in an effort to suppress the popular guerrilla forces of Sandino, who resisted the U.S. Marines sent to bodyguard the United Fruit Company and American mining interests in that country.'[8]

Those who today believe that the Americans are being reluctantly driven into imperialism in Vietnam by adverse force of circumstances and against the otherwise anti-imperialist tradition of American foreign policy ought seriously to take this record into account.

The nationalists and historians of India and Pakistan look back over a hundred years to their first 'war of national liberation'—the events recorded in British sources as the Indian or Sepoy Mutiny (1857). Nehru himself declared that it was

'. . . much more than a military mutiny, and it spread rapidly and assumed the character of a popular rebellion and a war of Indian independence.'[9]

But in fact the 'Mutiny' seems to have been nicely balanced between past and present. A recent historian remarks:

'The actual mutiny had definite religious motives behind it. The revolts, so far as they had definite direction, looked backwards to the defunct Mughal and Maratha régimes which in their day had bitterly clashed. The agrarian risings reflected grievances stemming from government action. Nowhere can be found any sign of forward-looking action towards a united India. *All the new Westernised class were on the British side.*'[10]

It should be noted that in an equivalent situation of unprecendented social upheaval (in this case the industrial revolution) the initial reaction of the British people was to look backward to an earlier social system by petitioning Parliament for legal protection, or by asking the justices to enforce the old Elizabethan statutes for the fixing of wages and the regulation of apprenticeship; the fashioning of more relevant instruments of struggle, such as trade unions, followed. But the interesting point from the Spear quotation is that concerning the role of the local Western-educated middle classes. In the Philippines, this group had, as we have seen, been actively campaigning against the abuses of Spanish rule *before* the Revolution broke out in 1896. It was only *after* the 'Mutiny' in India had been suppressed with sickening savagery by the frightened British that a middle-class nationalist *movement* began to develop (though there had, of course, been individual precursors); things were never to be the same again.

The vehicle of Indian independence was to be the Indian National Congress, founded in 1885. Although avowedly non-sectarian, Congress was predominantly a Hindu organization. There were many Muslims who feared that full co-operation in the attainment of freedom in and through Congress would be fatal to the distinctive characteristics of Islam, and it was for this reason that the Muslim League was founded in 1906. At first the nationalists most prominent in these organizations restricted their demands, as had indeed the leading 'Propagandists' in the Philippines, to internal reform and a greater degree of self-rule. They were, in other words, moderates. But more militant spokesmen were in the wings, and as the nineteenth century passed into the twentieth, it was their uncompromising definition of 'national liberation' which increasingly held sway; this unequivocally demanded the withdrawal of the British and the termination of their *raj*.

In the other Asian giant—China—the nineteenth century had brought a succession of unparalleled shocks and mortifications at the hands of the Western 'barbarians'. The failure of the old order to defend the rights and the honour of China; the contemptuous ease with which foreign armies and navies brushed aside the Imperial forces to march or sail into the interior to exact retribution or to ease the extraction of loot and profit; the condescending superiority of the Christian missionaries; the physical and moral deterioration of the people consequent upon the British-led campaign to make China a nation of opium addicts for the benefit of the coffers of the West; all these and numberless other affronts engendered in the intelligent young an attitude of radical rejection of the past and of determination to modernize the 'Middle Kingdom' and thus enable her to foil and repel her enemies. Already the peasantry were in turmoil as civil order decayed; the T'ai P'ing rebellion of 1850 to 1864 was a great peasant uprising of the kind that traditionally tolled the knell of a dying dynasty. At the end of a century of humiliation, the Boxer Rebellion (1899–1900), another peasant rising strongly antiforeign and markedly anti-Christian in declaration and deed, heralded the century of change which was to culminate in the successful Communist revolution of 1949.

The first generation of reformers, however, tried merely to make of China an industrialized power on the Western model with Western-style representative institutions. Notable among those who set out along this course was Sun Yat-sen. After several unsuccessful attempts had been made to end Manchu authority, a revolution in 1911 proclaimed China a Republic and made Sun Yat-sen provisional President. The following years brought further disappointments to the reformers, China remaining divided and racked by warlordism, political opportunism and corruption, aggravated by continuing weaknesses vis-à-vis the industrialized foreign powers (the governments and nationals of which did not hesitate to intervene in China's internal affairs if any advantage was to be derived thereby). Some economic development did occur, mostly in the coastal cities which had felt foreign influence longest, but its benefits were restricted to the small class of indigenous merchants and businessmen. For the peasantry, things went from bad to worse, and since they formed the overwhelming bulk of the Chinese population, 'improvements' which excluded them were hardly to be seen as *national* improvements. Sun Yat-sen towards the end of his life—he died in 1925 —had become disillusioned with the prospects of advance through bourgeois liberalism of the Western style, and was latterly interpreting his Three Principles of the People (*San Min Chu I*) in a more socialist way. His work was to be carried on by the young Mao Tse-tung, whose 'Analysis of the Classes in Chinese society' appeared in March 1926, to be followed in 1927 by the classic 'Report on an Investigation of the Peasant Movement in Hunan'. The definition of 'national liberation' was advancing to maturity.

Although it was not apparent at the time, either to people in the West or to the colonial peoples, the high-tide of classical imperialism had already by the first decade of this century deposited its ultimate wrack mark on the sands of time and begun to recede. The eighteenth century had seen the United States of America declaring her independence from British colonialism, but it had also seen the successful incorporation of India into the Empire. The early nineteenth century had witnessed the liberation struggles of the countries of Latin America against French, Spanish and Portuguese rule so that by about 1830 the familiar modern boundaries had more or less been drawn. The nineteenth century also saw the flourishing in Europe of a climate of opinion that colonies were not, in any case, profitable and that, therefore, they ought to be cast adrift; this was the logical conclusion of laissez-faire and free trade thought. It was indeed anticipated that Canada, Australia and New Zealand would move towards independence, albeit preserving with the mother country a 'special relationship'. But the *later* nineteenth century was remarkable for an upsurge of aggressive and assertive European colonialism which, in a matter of years, swept vast areas of the world into its fold. Great Britain during the years 1884 to 1900 acquired, for example, 3·7 million sq. miles of territory with a population of 57 million; France 3·6 million sq. miles with a population of 36·5 million; Germany 1 million sq. miles with a population of 16·7 million; Belgium 900,000 sq. miles and 30 million people; and Portugal 800,000 sq. miles with 9 million people. By 1914, 80 per cent of the world's area and 82 per cent of its population were in the white colonial sphere, either as metropolitan centres, colonies or virtual colonies (China, Turkey, Persia, etc.). Africa had been cynically and heartlessly divided up, and China itself seemed, in the aftermath of the Boxer Rebellion, to be about to share the same fate.

Moreover, the 'liberation' of Latin America was more apparent than real. 'Independence,' said Simon Bolivar, most famous of the liberators of that continent from the shackles of colonialism, 'is the sole benefit we have gained, at the sacrifice of all others.' But a recent writer comments:

> 'Yet many would have questioned even that judgement. Independence, in fact, meant little to the masses, since its main effect was the replacement of Spaniards by creoles in the seats of power, and this political change was unaccompanied by social and economic alteration within the states themselves.'[11]

The same author adds:

> 'Much more than those parts of Asia and Africa which were also colonial possessions of European powers, Latin America is an offshoot of Western civilization. First, the colonial empires in the other continents were of much shorter duration, in parts of Africa no longer than a man's lifetime. Secondly, though there are exceptions, Europeans went to Asia and Africa as traders, missionaries, soldiers and administrators rather than as colonizers, which they did from the earliest days in America. Hence, while in Asia and Africa political independence reflected the desire of native races to throw off foreign, white rule, in America it arose from the settlers' wish to direct their own affairs, rather than have them dictated by Madrid and Lisbon. Again, in Asia and Africa local people preserved much

of their traditional culture, religion, and government; in Latin America, where the natives were less numerous, the military and cultural shock of European conquest was far more sweeping. Finally, whereas in Asia and Africa the whites remained a race apart, in Latin America racial fusion between victor and vanquished began early and continued.'[12]

As the power of the United States of America progressively increased to the north, what freedom of manoeuvre the little states in the south did enjoy was progressively eroded and circumscribed; by 1914, Latin America had been effectively transformed into a new kind of colony, 'protected' and exploited by the military might and dollar imperialism of the USA. The relationships evolved provide an early model of post- or neo-colonialism, about which we will have much to say at a later stage. Finally, decolonised America herself became, as we have seen, a full-blown colonial power; her government made itself felt in the Philippines, Puerto Rico, Hawaii, Cuba, Panama and the Dominican Republic in the closing years of the nineteenth century and the opening years of the twentieth.

In all this, how are we to detect the high-water mark of imperialism? In fact, the writing was on the wall, or rather in the sands. The British 'forward movement' in Malaya, which had carried her proconsuls confidently into Perak, Selangor, Negri Sembilan and Pahang by 1874, and into Kedah, Perlis, Kelantan and Trengganu by 1909, stopped short of annexing the southern Malay-speaking states of Thailand. Notes a distinguished historian of Malaya:

'. . . there the matter ended, leaving Malaya with an unmarked, unsurveyed and rambling frontier, impossible to defend and difficult even to locate. . . . A wavering of British determination which might pass almost unnoticed in Paris or Berlin was instantly sensed in Shanghai and Hongkong.'[13]

Furthermore, the Chinese noted that the British did not even bother to fortify their last deliberate acquisition in China—WeihaiWei, at the tip of the Shantung Peninsula.[14]

More sensational by far were the resounding defeats meted out to Russia by Japan in their 1904–5 war. The repercussions of this victory by an Asian power over a white Western power that had been encroaching remorselessly upon Asia for centuries are incalculable. The Japanese fleet at one jump became a major consideration in the Pacific power equation. Britain, meanwhile, concerned at the growth of German naval power in the European theatre, and unable to meet threats on two fronts, had signed an agreement with Japan in 1902, and in 1905 more or less left the Pacific to her by withdrawing the British Far Eastern Fleet. It was never to return. The implications for European colonialism were ominous.

Asian nationalism responded to Japan's achievements with a dramatic surge of activity. In Indonesia, the first mass organization of the modern nationalist movement, *Sarekat Islam*, was founded in 1912 on a country-wide basis, following the proliferation of smaller nationalist bodies after 1905. In India, the crucial years in the first decade of the twentieth century saw a highly significant shift in the nature and scale of nationalist activity. A revealing episode was the campaign against the partition of Bengal (1905–11). 'The movement in Bengal,' writes an historian of India,

'. . . looked not to the ancient heroes but to local patriotism, to the myth of a wealthy and flourishing Bengal despoiled by foreigners. The opportunity came with the partition of 1905. Basically, the partition was a reasonable administrative measure. Calcutta, the capital of Bengal, was also (until 1912) the imperial capital, and this concentration of power in Bengal did not lend itself to efficient organization. It was proposed that a new province of Eastern Bengal, with its capital at Dacca, should be created. Logically, this proposition was supported by the existing religious division of Bengal, for west Bengal was predominantly Hindu, and the east Muslim. But partition struck at the belief in the Bengali "nation". The nationalists were thus supplied with a ready-made target, for on no occasion were the people most involved in the consequences of partition ever consulted by the government. For the first time, the nationalists had a single, specific issue over which to fight, rather than vague general beliefs in "freedom" and "rights". If partition could be reversed by agitation, a real victory would be achieved, and—on a much smaller scale—Russia's defeat by Japan would be paralleled upon Indian soil. Furthermore, partition supplied a rallying point for both moderates and extremists. . . . Two new weapons were to be used in the campaign, terrorism, and the economic boycott. The boycott began in August 1904. It was widely supported, especially by Indian mill-owners, and the wearing of homespun cloth became one of the manifestations of the struggle for freedom. Secret societies were formed amongst students; bomb-throwers and political assassins became popular heroes. . . . Terrorist activity was not confined to India and, in 1909, Sir Curzon Wyllie was murdered by a Punjabi at the Imperial Institute in London. This outrage at least brought home to the British public the existence of a nationalist movement in India. The partition of Bengal was revoked in 1911. . . .'[15]

But by and large the nationalist movements of Asia were still narrowly based in class terms at this time. In India, for example, at the time of the First World War it was

'. . . an urban middle-class movement dominated by English-speaking lawyers, journalists, and merchants who were concerned only with political objectives for the nation and had little appreciation of the economic miseries of the masses. Its politically ambitious members were more familiar with the struggle for democracy in England than with conditions in their own country.'[16]

Sarekat Islam in Indonesia had developed from an earlier association of Islamic businessmen and merchants. The alliance of elites and peasantry in pursuit of political independence had yet to be forged.

There then burst upon the world the 'European civil war'—known in the West as the First World War (1914–18). Its considerable impact upon Asian nationalism takes us into the next phase of the liberation struggle of the colonial peoples.

REFERENCES

1. L. Szekely: *Tropic Fever*, London, 1936, pp. 102–3.
2. Ibid, p. 158.
3. Mariano D. Manawis in the *Philippine Magazine*, January, 1934.

4. R. Segal: *The Race War*, London, 1966, p. 127.

5. W. F. Wertheim: *Indonesian Society in Transition*, The Hague, 1956, p. 41.

6. L. Wolf: *Little Brown Brother*, New York, 1960, p. 25.

7. D. Wurfel: 'The Philippines' in G. McT. Kahin [ed.]: *Governments and Politics of Southeast Asia*, Ithaca, 1964, pp. 685–6.

8. W. J. Pomeroy: *Guerrilla and Counter-guerrilla Warfare*, New York, 1964, p. 32.

9. Jawaharlal Nehru: *The Discovery of India*, New York, 1946, p. 324.

10. P. Spear: *A History of India, Vol. 2*, London, 1965, p. 143. Author's italics.

11. H. Blakemore: *Latin America*, Oxford, 1966, pp. 54–5.

12. Ibid., p. 7.

13. C. N. Parkinson: *East and West*, London, 1963, p. 233.

14. Ibid., p. 234.

15. M. Edwardes: *Asia in the European Age*, London, 1961, pp. 199–200.

16. C. A. Buss: *Asia in the Modern World*, London, 1964, p. 329.

CHAPTER FIVE
Nationalism

THE European civil war affected Asian nationalism in a variety of ways. It was not an edifying spectacle. The carnage was on a scale without parallel in human history, and deeply shocked those Asian intellectuals who had come, reluctantly or otherwise, to admire Western values and Western achievements (and perhaps even to concede some of the claims of the West to have a unique world role). At a different level, several of the imperialist powers sent levies from their colonies to fight in Europe and Western Asia (our 'Middle East'). These soldiers had an opportunity to see, even through the distorting perspective of war, just how much better the ordinary people of the free world lived compared with their counterparts in the colonies. As an agent of change the returning soldier was to play an important part in inter-war Asian affairs. Moreover, objective circumstances—inflation, poor harvests, the 1918 influenza epidemic and its aftermath—afforded a fertile seed-bed for general colonial discontent and radicalism.

The war had also, of course, profound implications for the future of Western Europe in the third world. At first sight, Britain and the victors had little about which to be apprehensive. Germany, the arch-rival in the colonial world, had been defeated, and America, potentially a serious alternative rival, retreated step by step into isolation. However, the reality was quite otherwise. Japan had used the cover of Western preoccupation with the European theatre insidiously to strengthen her position in the Pacific, and, by her threats and actions against China, had served serious notice of her future intentions. In addition, the Soviet Union had emerged as a result of the 1917 October Revolution as an anti-capitalist and anti-imperialist power dedicated to helping the struggles of the colonial peoples for independence. On the

other side of the power equation, the Western colonial powers
had suffered a grievous blow, however delayed the impact. A
whole generation of young men had been reduced by the slaughter
to pitiful proportions, fatally weakening the ranks from which
might be recruited the district officers and other necessary
cadres of colonialism. The damage, moreover, was not simply
in terms of death and injury; psychologically irreparable harm
had been done to the imperial idea. Plumed helmets had lost
their glamour beyond recall. The process of declining self-confidence, begun for Britain by the humiliating Boer War perhaps,
had been greatly accelerated.

The capacity for regeneration in societies must not be under-
estimated and two untroubled generations might well have seen
the ranks filled by fresh-faced and eager young recruits inspired,
as their great-grandfathers had been, by the white man's 'civiliz-
ing' mission. But there was to be no second chance and no respite
for the West. Once the immediate post-war problems had been
surmounted, a boom in trade and production promised to carry
prosperity in the northern hemisphere to dizzy new heights. But
the bubble grew, rose and glistened only to deceive. World
primary product prices began to decline after 1925, but for a
while continuing growth in the volume of exports tended to mask
this. Meanwhile, the manufacturing countries, both victors and
vanquished, were getting into all kinds of contortions and difficulties in the futile attempt to return to something like the pre-
1914 pattern of economic relations. Ominous signs of the
Nemesis to come were there for all who had eyes to see in the
shape of the German inflation, the British deflation and consequent bitter labour disputes, and the whole ludicrous reparations
muddle. Then, after a series of warning palpitations, the great
heart of the international capitalist economy—Wall Street—
seized up in 1929, and the whole system was accordingly pros-
trated from one extremity to the other.

Whole shelves of books have been devoted to the impact on
the countries of the West of the inter-war depression which
followed. Less publicized have been the consequences for Asia,
Africa and Latin America. Yet these were extremely serious.
Colonialism and economic imperialism engendered mono- or
oligo-culture, so that whole societies revolved round the prices
available on world markets for their staples. These world markets,

often physically sited in the Western world, were more sensitive to the expectations of the 'experts' than to the real tastes and needs of consumers, for the 'experts' could back their judgement with money, while all too often the consumers were deprived of the incomes to back up their demand by the decisions of other 'expert' businessmen not to invest, anticipated profits lacking sufficient attraction. In 1930, coffee accounted for three-quarters of the value of Brazil's exports, so that when unemployed men in Europe and North America cut down their purchases of coffee, the growers in Brazil were struck a blow which rocked the entire economy. The pattern of dependence on one or two chief primary commodities left the colonial and semi-colonial economies dangerously exposed, and few were in a position to avail themselves of effective protective clothing. The National Income of the UK, unemployment and depression notwithstanding, *rose* from £3,957 million in 1930 to £5,037 million in 1939, and per capita from £86 4s. to £105 8s. This was because Britain, like other independent developed countries, was able to defend herself against the chill winds of international stagnation by reverting to protection and semi-autarchy. Contrast this with the plight of the then Netherlands East Indies (now Indonesia). There, National Income as a whole *fell* from 3,478 million florins in 1930 to 2,022 million florins in 1939—at a time when the Indonesian population was rising from 61 million to 71 million; per capita income was accordingly roughly halved. 'Few countries,' comments an economist, 'suffered a more violent contraction of economic activity in the thirties than the Netherlands Indies.'[1] Nevertheless, the colonial world as a whole suffered as well.

The responses of the colonial authorities were less than adequate. The unemployed labourers suddenly released by the closing plantations and mines were thrown back virtually upon their own resources. Where they could, they returned to their native villages to add to the number of mouths dependent upon a given area of cultivated soil. Immigrants, having answered the lure of the boom times, were in a desperate plight. Many of the Indians and Chinese who had flocked to Malaya were simply repatriated. Those who had in the meantime contracted local attachments or responsibilities were left to their own resources. There was no redundancy pay, no unemployment benefit, and no attempt to provide work and income by carrying out needed public works. 'Many estates,' we are told,

'on instructions from agents or directors discharged their coolies to reduce expenses and later on were told to increase their force and resume tapping. These coolies being out of work for long spells wandered about ill-fed and like helpless children sleeping anywhere on road sides with the result that they became malarious and anaemic and when re-employed had to go to hospital to be re-conditioned. It was most expensive and disastrous economy for an industry employing labour of so dependent a type, encumbered as Tamils are by wives and children.'[2]

Far from taking measures to soften the impact of the depression on their colonial subjects, the imperialist powers actually used their political sovereignty to try to wrest advantage from the fortuitous dislocation. The various commodity control schemes, ostensibly designed to support prices by reducing output, in practice also discriminated harshly against the small producers in favour of the big enterprises in which important quantities of European capital were sunk. One planter gave the game away when he wrote unabashedly:

'Is it not time the governments concerned faced the situation and *prohibited* [sic] the cultivation of rubber by smallholdings? Briefly my argument is to eliminate the smallholder by legislation and then introduce a generally accepted restriction scheme. Only by this means can the rubber be protected and assisted to better times. The alternative is the survival of the fittest, who in the long run is sure to be the native smallholder.'[3]

Economic forces, then, were to be allowed to operate when they filled the coffers of the white man, but when they failed to do so, the white man insisted on invoking his political power in defence of his profits and privileges.

Faced with deteriorating circumstances, the mass of the people in Asia lent a ready ear to nationalist spokesmen. Capitalism had always been condemned by them as selfish, grasping, individualistic and contrary to Asian traditions and values. Now the interwar breakdown exposed it to the charge that it was also inefficient, wasteful, capricious and even unworkable. The gross injustices of the International Rubber Regulation Scheme were a frequent topic in the *Volksraad* (People's Council) in Indonesia, but unfortunately for the nationalists the Dutch never allowed this talking shop to assume any real measure of power or responsibility. It was outside the *Volksraad* that the nationalists pushed ahead with their propaganda and recruitment. Identifying the evils of colonialism with capitalism, nationalists adopted readily the vocabulary of socialism—and in particular of Marxism, the body of socialist ideas possessed of greatest scope and coherence:

> '. . . almost every significant organ of political expression in Indonesia—from the origin of its modern nationalist movement in the early years of this century—has been or has claimed to be socialist.'[4]

Despite this broad agreement in outlook, the Indonesian nationalists did not succeed in creating anything remotely resembling Congress in India. Indeed, political parties came, splintered, coalesced and disappeared with bewildering speed. From its foundation in 1920 until its temporary eclipse in 1927 the Communist Party of Indonesia (PKI) made the running. In 1927 leading Indonesian nationalists, including Sukarno, founded the Nationalist Party (PNI), in the hope of creating a united movement. In this they were unsuccessful, but the name and the initials survived as important political symbols, to be resurrected in the post-war period.

The PKI's downfall in 1926–7 was a result of staging an underprepared and premature revolt. The subsequent Dutch suppression inhibited not only the spread of communism in the Indies but also in effect mass political activity as such:

> 'The Communist debacle seemed to have finished popular hope that anything was to be achieved by political action, revolutionary or otherwise; and the Indonesian masses retired from the stage, not to return until Japan's victory over the Dutch proved once and for all that the white ruler was not invincible . . . the organizations founded by the new generation were restricted to the *élite*. Not only was the general population apathetic to political proselytising, but the government no longer allowed its opponents any benefit of doubt.'[5]

Elsewhere in South East Asia, the development of nationalist sentiment and organization proceeded at an uneven pace. In Burma, as in Indonesia, nearly all sections of the movement were socialist in tone. In both countries, such business as was not in the hands of the colonialists themselves was generally monopolized by alien entrepreneurs—in the one case by Chinese (Indonesia), and in the other by Indians. It was therefore possible even for would-be indigenous businessmen to be anti-capitalist: to be against, that is, 'sinful' (foreign or big) capitalism. The educated Burmese *élite* for their part bitterly resented the dominance of Indians in the professions, while the peasantry smarted under the loss of their lands to Indian moneylenders and the destruction of their traditional ways of life. Britain, it is true, had steered the country by a succession of careful steps to virtual internal home-rule by 1937—retaining the all-important control over finance, however—but the flimsy bandage of Western political institutions could not conceal the gaping wounds and scars on the body politic.

For different reasons, the nationalist movements of Malaya and the Philippines developed in quite another direction. In both countries there were opportunities for the indigenous *élite* to collaborate with the colonial authorities in capacities affording material rewards and prestige enough to encourage conservative attitudes. Malay aristocrat, Chinese big businessman, Filipino *compradore* or landlord or politician, all had cause to view colonial administration in a light quite different from that which struck the Malay peasant or Chinese proletarian or Filipino *barrio* dweller. But while in Malaya there had been little need for the British to move in the direction of self-government so small was the demand for it among the *élite*, in the Philippines the Americans had, as early as March, 1934, provided for independence after a transitional period of ten years during which the Filipinos were to be virtually self-governing. Influential in precipitating this decision were those agricultural interests in America whose livelihoods had been impaired by the depression, and who wished to restrict the entry of competing Filipino produce.

Not that the Philippines were without symptoms of deep social unrest. Indeed, even conservative Malaya could produce evidence of stirrings of revolutionary feeling; the Malayan Communist Party was formed in 1930, and in 1937 Chinese estate workers embarked upon a widespread series of strikes in the Federated Malay States (i.e. Perak, Selangor, Negri Sembilan and Pahang). In the Philippines, the traditions of the Revolution had not been wholly lost. Between the wars a number of peasant risings took place—for example, the Bucas Grande revolt in the Southern Visayas (1924), the revolt led by Florencio Intrencherado (1924–27), and the Sakdal revolt in Luzon (1935). Where the *élite* and the people were not united in common hostility to the colonial power, the peasants' and workers' movements could see more clearly how their interests diverged from those of the collaborating indigenous landlords, business groups and bureaucrats.

In Vietnam, then part of French Indo-China, the impact of the depression stirred this irascible and irreconcilable people to revolt. The year 1930 was marked by nationalist up-risings, led first by the Kuomintang-like Viet Nam Quoc Dan Dang (VNQDD—Vietnamese Nationalist Party), and later by the newly-formed Indochinese Communist Party (ICP), a body engineered by Nguyen Tat Thanh, alias Nguyen Ai Quoc (Nguyen the Patriot), better known today as Ho Chi Minh. (It is interesting that armed Vietnamese resistance to the French *officially* ceased in 1916, in the books of the colonial authority; but in fact French pacification of their colony was never complete —in 1917, for example, occurred the Thai Nguyen uprising, and sporadic clashes continued throughout the period—a fact which illuminates the present struggle against US occupation.) The French response to this upsurge of nationalism was to institute a reign of terror, imprisoning, exiling and executing without regard to whether the suspect was moderate or extreme in his political opinions. The ICP suffered with the rest, but showed better judgment and greater tenacity; by the end of the thirties, it had

'. . . come to dominate the revolutionary scene in Vietnam and had laid the foundation for its subsequent claims to historic leadership of the Vietnamese nationalist movement.'[6]

Meanwhile, to east and to west of South East Asia events were moving inexorably towards dramatic denouement. China's martyrdom continued, but leaders were emerging with definite and firm ideas for the regeneration of their society. In 1921, the

Chinese Communist Party was formed. Among its founders were
Mao Tse-tung, then a library assistant at Peking National
University, and Chou En-lai, at that time studying in Paris.
Such men might feel that they understood what was required in
order to unify and modernise China, but they had to move as a
minority in a maelstrom of clashing social and international
forces. Foreign interference in China's affairs was still all too
palpable, and there were always cynical and corrupt warlords
prepared to further foreign ends for a price. Something was
needed to rally a demoralized people, who could see for themselves
that the Revolution had brought China little if any benefit as yet.

Then on the 30th of May, 1925, students demonstrating in
Shanghai against the foreign-controlled police of the International Settlement were fired upon and a number were killed.
The incident swept China from end to end. It epitomized the
overweening presumption of the foreign imperialist.

'The Nationalist policy of "recovery of sovereign rights"
received an immense impetus and mass support. For the first
time since the revolution the whole body of the Chinese people
was stirred and roused. It remained for revolutionary leadership to give this great force its own goal.'[7]

The immediate result was the start of a campaign, which
developed irresistible momentum as it progressed northwards,
against warlords and others who stood in the way of national
unity and the national army. Because the communists were part
of the nationalist armies at this time, their progress was also
marked by the fomenting of peasant unrest against their landlords. But the primary urge was anti-foreigner, and there were a
number of incidents which seriously alarmed the Western
powers, fearful for the lives of their nationals resident in China
and for their factories and other investments there. Moreover,
the social forces released by Chiang Kai-shek's successful
northern expedition threatened to run away with those who
wished to keep them on some kind of rein. The workers in
Shanghai seized control of the Chinese part of the city in February 1927 under Communist leadership, an act alarming not only
to the foreigners in the International Settlement, but also to the
Chinese merchants, bankers, landlords and others with much to
lose if social revolution overtook them.

It was at this point that Chiang Kai-shek struck back. Although the communists had been among the most dedicated fighters in the nationalist armies, Chiang decided that he dare not risk any further co-operation with them, a co-operation which, by and large, benefited them, in the form of growing support in the rural areas, more than it did himself. In March, 1927, he moved on Shanghai, crushing the workers and slaughtering many of the leading figures of the Communist Party. At first all went well for Chiang, and it looked as if the right-wing nationalists whom he represented would be able to continue the process of unification of China without the two-edged support of the communists. However, in practice he had cut himself off from the really dynamic forces in Chinese society, and his suppression of workers' and peasants' movements confirmed that his power would have to rest on the support of landlord and business groups already compromised, and on the toleration of the leading Western powers, in particular the rising Pacific power of the United States of America. The Americans stepped up their supplies of war equipment to Chiang, detailed military advisers to help him, and generally underwrote his anti-communist activities financially and otherwise. The communists, for their part, took to the countryside, and there began the process of developing a guerrilla struggle which was to culminate in their sensational victories of the years 1948 and 1949. Mao Tse-tung and his lieutenants' experiences in the intervening years were to produce a classic corpus of writings on national liberation and people's war. Meanwhile, the Russian advisers, who had consistently pressed the Chinese communists to work with the Kuomintang and to await inevitable favourable changes—most importantly the growth of an industrial proletariat under bourgeois rule—retired, discredited, from the scene.

How was it that Mao's Red Army was able to maintain its existence and even progressively extend its influence in the rural areas? The first reason was an understanding of the crucial importance of retaining peasant support. Traditionally, armies had alienated the rural people by stealing or impounding food, by pressing young men into service, and by abusing the wives and daughters of hapless farmers. The Red Army changed all that by scrupulously observing certain rules of conduct, such as paying for food, and by identifying closely with the peasant, explaining carefully how his poverty was related to landlordism and imperialism and how the Communist Party planned to change society. The second reason was the natural advantage enjoyed by the guerrilla as against a regular army. This natural advantage arises from flexibility, mobility and the ability to merge if need be with the civilian population of the battle area. The third reason was that Chiang Kai-shek's policies failed in their objective of truly unifying the nation, and the continual splits in the ranks of the right-wing nationalists impaired their capacity to co-operate effectively. Nevertheless, by sending bigger and bigger armies, advised by foreign military personnel against the original Red Army strongholds in Hunan and Kiangsi Provinces, Chiang eventually forced it into undertaking—from October 1934 to October 1935—the famous 6000 mile 'Long March' into northern Shensi, where other sympathetic and allied red elements also converged from various parts of China to create a secure base area. But by this time, the most pressing political problem was the Japanese encroachment upon Chinese territory, and the communists launched an appeal to 'Stop the civil war; unite to resist Japan', an appeal aimed at the formation of a united front with the Kuomintang in the interests of halting Japanese invasion.

Meanwhile, the nationalist movement in India was experiencing a rather different fate. While Mao was materializing as leader of the Chinese people with his dictum that 'politics emerges from the barrel of a gun', and his successful putting of the dictum into practice, India produced Mahatma Gandhi and his doctrine of non-violent struggle or *Ahimsa*. Like Mao however, Gandhi succeeded in bridging the city-rural gap and in basing his movement squarely on the peasant masses who made up such an overwhelming majority of the population. As we have seen, a nationalist movement in its early years typically embraces only the educated *élite*, mainly urban-living and often Western-orientated. It requires an unusual personality, or an unusually favourable set of circumstances, or sometimes both together, to forge a workable unity in the struggle for liberation.

For India, the inter-war period started inauspiciously as far as future Indo-British relations were concerned. Rioting occurred in the early months of 1919 in several areas, and anti-foreigner racial feeling was present. Then there took place one of the classical colonial incidents, the name of which has since become a by-word and symbol—the Amritsar massacre.

'Amritsar, a city of some 300,000 inhabitants, and the chief religious centre of the Sikhs, stands about 250 miles north-west of Delhi. There, on 10 April, two nationalist leaders were arrested and deported. A large crowd attempted to enter the European cantonment and, on being turned back, began rioting in the city. Two banks were attacked, the railway station set on fire, four Europeans were murdered and others attacked, including a woman missionary who was left for dead. The military, under General Dyer, restored order and all public meetings and assemblies were declared illegal. On 13 April, a meeting gathered in a large enclosed space known as the Jallianwalla Bagh. On hearing of this, General Dyer went personally to the spot with ninety Gurkha and Baluchi soldiers and two armoured cars, with which he blocked the only exit. Then, without warning, he ordered his men to open fire on the densely packed crowd and, on his own admission, fired 1605 rounds before he withdrew, leaving the armoured cars to prevent anyone from leaving or entering the Bagh. Official figures of dead and wounded were given as 379 and 1,200 respectively. Dyer's action was approved by the provincial government. The following day, a mob rioting and burning at another spot was bombed and machine-gunned from aircraft. On 15 April, martial law was declared and not lifted until 9 June. During this period, Indians were forced to walk on all fours past the spot where the woman missionary had been attacked and, according to the report of the Hunter Commission, which enquired into the disturbances, public floggings were given for such minor offences as "the contravention of the curfew order, failure to salaam to a commissioned officer, for disrespect to a European, for taking a commandeered car without leave, or refusal to sell milk, and for similar contraventions." '[8]

Naked suppression of this kind marched uneasily with the phased programme of advancement towards Indian home rule within the British Empire. The Government of India Act of 1919 instituted a system of dyarchy in the provinces, whereby certain provincial portfolios were transferred to Indians, whilst the chief powers remained with the governor. This organization prevailed until 1935, when a further act extended the franchise, increased the Indians' share of responsible government both centrally and at provincial level, and sought—unsuccessfully as it happened—to create a federal India. But the nationalist movement, throughout the period dominated as before by Congress, eyed both the rate of progress towards independence and the real content of the 'self-rule' offered with suspicion. Indeed, despite the objective advance that was apparently being accomplished constitutionally, the nationalist movement made rapid progress among all classes, especially in the early twenties.

But although Gandhi's campaigns were an inspiration to the common people, who responded readily to such symbolic gestures as his sixty mile walk to the sea at Dandi to make illicit salt or such Hindu holy traditions as fasting, the path to effective national *unity* was not an easy one. After cooperation occasioned by the *Khilafat* movement, and by Gandhi's insistence on Muslim-Hindu unity, relations between the two religions began to deteriorate, and when Mr. Jinnah took over leadership of a revived Muslim League, more and more was heard of a separate Muslim state. Again, Gandhi's economic ideas, based on village industry, clearly clashed with the interests of the Indian manufacturing bourgeoisie, whose ability to compete with British capital was enhanced after the inter-war depression, and whose appetite was thereby whetted for political independence which would afford them an opportunity to further attack the hold Britain had on the Indian economy. Younger nationalist leaders, led by Jawaharlal Nehru, although devoted to Gandhi, saw that a modern prosperous India necessarily called for comprehensive economic planning of a socialist kind. As Indian industry developed, a further element in the nationalist struggle was added—labour organized in the trade unions. Although Marxist influences were present among intellectuals and in the labour movement, communism made little impact nationally at this time. There were, too, from time to time peasant disturbances and risings, but the whole weight of Gandhism was consistently tipped in favour of non-violence, and there was no dedicated armed force in India, such as the Red Army in China, to move among the peasantry, encouraging their defiance of feudalism and imperialism and affording them some prospect of protection from retaliation.

Gandhi's dominance ensured the dominance of Congress. Tactics veered from non-co-operation to seeking elective office. He was always astute enough to isolate and frustrate any group inside Congress which threatened to tip it too sharply in one direction and therefore upset the balance. It looked as if real progress was at last in the offing when, between 1937 and 1939, Congress ministries or coalition ministries in which Congress dominated were installed in eight of the eleven provinces, following elections. But here, as elsewhere in Asia, the second world war suddenly and dramatically intervened diverting the course of history precipitately into new channels.

The reasons that drove the Japanese into their ill-fated Asian adventure need no lengthy elaboration here. It ought to be pointed out, however, that disastrous as the consequences were in practice, Japan's leaders had reasons for being attracted to imperialism in Asia. They over-estimated the prospects of German victory in Europe, under-estimated the prospects of American intervention in the shape of all-out commitment to the unconditional defeat and surrender of the Axis powers, and in consequence made far too light of the problems involved in actually extracting the wealth of Asia to feed industry in Japan. The great Western 'forward movement', which had extended empire so widely in the last quarter of the nineteenth and the first quarter of the twentieth centuries, had been a comparatively unimpeded process. The Japanese, having attained something like a comparable phase of economic development in the inter-war period, saw that the need for markets, investment outlets, and raw materials which had inspired Western expansion was now an objective need for their own economy. The First World War had afforded Japan an opportunity of undertaking exploratory territorial expansions in Asia—for example in China—and in addition had allowed her export industries to bite into traditionally Western markets throughout Asia. The inter-war depression drove all the white colonial powers into autarchic protectionist policies in their overseas possessions, thus threatening Japan's rapidly growing and increasingly important international trade. Two other factors weighed in the calculation of whether to undertake an imperialistic adventure. Firstly, the self-confidence of at least the European colonial powers was visibly waning—something it was possible to detect not only in their appeasement policies towards the European fascists but also in their art, literature, politics and culture generally. Secondly, aside from the terrible struggle which developed in China after the outbreak of full-scale hostilities in 1937, Japan's previous imperial adventures (such as the take-over of Manchuria in 1931) had not been expensive affairs either in terms of money or of men, and, moreover, as it happened, large military expenditures were an appropriate Keynesian response to the threat of involvement in the general international Depression.

The early part of the Pacific war, in 1941 and 1942, seemed to vindicate the Japanese 'hawks'. China admittedly remained intractable and an expensive commitment, but, by-passing it, Japan's armies cut remarkably quickly through South-East Asia, encountering unexpectedly feeble resistance, and only grinding to a halt almost within sight of India herself. Far from the Western Allies crumbling under such a series of reversals, however, and suing for a negotiated peace, counter-attack was soon under way, and the long-term prospects for Japan's vaunted 'Greater East Asia Co-Prosperity Sphere' progressively deteriorated. Total surrender followed the dropping of the world's first two atom bombs on Hiroshima and Nagasaki in 1945, after a campaign on a number of fronts characterized by bitter fighting.

But although the Japanese 'empire' in Asia was shortlived indeed, its consequences for the development of Asian nationalism, and for the future of the region politically, were incalculable. Coming at a critical juncture in the development of national consciousness, Japanese intervention greatly accelerated certain tendencies and in general irretrievably shook up the pre-existing pattern. With the arrival of Japanese power, we reach the period when the movements for political independence in Asia matured.

REFERENCES

1. B. Higgins: *Indonesia: The Crisis of the Millstones*, New York, 1963, p. 64.
2. J. N. Parmer: *Colonial Labour Policy and Administration*, New York, 1960, p. 230, citing a Malacca Agricultural Medical Board Report.

3. *India Rubber World*, September, 1930.
4. Jeanne S. Mintz: *Mohammed, Marx and Marhaen*, London, 1965, p. 6.
5. Ruth T. McVey: *The Rise of Indonesian Communism*, New York, 1965, p. 354.
6. R. Jumper and Marjorie W. Normand: 'Vietnam' in G. McT. Kahin (ed.): *Governments and Politics of Southeast Asia*, New York, 1964, p. 390.
7. C. P. Fitzgerald: *The Birth of Communist China*, London, 1964 p. 62.

CHAPTER SIX

War and Revolution

THIS chapter begins with Japanese fascism rampant and apparently at China's wind-pipe, and ends with the triumphant conclusion twelve years later in that same China of the first fulfilled national liberation struggle in the exploited and downtrodden Afro-Asian-Latin American world. General war between China and Japan broke out in July 1937, although there had been many incidents and Japanese transgressions in the previous four decades. Mao's skilful tactics in launching his patriotic slogan had persuaded many non-communist nationalists that Chiang was more anxious to attack the communists than to halt the Japanese, and it was they who eventually put pressure on the Kuomintang leader to enter (reluctantly on his part) into a common front with the Red Army against the invader. From that point until 1945 and the defeat of the Japanese by the allied armies the KMT and the communists co-existed in uneasy harness, each seeking to wrest advantage from the other while extracting the maximum of prestige from engagements with the common enemy. The nationalists tried to prevent allied aid and equipment reaching the red armies; Mao and his lieutenants constantly sought to build up their strength among the peasants and to extend the area which they effectively controlled and administered. The nationalist leaders grew wealthy and corrupt on the scarcities inevitably associated with war and semi-siege with few supply routes; the communist leaders, in contrast, continued their education in privation and dedication in preparation for the anticipated post-war struggles. The peasants and workers, themselves hungry and hard-pressed, could draw their own conclusions; and in their midst moved devoted communists carefully explaining and educating. The KMT generals treated their peasant conscripts with contempt and callousness; the Red Army leaders lived with and like their own men. In this way, the seeds were being sown for the crucial post-war years.

But during the time of the actual Pacific war (1941–45), the Chinese theatre was relegated to the wings, the parties to a large extent bogged down in situations that only fluctuated within certain narrow limits. The telling changes in fortune were registered elsewhere in Asia. The Americans' island-hopping campaigns and the British struggle in Burma do not directly concern us here, but it is imperative to look round the individual countries of South and South-East Asia and to assess the impact of Japanese control of a large part of the region.

'The Japanese period was important for a variety of reasons. First of all, the speed and decisiveness with which the Japanese forces defeated and humiliated the European armies made an indelible impression on the peoples of the region. The myth of white supremacy had been dealt a death blow, and it would never again be possible for a handful of white troops and administrators to hold down millions of Asian subjects. The Japanese rammed home the point by publicly exposing European prisoners to the most menial of tasks. Second, the Japanese presence gave the nationalists training and experience in the use of arms. This was partly by intention, as with the Indonesian-manned and officered auxiliary armies of Java, Sumatra and Bali, and the Burmese Independence Army. But it was also a result of the resistance movements that grew up throughout South-East Asia as the initial goodwill or at least neutrality towards the Japanese gave way to disillusion and hatred. Naturally, it was allied policy to help these resistance movements . . . and this was an extremely useful source of arms. . . . A third important result of Japanese occupation was the precipitous promotion of layers of South-East Asian administrators, who had, under the colonialists, been restricted to the lower echelons of the service. This was important training for the tasks that lay ahead. . . . A fourth factor was the encouragement, direct and indirect again, given to the development of local nationalism. . . . Finally, the Japanese afforded the South-East Asian Communists an opportunity which they grasped to some effect.'[1]

Resistance to the Japanese was fiercest, and arose with the greatest spontaneity, in the Philippines. The Commonwealth of the Philippines had been inaugurated in 1935, with Quezon as President and Osmena as Vice-President. Proximity to the increasingly militaristic and expansionist Japanese had aroused apprehension in the Philippines, and the Americans had done nothing to allay this; indeed they had in the vicinity quite inadequate armed forces, and yet resisted Filipino pressure to train, arm and supply a strong indigenous army. The reason was not far to seek. Peasant and worker organization had proceeded apace in the thirties. Prices had risen more rapidly than wages, and the resulting poverty and distress contrasted strongly with the wealth of the landlords and urban middle-classes, including the politicians. Moreover, many of the trade unions were modelled on the worst American pattern, with officials more concerned with personal gain and advancement than with the welfare of their members. In these circumstances, it was not hard for genuine socialists like Pedro Abad Santos and Luis Taruc to rouse the people in the rural areas and in the city slums. There were, as we have seen, strong traditions of insurrection in the Philippines, and the rise of such revolutionary bodies as the League of Poor Labourers (*Aguman ding Maldang Talapagobra*— AMT) and the National Peasants Union (*Kapisang Pambansa ng Magbubukid sa Pilipino*—KPMP) was an alarming symptom for both the Filipino *élite* and their American backers. In 1938, the Communist Party of the Philippines was founded by a merger of socialists and communists.

When war finally broke out, both Americans and Filipinos fought heroically before they were overwhelmed, but resistance continued in the form of guerrilla warfare.

'Because of this spirit of resistance, manifested by more acts of sabotage and open defiance than anywhere else in South-East Asia, the Japanese reserved some of their cruellest atrocities for the Filipinos. Nevertheless, it can be said that there was less disruption of the social structure and of the composition of the political *élite* as a result of Japanese occupation than in any other country of the region except Thailand. There was a substantial proportion of the *élite* which collaborated with the Japanese . . . a large percentage of the officials of the Commonwealth government served also under the Japanese.'[2]

Quezon and Osmena, it is true, fled to the States and there headed a government in exile, but the Japanese had no difficulty in finding puppets to work through. One, a former Associate Justice of the Supreme Court, Jose Laurel, became President of an 'independent Republic' in 1943.

The working class movement, in contrast, spear-headed resistance. Its main vehicle was the *Hukbo ng Bayan Laban sa Hapon*, usually contracted to Hukbalahap or Huk movement. Based as it was securely on the preceding peace-time peasants' and workers' organizations, the Huk movement did not restrict itself to harassing the Japanese. As Mao's red armies had done in China, so the Huks in the Philippines during the war propagandised among the peasantry, and undertook constructive steps to show them how their lives might be transformed. Through the Barrio United Defence Corps (BUDC), set up in liberated areas, the Huks

'. . . brought a hitherto unknown phenomenon into the barrios: democratic government. After centuries of *caciquism* the people were given the opportunity to rule themselves. A BUDC council, in a large barrio, had up to twelve members; smaller barrios had as few as five members. . . . The members included a chairman, a vice-chairman, a secretary-treasurer, and directors of recruiting, intelligence, communications, education, sanitation, agriculture, and a chief of police. . . . All offices in the barrio were elective. . . . In those regions where the pre-war peasant unions had been strong and had accustomed the people to organization and struggle, we had almost complete mass support from the beginning.'[3]

This quotation draws attention to two essential components of successful revolutionary guerrilla fighting, namely the need to construct alternative government in the protected areas, and the prerequisite condition of an already favourably-inclined mass base which has been the subject of previous political agitation and organization. 'The most effective guerrilla movements,' writes one commentator,

'have been founded on prolonged experience of peasant

union and trade union struggles and of previous anti-imperialist nationalist movements. Oriente Province in Cuba, where Castro landed with his nucleus, had for decades been the centre of militant worker and peasant struggles. The Mau-Mau followed in the path of the rural and urban unions around Nairobi and of the nationalist Kenya African Union. In the Philippines, the Huk guerrilla movement's base and its framework were in the earlier Filipino peasant unions. In Malaya, the Malayan Races Liberation Army arose from an outlawed trade union federation. The Viet Minh could not have come into existence and have grown without a long history in Indo-China of trade union, peasant union, student and nationalist organization. This pattern can be traced in every colonial area, and is the meaning of a "mass base" for guerrillas.'[4]

But it wasn't everywhere in the Philippines that peasant unions had flourished in the pre-war period, and the Huks by no means had things their own way. There were several contending forces. The leaders of the 1930's Sakdal peasant movement had looked to the Japanese for arms and support, and during the occupation the successor movement became the core of the Japanese-sponsored terror organization Makapili. On the other hand, the United States Armed Forces of the Far East (USAFFE) supported guerrilla bands which were 'safer' politically than the Huks. It was to these more purely 'resistance' groups, dedicated to restoration of the *status quo ante* and not to social revolution, that US aid flowed. Evidence of the extent of American concern for the post-war situation in the Philippines is to be found in the frequency of clashes between the USAFFE-backed (and often USAFFE-led) guerrillas and the Huks. Indeed on occasion, according to Louis Taruc, leader of the Huks, there was an unlikely alliance:

'A Huk squadron engaged a force of the PC (Philippine Constabulary—Japanese-puppet police), which was suddenly reinforced during the fighting by a group of USAFFE troops! The Huks managed to drive away both groups (capturing 12 arms, including an automatic rifle) but the co-operation between puppet troops and a supposedly anti-Japanese guerrilla unit was cause for concern. This was an entirely new situation which bore within it seeds of a major threat to the people's movement.'[5]

Taruc also charges that USAFFE guerrillas were instructed to safeguard American property, even if the Japanese were making use of it for the time being.

It was not to be anticipated from their history that the Vietnamese people would lie down easily under the Japanese yoke (albeit disguised behind a pretence of French sovereignty until nearly the end of the war). In fact, in the early stages of the war the Indo-Chinese Communist Party took the initiative in convening a meeting of nationalist organizations and individuals at which it was decided to launch the Vietnam Independence League (*Viet Nam Doc Lap Dong Minh Hoi*—Viet Minh). Its aim

'. . . was to organize all patriotic Vietnamese for the seizure of political power when the Franco-Japanese régime collapsed. The closely-knit Communist group were from the first the leaders, inspirers, organizers and pace-setters of the whole Viet Minh movement. One of the leading Communists, Vo Nguyen Giap, was given the task of organizing the military side of the resistance and the revolt; and to prepare himself for this he went off to study the methods of revolutionary warfare perfected by Mao Tse-tung.'[6]

But here, as in the Philippines, there were cross-currents obstructing the straight-forward fight for political independence. General Chiang Kai-shek in China, worried about the formidable and growing strength and influence of his own Communist challengers, attempted to sponsor a rival Vietnamese independence movement of more amenable and acceptable complexion, and imprisoned Ho Chi Minh, the unquestioned leading spokesman for the Vietnamese people. This status later brought his release, and an invitation to join the Chiang-backed 'Provisional Government'. However, it was the Viet Minh which bore the brunt of organizing the people inside Vietnam, and by 1944 General Giap and Ho were there, firmly established in liberated areas, and ready to call on the Viet Minh cadres throughout the land, north and south, to lead the people in asserting their right to independence. The grant of 'independence' to Vietnam by Japan via the puppet Emperor Bao Dai in spring 1945 was something of an irrelevance.

The Japanese were not everywhere received with the same coldness or hostility by the bulk of the population as they were in the Philippines and Vietnam. The Vietnamese, of course, had a long tradition of resistance to foreign occupation. In addition, the communists had a preponderance in the nationalist movement of Vietnam which they did not enjoy elsewhere in South-East Asia. This gave the nationalists a strongly anti-fascist consciousness and orientation. The reasons were slightly different in the Philippines, although here too there was a strong tradition of resistance to alien domination. On top of this, Japan was very much nearer the Philippine islands than any other part of South-East Asia, and awareness of imperialistic Japanese ambitions was accordingly sharper. In the inter-war period, the Japanese had settled in the Philippines and had come to play an important, and locally resented, role in the commercial and business life of the islands.

In contrast, elsewhere in South-East Asia insurrectionary traditions were weaker, and, more important, anti-sinicism complicated the picture. Mostly, it was the overseas Chinese whose control of trade and business was resented by the local people who regarded themselves as the original indigenous inhabitants of the area. When the Japanese invaders arrived, the Chinese communities generally bore the brunt of their victimization, as a corollary of the war which had been raging for some time in China, and the other local people could hardly fail initially to derive a certain amount of satisfaction from witnessing this persecution of their erstwhile economic exploiters. Indeed, there were those in South-East Asia who enthusiastically helped the Japanese to hunt out and harry the Chinese—Sikhs and Malays in Malaya, for example. As the occupation lengthened, however, Japanese brutality tended progressively to alienate all sections of the local populace. [7]

Another relevant factor was that after the Russo-Japanese war, a number of South-East Asian nationalists had been educated in Japan and naturally tended to be pro-Japanese in outlook, anticipating that a Japanese defeat of the European colonial powers would indeed lead to independence. An interesting adjustment to the situation of Japanese occupation was found in Indonesia, where part of the leadership ostensibly collaborated (extracting what advantage they could from the situation for the Indonesian people), while others retreated into the resistance, the two wings keeping communications open by one means or another.

Indonesian nationalism was too strong for the Japanese to ignore. In Malaya matters were otherwise:

'Up to 1942 the forces of tradition in Malaya were rather stronger than in many other Asian countries then under colonial rule. The British régime, unquestioned in its authority and success, had reached a satisfactory accommodation both with the aristocratic leaders of the Malay community and with the still influential Chinese merchant class. The events of the inter-war years had not seriously damaged this understanding. There was no educated middle-class in revolt against these forces. With the important exception of the MCP (Malayan Communist Party) no radical or left-wing group had achieved significant influence with the mass of the people though stresses and strains were beginning to arise from economic and social causes. The preponderance of conservative and traditional forces regulated the pace of change to a walk rather than a run and the influential spokesmen of incipient nationalism were the well-to-do rather than the revolutionaries.

'The significance of the short period of Japanese rule consisted in its being a violent upset of the status quo which altered the balance between conservatism and change. The Malayans were thrown in on themselves, deprived of their familiar protecting power and of their confidence in such protection. They were isolated from the world and obliged to think of their own salvation rather than of the fortunes of distant countries. If they were to manage their own affairs in Malaya in future the Malayan communities must achieve a minimum of accommodation between themselves. It was a novel idea and one which found general acceptance only after a decade (1942–52) of much struggle and bitterness. Yet it was the key which unlocked the door to the making of a new nation.'[8]

The same author adds[9] that it was perhaps most significant of all that at the end of the war, the British referred to the 'liberation' of Malaya, but that the Malayans 'quietly persisted in calling it the "reoccupation" '.

Such armed resistance as there was during the occupation in Malaya came from the Malayan People's Anti-Japanese Army

(MPAJA), an almost wholly Chinese force, which had a certain amount of British army backing and help. Its core was the MCP. It should be noted that the British, like the Americans in the Philippines, were well aware at the time of the dangers of encouraging a pro-communist resistance movement with the post-war period to consider. It was therefore British policy, in developing contacts with the MPAJA, to employ known pro-Chiang Nationalist Chinese; this was not calculated to make Allied-MCP co-operation 100 per cent efficient. Malay left-wingers were permitted by the Japanese to form their own para-military force (PETA); this subsequently developed secret links with the MPAJA.

Across the Straits of Malacca in Indonesia, the impact of Japanese conquest was uneven. It is true that the humiliating collapse of Dutch power was observed everywhere, and was to frustrate post-war attempts to reassert their rule by force of arms. But the Japanese administered the East Indies as three entities. The island of Java was under an Army command which permitted Indonesian nationalism a reasonable degree of latitude; Sumatra was under a separate and less sympathetic Army command; and the eastern islands were subject to the Navy, which in general adopted a repressive policy.

Two of the most prominent Indonesian nationalist leaders, Sukarno and Hatta, released from Dutch captivity by the Japanese, were among the ostensible collaborators. Others, such as Sjahrir and Sjarifuddin, led the underground. Many Indonesians found themselves suddenly promoted to fill posts vacated by the Dutch, who had fled or were interned. But the occupation weighed heavily on the majority of the people. The Japanese were arrogant and overbearing and brutal wrote an observer of their rule;

'... in Bali and in Java they had been rounding up thousands of Indonesians—men and women alike—from the kampongs and sending them into slave labour in other countries. Large numbers had been sent to Malaya and Burma. And there was the question of food. Everywhere the Japanese were confiscating the rice crops and shipping them to support the Japanese troops throughout South-East Asia. The Indonesians were beginning to hunger. ... Resistance movements were spreading, consolidating. There had been many uprisings in Java, Sumatra, Borneo, and an especially violent outburst against the Nipponese in Blitar, in Java.'[10]

The official Indonesian resistance did not itself harass the Japanese by the use of armed attacks or sabotage, but the organization was to prove the framework of post-war resistance to the return of the Dutch. Meanwhile, the collaborators such as Sukarno and Hatta were allowed much leeway.

'The use for propaganda purposes of prominent figures . . . was intended to reduce opposition to Japanese authority. In fact it gave such leaders a vantage point from which radical nationalist consciousness could be developed among the masses of the population.'[11]

One of the ways in which national consciousness was conspicuously advanced was in the promotion and use of *Bahasa Indonesia*, the national language. Sukarno also made violently anti-imperialist speeches which simultaneously undermined both Western and Japanese aspirations.

Finally, the Japanese trained and armed several local military and para-military organisations, thus affording useful experience to many who were shortly to be plunged into conflict with the returning colonialists. Towards the end of the war, these Japanese puppet organisations were increasingly penetrated by underground elements. There *were* Japanese officers who were genuinely sympathetic to Indonesian nationalism, and as defeat loomed the administration itself pushed ahead with preparations for granting Indonesia 'independence', but Sukarno and Hatta in the end, under pressure from the anti-Japanese resistance, proclaimed independence without the permission or pre-knowledge of the Japanese.

Burma to the north-west suffered acutely from the war, as a country fought over by the rival armies, both intent as they retreated in turn on destroying anything likely to be useful to the other side. It is estimated that about half of Burma's pre-war capital (excluding land) was destroyed in this way.

'Faced with Allied harassing tactics and threat of reinvasion, the Japanese tried to win the support of the people by promising them freedom. The Japanese sponsored an indigenous army commanded by Burmese. Led by Aung San—who secretly trained in Japanese-occupied Hainan island with twenty-nine other "heroes"—the Burmese Independence Army followed the invading Japanese from Thailand to Burma, adding recruits as it progressed. Although the name of the Burmese army changed . . . it remained an indigenous product and on March 27, 1945, revolted against the Japanese and joined forces with the Allies.'[12]

The Japanese actually conferred 'independence' on Burma in 1943. As in Indonesia, many local people had willy-nilly to be promoted to posts of great responsibility, and the experience was to prove a valuable training for real independence after the war. During the period of the Japanese-sponsored 'independence', a true national resistance movement arose, the Anti-Fascist People's Freedom League (AFPFL). It was the AFPFL which succeeded in uniting the people of Burma, and, as we have observed previously, objective conditions dictated that its policies should be left-wing and Marxist-influenced. Its unity and popular backing presented the returning British with a delicate problem.

Meanwhile, in India the war had not failed to divert the nationalist movement from the paths along which it had seemed set in peacetime just because actual Japanese occupation was avoided. There was, in fact, a Japanese-backed Indian National Army. Its leader was Subhas Chandra Bose, who had been President of Congress in 1939 until schemed out of power by Gandhi. Bose made his way during the war first to Germany, and then to Singapore, where he recruited among the overseas Indian population. A 'Provisional Government of Free India' was declared in 1943, and the Indian National Army saw action briefly with the Japanese on Indian territory the following year. As the Japanese were rolled back, however, Bose's influence declined pari passu; he was killed in an air crash at the end of the war.

Inside India, the way in which Britain had declared war on India's behalf without consultation led to a sudden and almost complete withdrawal of Congress from the administration. Gandhi followed this up by launching a campaign of non-violent resistance to the war. The sudden reversal of policy on the part of the Hindu politicians from co-operation to non-co-operation was widely welcomed by Muslim leaders, who saw in it a chance to extend their own influence with the British in preparation for the obviously imminent negotiations. During the war the goal of Muslim League policy gradually hardened into a definite demand for a separate Islamic state of Pakistan, thus laying the seeds for post-war partition.

Despite strenuous efforts on the part of British negotiators to reconcile Congress to imperial rule at least until the cessation of hostilities, Gandhi and his followers remained obdurate. The failure of Sir Stafford Cripps in 1942 to convince the Indian leaders that it would be worth waiting until immediately after the war for a promised negotiated independence led Gandhi to launch his next campaign:

'. . . Gandhi now declared that the British in India were a provocation to the Japanese. With his usual skill he invented the "Quit India" slogan and demanded British withdrawal on pain of new civil disobedience which might well coincide with a Japanese advance in the autumn. "After all," he said, "this is open rebellion." So also thought the government . . . (and) . . . the whole Working Committee was interned. . . . There followed a short but sharp outbreak by left-wing elements of the Congress. For a time communications were disrupted in Bihar and the United Provinces. About a thousand lives were lost and 60,000 were arrested by the end of the year, and damage worth a million pounds inflicted. The government called this a Congress rebellion, while the Congress claimed it as a spontaneous reaction to the intolerable strain to which the government had subjected the people.'[13]

It is true that the war brought hardship to the people owing to the cutting off of Burmese rice supplies and the clogging of the transport system by the needs of the military. There was a severe famine in Bengal in 1943, during which three and a half million people died, for these reasons. On the other hand, two million Indians were recruited into the forces, many of whom saw service overseas and learned skills they would never otherwise have acquired. War needs also triggered off a rapid and significant growth in Indian industrial capacity. The bitterness and intransigence of Congress was not therefore mirrored throughout

society. Furthermore, the grievances of the peasant masses, one
social stratum that was in general adversely affected by the war,
resulted in no cohesive protest. Gandhi had demonstrated his
undoubted power to appeal to the rural people in the past, but
he had always invoked non-violence and other pacifico-religious
concepts whenever peasant awareness threatened to turn into
violent social revolution directed against landlordism and feudalism as well as against imperialism. By doing so, Gandhi served to
deflect and stifle the energies of the peasant class where Mao
Tse-tung in China succeeded in tapping them.

The Indian Communist Party, for its part, had concentrated
in a doctrinaire fashion on the urban proletariat in the twenties
and early thirties. By the end of the thirties, although increasingly
conscious of the urgent need to work among the peasants, the
Communist Party leaders were tied to a 'popular front' line which
limited the extent to which they were willing to criticize their
socialist colleagues on the All-India *Kisan Sabha* (Peasant
Congress—AIKS), colleagues whose inclination was to avoid
stirring up the poorer peasants against the richer. It is perfectly
true that Communists were to be found in the van of local and
spontaneous peasant uprisings and struggles when they occurred,
but the official leadership tended to adopt an

'. . . essentially "Menshevik" view of the revolutionary
perspective in India . . . it was argued that because of an in-
sufficiently developed industrial base an indefinite period
would elapse between the "bourgeois-democratic revolution"
and the "socialist revolution" in India. In effect this meant
that the task of organizing the rural proletariat and the poor
peasants did not have any urgency for them.'[14]

The contrast with China is striking. As we have seen, the
1926–27 revolutionary upsurge had been frustrated by Chiang's
break with the Communists, and by his increasing co-operation
with the foreign industrial capitalist powers. However, although
conditions for the peasantry remained virtually unchanged—
exploited by rapacious landlords and destined for life-long
poverty—there was now a strong and growing power dedicated
to the elimination of landlordism and the elevation of the rural
poor, namely the Red Army. Throughout the war, by extending
the areas of effective Communist rule, the Red Armies taught

more and more peasants in the north the advantages to them of living in, and actively defending, 'liberated areas'.

Several other factors worked in Mao's favour during and immediately after the war. First, his forces, trained and experienced in guerrilla war, were far more active against the Japanese than the Kuomintang armies. The latter were well satisfied with stalemate, and indeed there was even a degree of fraternization with the Japanese invader, to the mutual economic advantage of the two parties. The Communists in contrast harried and harrassed the occupying forces without mercy or remission, and in this way established a favourable reputation with uncommitted Chinese, concerned only for the freedom of their country and appalled by the corruption and inaction of the KMT forces and their leaders. Second, Allied policy following the surrender of Japan convinced many otherwise neutral Chinese that Chiang was a Western puppet and that the Communists were the only true nationalists.

The position that prevailed at the moment of Japanese surrender was as follows. The Kuomintang had been virtually eliminated as a political force north of the Yangtze. The Communists controlled all but the invested major cities of the north. Beyond lay Manchuria's wealth and decisive strategic location. The allies recognized Chiang as the legal head of all China. But he had no prospect of regaining actual control without allied help. This the Western powers proceeded to supply, flying KMT troops into the cities of the north, beleaguered islands in a sea of Red power. There, joined by the former Chinese collaborators with Japan (and indeed at first by the Japanese themselves), the Kuomintang, assured of all-out US support, set about its Sisyphean task of rolling back communism. Russia, as one of the allies, had meanwhile invaded Manchuria. Had the Russian rulers now proceeded to hand Manchuria over to Mao Tse-tung and his armies, the issue of the impending civil war would surely have been decided there and then. Stalin, however, recognized Chiang, and, after stripping Manchuria of its movable industrial capital, handed over the cities to KMT troops flown in by the Americans. The Chinese communists had already penetrated the surrounding countryside. The stage was set for the final scenes of the long Chinese civil war.

The majority of non-partisan Chinese saw that the consequences of a prolonged civil war would be catastrophic; everything that the anti-Japanese war had fortuitously spared would now be destroyed. Reasoning thus, a growing majority favoured a coalition solution, some compromise whereby the venality of the Nationalists might be curbed and the revolutionary zeal of the Communists contained. Attempts were indeed made to reach such an outcome, but Chiang Kai-shek himself as well as his closest relations and advisers, and a substantial body of influential American opinion, were utterly opposed to any truck with the devil of Communism. On the other hand, the Communists were not alone in interpreting Chiang's intransigence and the consequent rapid build-up of American military and financial aid to his régime and armies as an imperialist plot to re-subject China to foreign domination, and to reverse, on behalf of the Chinese landlords, bankers, compradores and other privileged groups, the social revolution promoted so whole-heartedly by Mao and his followers in the countryside.

The great powers without exception proved singularly in-accurate in their interpretation of events. The Russians almost to the very end retained contact with Chiang Kai-shek and coun-selled caution to the Red armies. They believed, extrapolating from their own experiences, that for the socialist revolution in China to have any prospect of success, Chinese industry and therefore the Chinese proletariat would have to develop under bourgeois aegis at least to the level attained in Russia in 1917. The Americans increasingly saw developments in China as an alarming microcosm of the Cold War which had already settled over Europe partly as a result of Anglo-American interventionist and 'containment' policies. Europe was to be shored up by Marshall Plan aid, and Asia by aid to Chiang and the Nationa-lists.

In point of fact, the Chinese peasantry, emboldened by the obvious strength and high morale of Mao's Red armies, and spurred on by the feel of land and the promise of perpetual emancipation from the yoke of landlordism, had already made up its mind. The progressive alienation of the Chinese intelligentsia from the Nationalist cause merely hastened a process largely decided in the countryside. As this social group moved with varying degrees of fatalism or enthusiasm to the Communist side, Chiang's fate was finally sealed:

'The revolution of 1926–7 was an explosion, violent and evanescent; the revolution of 1948 was an avalanche, ponderous, irresistible, and conclusive. In 1926–7 the revolution had no assured aim; to some it meant the simple expulsion of foreign influence and privilege, to others widespread reform, to the Communist minority, social revolution. It had no unity of purpose and therefore no certainty of operation. In 1949 the revolutionary forces were wholly under the control and leadership of the Communist party; they worked towards an accepted aim, their operations were coordinated and they had come to a clear realization of what objectives were significant and what could be ignored.'[15]

In these circumstances, American military advisers and American military equipment were impotent to buttress the crumbling dykes of Kuomintang power. As Mao Tse-tung had foreseen,

'. . . several hundred million peasants in China's central, southern and northern provinces will rise like a tornado or tempest—a force so extraordinarily swift and violent that no power, however great, will be able to suppress it. They will break through all trammels that now bind them and push forward along the road to liberation.'[16]

The long-awaited moment had now, in 1948 and early 1949, come, and the consequence was just as Mao and his lieutenants had long foreseen—the remarkably precipitous and complete collapse of the opposition, a framework of American steel hollowed out and gutted of all Chinese substance by corruption and dissolution. In the van of the peasant struggle were the seasoned and battle-tough soldiers of the Red armies. Against their combined assault the effete and hunger-weakened city garrisons of the major KMT-held cities had neither the means nor the will to resist, and one by one the fortresses went down.

An expert concluded that the

'. . . Chinese civil war of 1946–9 is unquestionably one of the most striking examples in history of the victory of a smaller but dedicated and well-organized force *enjoying popular support* over a larger but unpopular force with poor morale and incompetent leadership.'[17]

And certainly popular support was essential to the Communists. At the end of the Long March, in 1935, Mao's total forces had numbered only some 15,000 in contrast to the millions under the colours of Chiang Kai-shek. Gradually over the years the balance had tilted, until in 1949 when the remnants of the Nationalists armies sought refuge on the island of Taiwan (Formosa) they numbered but 300,000, while it was under the Communist banner that the millions marched on the mainland. Moreover, whereas the Kuomintang had altogether received over £1,575 million in American military and economic aid, the Communists had had to accomplish their victory without substantial external assistance, and frequently shut off completely from the outside world. When the Red Army marched triumphantly into Peking on the 3rd of February 1949, the parade

'. . . was exceedingly well controlled and carried out in perfect order. The troops, veterans, instantly recognizable to all who saw them as real soldiers, not the ruffians in uniform who had so long disgraced the name of China, were under firm and rigid discipline. Their weapons were well kept and clean, and they were of *Japanese or American make* in almost equal proportions. To the surprise and disappointment of some observers, who had fixed ideas on the subject of Communists, no Russian weapons and no Russians were to be seen.'[18]

The support of the people and self-reliance in ordnance—on these two basic principles Mao had made his revolution. The Red armies had adhered rigorously to the code of behaviour promulgated by their leaders, and thereby had won the confidence and gratitude of the people. Everywhere the Communist forces went, they paid for their requirements, respected life and property, and in addition did whatever was feasible to alleviate the circumstances of the people, by importing food if there was shortage, by setting up first-aid clinics, by removing local tyrants, and generally by identifying themselves with the people and acting on their behalf, working along-side them in the fields if need be. In contrast, the KMT forces had ravaged the countryside, press-ganging men into their ranks, expropriating grain, disrupting production and generally earning hostility and resentment. Then again, whereas the Communists had necessarily husbanded their firearms carefully, cherishing each gun with lavish care and protection, the KMT could afford to be prodigal with their resources, flinging away weapons if they impeded flight, because the American Treasury with its seemingly inexhaustible funds could quickly made good any losses.

That the Chinese people had backed the Communists and that the revolution was a genuinely indigenous phenomenon was not, of course, accepted in many circles in the West. The new régime was accused, especially in America which had staked so much on Chiang Kai-shek's leadership, of having come to power through a combination of ruthless terrorism of the people and the active and massive support of international communism. It was totally inconceivable to many Americans that the Chinese people should, without coercion, opt for Communism in preference to 'democracy', 'freedom' and the American way of life. The facts were, however, as we have seen, quite at odds with the widely accepted Western explanation, and, if anything, even more ominous for the prospects of perpetuating Western power and privilege in the third world than if it *had* been the case that Communism had spread in China by means of coercion and subversion. For the first time, a largely peasant nation of the non-white world had decisively struck away the shackles of feudalism and imperialism and embarked upon a course of autonomous economic and political development, beholden to no external power, and uncompromisingly committed to the cause of the rural masses so long the victims of domestic oppression and foreign exploitation. On the success or failure of Mao's régime the eyes of the peoples of Africa, Asia and Latin America would inevitably be turned. Already by 1949 and 1950 the repercussions of the revolution had been widely felt outside the borders of China, and the impact was destined to grow with the passage of time and with each successive achievement of the new Chinese People's Republic, formally proclaimed on October 1st 1949 by its Chairman, Mao Tse-tung.

REFERENCES

1. Malcolm Caldwell: 'Problems of Socialism in South East Asia', in R. Miliband and J. Saville (eds.): *The Socialist Register 1966*, London, 1966, pp. 288–9.

2. D. Wurfel: 'The Philippines' in G. McT. Kahin (ed.): *Governments and Politics of Southeast Asia*, New York, 1964, p. 696.

3. L. Taruc: *Born of the People*, New York, 1953, p. 117.

4. W. J. Pomeroy: 'The Myths of Counter-Insurgency' in *New Left Review*, September–October 1964, pp. 92–3.

5. L. Taruc: *Born of the People*, New York, 1953, p. 148; see also pp. 149 et seq.

6. W. Warbey: *Vietnam: The Truth*, London, 1965, p. 21.

7. See, for example, F. Spencer Chapman: *The Jungle is Neutral*, London, 1965, p. 149 et passim.

8. J. M. Gullick: *Malaya*, London, 1963, p. 78.

9. Ibid, p. 83.

10. K'Tut Tantri: *Revolt in Paradise*, New York, 1960, pp. 119–20.

11. J. D. Legge: *Indonesia*, New Jersey, 1964, pp. 131–2.

12. J. Silverstein: 'Burma' in G. McT. Kahin (ed.): *Governments and Politics of Southeast Asia*, New York, 1964, pp. 83–4.

13. P. Spear: *A History of India, Vol. 2*. London, 1965, pp. 219–20.

14. Hamza Alavi: 'Peasants and Revolution' in R. Miliband and J. Saville (eds.): *The Socialist Register 1965*, London, 1965, p. 264.

15. C. P. Fitzgerald: *The Birth of Communist China*, London, 1964, p. 64.

16. S. Schram: *The Political Thought of Mao Tse-tung*, pp. 179–80.

17. S. Schram: *Mao Tse-tung*, London, 1966, p. 242; author's italics.

18. C. P. Fitzgerald: *The Birth of Communist China*, London, 1964, p. 116; author's italics.

CHAPTER SEVEN

War and Independence

SHORT as the Japanese assault on Asia had been, and total as was its collapse, yet things could never, and would never, revert to their pre-war pattern. It will be necessary in this chapter to go back from the victory of the Chinese revolution to consider the derivation and determinants of the post-war configuration that was to emerge. America's predominant position in the West had been massively underlined by the war and initial post-war period, but at the same time there had been a significant extension of the Communist world, and third world nationalism had received a boost that had transformed its quality and prospects. Political and popular opinion was slow to grasp the essential elements of the new international chemistry and so to elaborate in anything like a realistic way its short- and long-term implications. Towards the end of the war, for example, the editor of the *Economist* wrote:

'. . . for Britain, and in similar measure for France and Holland, the Far East is a *necessity* of greatness and wealth. . . . The conception of the (Japanese) Co-Prosperity Sphere was an inconvenience to the US. To Britain, to the Netherlands and to France, it was a death sentence passed on their fundamental way of life . . . none of them has any intention of abandoning its colonial empire, but on the contrary regards the restoration of Malaya to the British, the East Indies to the Dutch, and French Indo-China to the French as an *essential* part of the destruction of the Japanese. . . .' (16/9/44).

Yet at first glance much seemed to favour the national liberation aspirations of the peoples of the non-white world. After all, the war *had* been a war against fascist-racism, and racist views were in greater disrepute than at any previous period in human

history. After the first world war there had been a heady season
of talking about national self-determination, but the countries of
Asia had quickly discovered that there was an unstated premiss
in all this talk that self-determination was for white men only.
And there was no pretence at that time by the white powers that
they accepted even the principle of racial equality; when the
Japanese delegation at the League of Nations tried to obtain
world acceptance for that principle the

> '. . . Australian prime minister stated frankly that if "racial
> equality is recognized in the preamble of any article of the
> Covenant, I and my people will leave the conference bag and
> baggage." '[1]

The UNESCO statement on race, in contrast, said that

> 'Scientists have reached general agreement in recognizing
> that mankind is one; that all men belong to the same species,
> *Homo Sapiens*. It is further generally agreed among scientists
> that all men are probably derived from the same common
> stock . . . (and) . . . given similar degrees of cultural opportun-
> ity to realize their potentialities, the average achievement of the
> members of each ethnic group is about the same. . . . For all
> practical social purposes "race" is not so much a biological
> phenomenon as a social myth.'[2]

An additional favourable omen initially was the attitude of the
wartime President of the United States, Franklin D. Roosevelt.
Whatever the attitude of the leaders of the European colonial
powers, Roosevelt seemed to want in the post-war world to extend
the benefits of self-determination to the peoples of the non-
Western world. Nor were there lacking American business interests prepared to back this policy, for the elimination of British,
French, Dutch and Portuguese colonies promised excellent
opportunities for improving the marketing and investing prospects of American companies at the expense of their European
rivals. There was an excellent and most apposite historical pre-
cedent in the fate of Latin America; after the expulsion of European colonial authority, the United States had progressively
strengthened her economic position *vis-à-vis* the countries of
Central and South America, to the point that they had become
virtual economic dependencies or 'neo-colonies'.

'The essence of neo-colonialism is that the State which is subject to it is, in theory, independent and has all the outward trappings of international sovereignty. In reality its economic system and thus its political policy is directed from outside.'[3]

Circumstances could hardly have been more propitious for the earliest experiments in neo-colonialism than they were in the Latin America of the later part of the nineteenth century, and it is not hard to see why the US was able to establish her continental hegemony. The European powers—possible rivals—were geographically remote, and because of African and Asian involvements increasingly inclined to leave the field to the United States. It was not therefore necessary to undertake pre-emptive colonization along traditional lines. Also Latin America was 'balkanized'—a classical condition for the imposition of neo-colonialism according to Kwame Nkrumah. Because the states were tragically at odds with each other, the US could deal with them severally without fear of facing united opposition. Moreover, each state was woefully vulnerable and divided, with a volatile *élite*, itself subject to internal dissention, and cruelly suppressed and exploited peasant masses devoid of rights (but cynically harnessed from time to time for the purpose of replacing one authoritarian caudillo by another).

The United States soon saw the chances of profiting from such circumstances. Texas, California, New Mexico, Arizona, Nevada, Utah and part of Colorado had been carved out of Mexico by the middle of the century. But consummation of the neo-colonial empire further south had to await upon two things: the Civil War (1861–65) and completion of the internal railway network of the United States; for only with the country united and the major capital-absorbing project of the century completed was American capitalism in the position and in the frame of mind to embark upon intensive world-wide economic imperialism: 'A new consciousness seems to have come upon us,' stated the *Washington Post* in an editorial in the 'nineties,

'the consciousness of strength—and with it a new appetite, the yearning to show our strength. . . . The taste of Empire is in the mouth of the people even as the taste of blood in the jungle.'[4]

But although American troops were indeed very soon to see
bloody battles in two continents, notably in Cuba and the
Philippines, and large territories were to be incorporated in an
old-fashioned looking empire, the major thrust of aggressive
American capitalism was to be neo-colonial—manipulating
governments by bribes and threats, penetrating countries
economically and exploiting them by virtue of incomparably
greater financial, organizational and technological resource, and,
in general, directing the economic and political affairs of nominally independent sovereign powers for the benefit of the USA.

The system of economic and military relations which came into
being on the American continent foreshadowed in a remarkable
way what was to develop only after the second world war in
'free' Asia. From time to time the smooth operations of the system whereby the potential investible surplus of the countries of
South and Central America was largely transferred to the United
States were threatened by the appearance of nationalist rebellions,
which required direct US military intervention to put matters
right; it was thus that the Dominican Republic was occupied
from 1916 to 1924. In general, however, it was possible to work
through indigenous puppet rulers, often military figures, and
always reliably conservative, and until the Cuban revolution in
1958, only in Mexico did the people succeed in carrying out a
significant measure of social revolution and largely emancipating
the country from feudalism and economic imperialism. Elsewhere, United States capital was free to rampage at will. Big US
corporations took what opportunities there were for profit,
secure in the knowledge that ultimately overseas assets were
underwritten and protected by US military power. President
Theodore Roosevelt told Congress that:

> 'Chronic wrongdoing ... may in America, as elsewhere, ulti-
> mately require intervention by some civilized nation, and in the
> Western Hemisphere, the adherence of the United States to
> the Monroe Doctrine may force the United States, however
> reluctantly ... to the exercise of an international police
> power.'[5]

As time passed, the scale of United States business involvement
in the economies of South and Central America increased and
therefore the magnitude of the capital at risk and *therefore* the

concern of business in general to ensure prompt and effective US government intervention to safeguard investments.

The unilateral assumption of continental police powers by the United States did not go unchallenged, of course. From time to time it *was* necessary for the US government actively to intervene to ensure the survival of a tractable ruler or to unseat an intractable upstart. However, the system as a whole normally functioned satisfactorily. It was, then, with this model in view that the US approached the problems of the post-war world. Of course, it was recognized that there were complications. South and South-East Asia could not be shifted half way round the world and secured in the home stockade of the Monroe doctrine: geographically and strategically the emerging Asian nations were clearly much more vulnerable; and communism posed a much more serious problem in Asia than in Latin America. The countries of Latin America had come to independence in the early nineteenth century, and their characteristic form of élitist government had become stabilized under the United States umbrella long before the Russian Revolution. It is true that thereafter communism gained footholds among urban workers and the intelligentsia but this

'. . . did not seriously challenge the traditional order on a continent still overwhelmingly rural. As the Mexican revolution was revealing, only the aroused peasants possessed the potential to change the basic social structure.'[6]

The great majority of the *élite*—in the armed forces, in politics, in administration, in the business world, and in the educated classes generally—were naturally implacably opposed to a social force which threatened to cut at the very roots of their power, wealth and privileges. In contrast, the dispossessed *élite* of Asia, shut out from the highest positions (in terms of power, status and the chances for self-enrichment) in their own societies by the capitalist-colonialist whites and their frequently alien intermediaries and compradores, had become widely imbued with Marxist ideas, and at least in pursuit of political independence found common ground with the urban and rural masses. One should note, too, the role of the Catholic Church in Latin America as a reactionary bastion against the spread of socialist ideas; only in the Philippines is Catholicism a major social force in Asia.

There had, then, to be modifications in applying neo-colonialism to an Asia in nationalistic ferment as a result of the second world war and profoundly permeated by socialist ideas. President Franklin Roosevelt's expressed sentiment that the peoples of Asia deserved better than to be handed back to their old colonial masters after the war was no doubt genuine and reflected a real strand in American thinking, both public and official. But it was by no means as simple as that. Roosevelt himself died in 1945, before the end of the war, and was replaced by Harry Truman, a precocious and inveterate 'cold warrior'. Truman and his closest political allies were determined to halt the advance of communism and social revolution. It was therefore absolutely essential from their point of view to see sovereignty transferred from the European colonial powers to indigenous nationalists of a safe political hue, and not to allow the struggle for political liberty to gather momentum into a struggle for radical social change. Yet at first Truman had to move slowly, for it would have been quite impracticable to have abruptly reversed U.S. policy towards the Soviet Union as soon as the war ended. The 'Truman Doctrine' was not, in fact, enunciated until early 1947, when the President in effect declared Greece and Turkey American protectorates, and indicated that the United States would consider it a national obligation to defend 'free people' (i.e. the governments of countries with capitalist economic institutions) everywhere in the world if these were threatened with 'subversion' or 'aggression'.

By 1947 the Cold War was well under way. The following three years were to prove of decisive importance in shaping the Asia of the subsequent two decades. Europe had experienced a 'year of revolutions' in 1848; now exactly a hundred years later it was to be the turn of Asia. From end to end of the continent the peasants and workers were in a state of unrest and in parts in actual armed revolt. The communists everywhere moved to instigate such risings or at least to associate themselves with them. It was an alarming picture for the Western powers, especially with the success of the Chinese communists as a background. The following year, 1949, saw the triumph of the revolution in China and the routing of Chiang Kai-shek, despite massive US aid. It seemed as if all Asia was suddenly at risk. Then in 1950 came the Korean war and America's massive direct intervention under the convenient cover of the United Nations' colours. The problems of shoring up the status quo took on a new urgency, and it was in the light of this that the decision was taken that year to step in and help the French to retain their colony in Indo-China against a nationalist movement dominated by the communists. Just a year before, the United States had used its influence to persuade the Netherlands to grant independence to Indonesia. No further risks could be taken. If independence could not be granted to nationalists of a co-operative and congenial political character, such as those in the Philippines, it was henceforward not to be granted at all. The front lines of the American empire in the 'free' world had been determined.

Within the boundaries of the 'free world', the typical institutions and arrangements of neo-colonialism were being elaborated and perfected. The Chinese revolution had forcibly directed the attention of the American government to the weakness of that flank, and in consequence there was a rapid extension to Asia of policies already successfully implemented in the European theatre. It is worth considering this point briefly. The overall policy had three principal elements. The first was provision of economic aid. The second was construction of military bases and alliances. The third was direct armed intervention to help anti-communist and pro-capitalist governments to crush left-wing movements if these threatened to overturn the status quo. Aid, in the form of the Marshall Plan, had successfully rehabilitated the economies of the West and in doing so had pulled the teeth of the dangerously large communist parties of Italy and France. NATO formed the core of the military system in the area. An example of the interventions was the suppression of the left in Greece in order to instal a reliable anti-communist régime in favour of private enterprise.

The aid poured in by the United States to bolster Chiang Kai-shek had not achieved its purpose. But lessons had been learnt from the failure. The aid programme was now to be co-ordinated with and indeed made subordinate to the military aspect, which in turn was to be far more closely supervised by the United States, and to have a very much higher direct participation by US forces. The first steps were quickly taken. Support was forthcoming for the French struggle in Indo-China. Huge US forces entered Korea to sustain the pro-Western South. The

Kuomintang remnants in Formosa were guaranteed immunity from invasion by the Communists by intercession of the US Seventh Fleet. Whereas previously there had been general agreement in Washington that Formosa was part of China, although there had been a strong pro-Chiang lobby including General MacArthur, a new line was now stated by President Truman, two days after the outbreak of the Korean war in June, 1950:

'. . . the occupation of Formosa by the Communist forces would be a direct threat to the security of the Pacific area and to United States forces performing their lawful and necessary functions in that area. Accordingly I have ordered the Seventh Fleet to prevent any attack on Formosa.'[7]

Finally, a separate peace-treaty and a mutual security pact with Japan were rushed through, in order to secure the United States position there; the ANZUS Pact was concluded with Australia and New Zealand; and a mutual security pact was signed with the Philippines. All these arrangements were made in the course of 1951. The United States was now guaranteed a complex of bases and puppet armies in a great curve 'containing' China.

Before considering how successful the US policy of containment was to prove in practice, let us now trace early post-war developments inside the frontiers of the 'free' world as defined by Washington.

Post-war readjustment was not a smooth process anywhere in formerly Japanese-held Asia; in the Philippines the problems were immense. The economy had been laid low by the fighting and by inflation, and politically there was division between those who had collaborated and those who had resisted. American policy was to hand over independence as quickly as possible to trusted Filipinos, but to secure at the same time certain vital national objectives. These included, first, permanent bases in the Philippines; second, favourable trade and economic relations; and, third, the exclusion of the left from constitutional political life in the Philippines and the extirpation of radical movements of social protest such as peasant unions. All these were in large measure accomplished, although, as we will see, it has never proved possible to crush completely peasant protest and armed struggle. Independence was achieved on July 4, 1946. The first

President was Manuel Roxas, who had organized rice collection on behalf of the Japanese during the war, and who had subsequently been rehabilitated by his friend General MacArthur. Although collaboration had been an issue, in practice no important collaborator was ever convicted for his part in helping the Japanese during the war, and Roxas declared a general amnesty in 1948. The real target of US policy was not the collaborators, who were generally malleable politically and favourably inclined to private enterprise (their own and that of others), but the left-wing guerrillas, with whom there had been conflict even during the war, as we have observed above.

The necessary bases were obtained by the agreement of 1947, under the terms of which the US acquired a 99-year lease over 23 bases and, in addition, was conceded legal jurisdiction over the bases and their personnel. The distinguished Filipino Senator and statesman, Claro Recto, claimed that the terms of this agreement, which in essence was dictated to the Philippines by the United States, made the new nation a 'military protectorate.' The agreement was re-negotiated in 1959 and some concessions made to Filipino nationalism. Nevertheless, the United States preserved the essentials.

The tactics which the Americans employed to force their economic terms on the Philippines were also an affront to nationalism. The US Congress made implementation of the Philippine Rehabilitation Act, which provided for economic assistance to reconstruct the war-devastated economy, conditional upon Filipino passage of the Bell Trade Act. The latter extended free trade between the countries for eight years after independence and special trade terms for 20 years thereafter and granted US businessmen equal rights with Filipinos in exploitation of the natural resources of the country until 1974—a provision in direct contradiction to an Article in the Philippines Constitution. The necessary legislation was only narrowly passed by the Philippine Congress after a number of congressmen had been refused their seats on spurious grounds. Among these were important leaders of the Filipino left. Moreover in the subsequent approving plebiscite, barely 40 per cent of the electorate voted. Recto branded the consequent economic relations between the United States and the Philippines as those characteristic of a metropolitan power and an 'economic colony'.

The final task facing the United States was the elimination of the left as a significant political force in Filipino national life. The war-time Hukbalahap decided on disbandment on the return of peace in order that members and supporters might concentrate on legitimate constitutional political activities. A new party— the Democratic Alliance—was formed to seek representation in Congress, and simultaneously organizations were fostered among rural and urban workers, as a result of which increasing numbers were enrolled into the PKM (National Confederation of Peasants) and the CLO (Congress of Labour Organizations). But the US and her local collaborators did not stand back idly. Despite the anti-Japanese record of the Huks, they did not share in the post-war gratitude of the US:

'. . . at the same time that most guerrilla organizations were given recognition for services rendered to the American cause, Huk leaders Luis Taruc and Casto Alejandrino were imprisoned by the US army. US military police assisted the Philippine constabulary and the private landlords' armies, called "civilian guards" or "temporary police", in restricting left-wing political activity . . .'[8]

Nevertheless, not only did the Democratic Alliance secure six seats in the 1946 elections (including one fought by Taruc) despite widespread use of bribery and terror by Roxas, but both the PKM and the CLO were making significant gains, the former having forced through a crop-sharing tenancy act against the opposition of the landlords, and the latter having begun creating militant unions in US-owned industries. The response was therefore stepped up:

'Acting at imperialist instigation (Filipino military forces were still under the command of American officers), the government launched a suppression policy against these legal forms of expression for the Filipino masses. . . . The terror fell with particular savagery upon Central Luzon where, in the attempt to break the strong mass movement, indiscriminate killings, murder, torture, mass arrests, and the wholesale razing of villages were employed. It was here that the armed struggle began, as a defensive measure during attacks upon villages by government troops and by private landlord-hired fascist units. In the face of these mailed-fist blows, the Huk armed forces regrouped and fought, spontaneously and virtually without central guidance. The Communist Party, which had provided much of the leadership of the movement during the Japanese occupation, was at this time disorganized, without unity on strategy and tactics, and with no clear perspective for the period ahead. At best, provincial organizations of the Communist Party, of the Democratic Alliance, of the PKM and the CLO, largely on their own, were giving direction to peasants arming themselves and fighting back against suppression. . . . Only the heroism and fighting capacity of the people, with leaders who fought largely on their own initiative, frustrated and turned this phase of the imperialist-ordered suppression into a failure.'[9]

It is worth quoting this author at length, as he himself was involved in the post-war Huk revolt in the Philippines. Moreover, the point he is making about this period (1946–8), namely that armed struggle was already under way, confutes the common allegation that the post-war uprisings in South-East Asia were undertaken at the instigation of Moscow, the orders being conveyed to local parties via the South-East Asia Youth Conference at Calcutta early in 1948. That a more militant line in the Communist world was apparent by 1948 is certainly true, but hardly to be wondered at in view of the growing militancy of United States policy as typified by the Truman speech of March 5, 1947, and the subsequent brutal intervention in Greece to sustain the oligarchy against the threat of social revolution (Truman's new doctrine was reported in the *New York Herald Tribune* under the headline 'President Says Americans Love Free Enterprise More Than Peace'). As we will see, constitutional openings for the socialist and communist left in Asia had been or were being rapidly closed in much the same manner as in the Philippines.

By mid-1948, some degree of organization had become more apparent in the turmoil of Central Luzon. A re-shaped HMB (Hukbong Mapagpalaya ng Bayan—National Army of Liberation) undertook recruiting and the articulation of policy. It was still hoped to attain the right to contest political power by orthodox means, and efforts at reconciliation with the government were made. The Huk leaders were not, however, successful in this, encountering fraud and terror at every turn. Therefore in January, 1950, the Huk leaders called for the armed overthrow of the 'imperialist-puppet régime'.

Fierce fighting ensued, in which at first the guerrillas scored signal successes; for a time two of the provincial capitals in Central Luzon were held, and much of the rice produced in the region was effectively in Huk control. By 1955, however, the up-rising had been broken. American experts regard this achievement as the paradigm of how the 'free world' can repel 'subversion'. According to this view, the problem was attacked in two ways: by giving military aid and advice, and by encouraging the Philippine government to undertake effective reforms to cut away peasant support for the guerrillas. A further important element was the emergence of an effective military leader and national figure in Ramon Magsaysay, one-time Secretary of National Defence, who became President in 1953 after a campaign partly financed by American backers. It is argued from this experience that similar steps can be made to succeed against national liberation movements elsewhere. Comments Pomeroy:

> 'The assumption is false. . . . While steps were taken to minimize fraud and terrorism in elections, beginning in 1951, reforms were superficial, were almost wholly of a propaganda nature, and had little if any effect on the lives of the peasantry and the workers. So-called agrarian reform laws that were passed during the Presidency of Ramon Magsaysay (an absolute puppet of the American military advisory group) . . . caused no changes whatsoever in the conditions of the peasantry, who actually suffered a worsening of their circumstances after they were adopted. The principal factor in the setback to the Huk movement was ruthless military suppression, carried out with vast quantities of US military aid, by an army equipped, trained and supervised by an American military advisory group. Even this, however, would have been ineffective but for deficiencies within the Huk movement itself.'[10]

These deficiencies included, according to this participant, inadequate security (leading to the arrest in Manila in 1950 of the entire top leading committee and all its files); neglect of the lessons of previous guerrilla struggles, such as that in China;

poor equipment and inexperienced military leadership; and isolation:

'No aid of any kind, whether in the form of arms, funds or training facilities, was available from outside the Philippines, where the struggle was conducted in isolation from allies or sympathisers from abroad. No groups or committees, to inform the world of what was happening or to rally international support, existed anywhere, unlike the circumstances of other liberation struggles.'[11]

In spite of all this, US military aid had reached nearly $1 billion by 1956, and still there were Huk units in the field, necessitating large-scale operations by the US-advised Philippine Army. Poverty, unemployment, rural indebtedness, terrorism by the security forces, all combine to provide fertile soil for a resurgence of Huk activity from time to time.

Elsewhere in South-East Asia after the war there were armed struggles. The case of Vietnam is particularly well documented (see note p. 181). In three other cases—Malaysia, Burma and Indonesia—important enough lessons are to be learnt to justify brief consideration of each.

The abrupt termination of the Pacific war after Hiroshima and Nagasaki caught all parties unprepared. As far as Malaya was concerned, there was an interval before official British forces could return to the country to take over administration from the Japanese. There was some fear at South-East Asia Command Headquarters that

'. . . the guerrillas (i.e. the Malayan People's Anti-Japanese Army) would usurp the functions of the government and take the law into their own hands, but the fact remains that the MPAJA with its Force 136 (British) liaison officers, apart from the Japanese, was the only organized body in the country at that time. During the period between the publication of the Japanese surrender and the arrival of British troops—in remote areas a period of several months—only two serious clashes occurred with the Japanese. This is the more remarkable considering what the MPAJA had suffered at the hands of the Japs, and says a great deal for the discipline and order which existed.'[12]

However, the fact that the largely Malay police force had collaborated so thoroughly with the Japanese against the Chinese did lead to MPAJA reprisals against those held to be guilty; this in turn led to reciprocal terror, so that in

'. . . west Johore there was almost a Sino-Malay civil war in miniature. In the interior of Negri Sembilan Malays fell on Chinese villagers, mainly women and children, and slaughtered forty of them. In Perak the Chinese set upon the Malays. Each act of vengeance was like a pebble dropped in a pond. The widening ripples of fear and hate spread rancour and panic for miles around.'[13]

This heightened communal tension was to prove an important asset in the long run to the returning colonial power, for it made containment and eventual defeat of the mainly Chinese left-wing uprising easier when it came, and it simultaneously frightened the *élite* of the two races into effective political co-operation in order to attain political independence under British tutelage.

At first, the MPAJA responded to the call of the returning British authorities and surrendered a major part, but by no means the whole, of their arms. It was the hope of the MCP (Malayan Communist Party) to extend its influence by constitutional means. The conventional account then goes on to claim that after the February 1948 Calcutta Youth Conference the Party

'. . . received new instructions from Moscow . . . (and) . . . like other parties in South-East Asia, was summoned to revolt.'[14]

But Gullick himself shows elsewhere that this is far too simplified an account, and he concedes in a footnote that other authorities do not consider the connection between Calcutta and the start of the Malayan 'Emergency' as, in fact, proven.

Progress was to be made on two fronts—political and industrial. High-point of MCP success in the first respect was the brief PMCJA–PUTERA coalition, combining Malay and non-Malay opponents of the constitutional steps being taken by the British authorities with the co-operation (after defeat of the Malayan Union idea) of the Malay aristocracy. The Federation of Malaya which succeeded the British-dominated Malayan Union in early 1948 had the backing of the Malay upper classes, and therefore of the conservative and loyal majority of the Malay peasantry, because its constitution effectively relegated the Chinese to second-class citizenship, denying many of them the right to vote, while perpetuating Malay privileges. Moreover, like the Malayan Union before it, it excluded Singapore, with its large Chinese and Indian communities. With the launching of the Federation, much of the backing of PMCJA–PUTERA melted away: the Chinese (and Indians) in the Federation had to accept their inferior position and to try to make the best of it, while those in Singapore now had a separate and different task—the attainment of independence for the island itself. 'Divide and rule' had again been shown to be an astute imperialist tactic.

On the labour front, despite early MCP successes, including the general strike of January, 1946, the British again gradually got on top. The security network was restored to its former pre-war efficiency, trade union legislation was stringently tightened in May, 1948, and hundreds of labour leaders were imprisoned or deported. Strikes and industrial clashes in mining and plantation areas became increasingly violent, and British-officered Gurkha troops were sent in to police the rubber plantations of Johore. On 16th June, 1948, following the murder of three British and two Chinese planters, a state of 'Emergency' was declared by the colonial administration for the states of Perak and Johore. This was subsequently extended, in July, to the whole country. On the night of June 20–21, the Special Branch moved:

> '. . . more than 600 political leaders and activists of all nationalities were arrested; more than 300 trade union and mass organizations were closed down. By the end of the year, i.e. within six months of the proclamation, 13,341 persons were put in prison, or deported, and nearly 400 persons murdered. In December 1948 the Central Executive Committee of the MCP met and decided on a counter armed struggle.'[15]

British tactics were certainly not kid-glove. The active wing of the new Malayan Races' Liberation Army (MRLA—known to the colonial authorities as CT's—that is Communist Terrorists) probably never exceeded 10,000 at its peak, and is generally numbered at about half that strength in British sources. Against them were ranged 40,000 regular troops (25 battalions of British,

Australian, New Zealand, Fijian, East African and Malay troops), supported by aircraft, artillery, and naval vessels, some 70,000 armed police, and 350,000 Malay 'Home Guards'. Plantations and mines frequently raised and supported their own 'armies' made up of Malays from the villages and rather more dubious adventurers recruited from the towns. Regulations gave the British and their Malay auxiliaries sweeping powers:

> 'The police could detain suspects for periods up to two years without trial . . . control the movement of traffic and food along the roads and on the railway, impose 24-hour curfews, and search without warrants. A much-criticized measure enabled the Government to fling into detention the residents of an entire village, area or district on merely satisfactory evidence of aiding, abetting or consorting with the terrorists.'[16]

But perhaps the crucial step in enforcing control was the plan to 'resettle' the squatters.

These squatters were the product of the worst years of the inter-war depression (1931–4) and of the Japanese occupation when employment opportunities had shrunk drastically. Tens of thousands of Chinese had moved out to remote areas, beyond the effective jurisdiction of authority, to clear jungle-fringe land for subsistence agriculture, with a slight surplus in many cases for sale in nearby or accessible urban areas. It was among these squatters that the *Min Yuen*, the civilian wing supplying the MRLA with recruits and food, had its strength; perhaps families numbering in all half a million people were involved. At first, British policy was simply to round up suspects and intern them, with a view to deportation. Half a million was, however, too many to be handled in this way. The essence of the new plan, devised by Sir Harold Briggs, was to re-group the squatter population in resettlements, or 'new villages', wherein the government could exercise close and effective supervision of all comings and goings. At first, undue haste and brutality marked the attempt, and the 'Emergency' took on the aspect of a war by the British against a whole people (one in five of all the Chinese in Malaya were involved—one in ten of the whole population of the country). The early camps were often badly sited, and inadequate provision was made in all material respects. Nevertheless, by surrounding each camp with high barbed-wire fences, and by making each vulnerable to a heavily-armed police post within the perimeter of the wire, it proved possible to choke off in time the vital food supplies of the MRLA. A rigid night curfew was imposed, and the *Handbook to the Emergency* declared that

> 'Anyone found with food beyond the wire fence, will be considered as aiding terrorists and under Emergency Regulations liable to penal servitude, or to death. . . .'[17]

Faced with such tactics, the MRLA—so dependent upon the Chinese rural community (now largely incarcerated)—had to resort to other means to ensure its supplies. These included armed robbery, further alienating the other communities, and retreat into the remote jungles to grow their own food. Meanwhile, the British forces were bit by bit mopping up and declaring 'white' area after area. Moreover, progress towards independence was being made much more rapidly than had at one time looked likely in view of the terrible disruption and difficulties created by the Emergency. In 1955, Malaya attained virtual self-government and, two years later, independence. This was made possible by co-operation of the conservative majority of the Malay community, organized in UMNO (United Malays National Organization), with the leaders of the Chinese business community, organized in the MCA (Malayan Chinese Association). That the resulting new nation had a distinctly neo-colonial character, as indeed suggested by such co-operation, underlines yet again the failure of the MCP to harness and build on the genuine economic and nationalist grievances of the peoples of all communities. Throughout the period, there was apparently a certain lack of flexibility on the part of the MCP leadership. In addition, whatever their dedication and courage—testified to in a variety of sources—the guerrillas were militarily inexperienced. The Vietnamese and the Filipinos both had long traditions of armed insurrection; the peoples of Malaya had not. Spencer Chapman, in his contacts with the MPAJA during the war, found the Chinese un-military and poor shots, a judgement reinforced by observers of the MRLA in action.

With all these failings and disadvantages, the MCP conducted a surprisingly long war. The Emergency was not formally lifted until 1960. In twelve years, approximately 11,000 persons—terrorists, civilians, security forces—were killed, and the approximate cost to the administration was £200 million. Moreover, the guerrillas were never entirely stamped out, and even after 1960 it was necessary for there to be security operations in the northern states, the hard core having taken refuge in southern Thailand. During the short life of the ill-fated Federation of Malaysia, including Singapore, there was a marked upsurge in Communist activity, facilities for training being available in hostile Indonesia. Indeed, Lee Kuan Yew, the Singapore Premier, argued that if Malaya and the island had not parted company in August 1965 there would have been

'... a communist resurrection ... a civil war ... in which all the non-Malays would have backed the Communist Party. ... It would have happened within six months.'[18]

The statement underlines again the racial bases of present Malaysian politics. But the truth of the matter is that Malaysia's real problems are her lack of economic autonomy—a product of the colonial past and the neo-colonial present—and the poverty of the mass of the people. The current weakness of the Left is not a tribute to the success of Western counter-insurgency, but a result of the local failure to forge a truly multi-racial, anti-imperialist, anti-feudal and anti-compradore front.

The implementation of a 'left' policy in Burma was, on the contrary, aided by a racial factor. The demand of the Burmese people for independence was quickly met. The country had been devastated by war, and promised no such economic advantage to Britain as did Malaya.[19] Moreover, the people were well armed and united, and India and Pakistan, with whose progress Burma had been associated during the colonial period, were themselves moving rapidly towards independence. Burma became free, in fact, in 1948. Since then, developments have been complex and in recent years difficult to follow because of the progressively more stringent regulations governing contacts with the outside world. However, it is clear that the almost total departure or expulsion of Indians from the country and expropriation of their wealth during and since the war radically altered the land problem, since so much of the best land in the country had passed into their hands under colonialism.

The immediate post-war years witnessed a mass wakening of the people in the ferment of change and expectations induced by

the war and the post-war prospects. This 'social revolution' of
the years 1946 to 1948 was

'. . . stunted when the British freely transferred power to an
indigenous *élite* and the latter was unable to act creatively in
the face of revolt and threats of secession. Although the new
leaders maintained the slogans and organizations of revolution,
the people drifted away, returning to their traditional pursuits
and retaining their religious and social customs and traditions.'[20]

The *élite* was, in fact, a coalition of interest groups, united in the
pursuit of independence, but now in power divided among themselves. Almost at once the great difficulties facing them—communist insurrections, uprisings of minority hill peoples, restoration of pre-war levels of production—exposed their weaknesses.
Socialism remained an agreed goal, but in practice policy had to
be based on expediency. The army finally moved in in March,
1962, and assumed power in a Revolutionary Council.

The Revolutionary Council has sought to guide Burma in a
socialist direction, in accordance with its programme, the *Burmese
Way to Socialism*. In 1963, widespread nationalization was undertaken, the role of private businessman being virtually eliminated.
In addition, major measures of rural reform were launched,
protecting the peasant from losing his land and implements as a
result of bad debts, offering credit from the government as an
alternative source to the traditional moneylender, and encouraging the formation of rural co-operatives and collectives. The
success of the régime in this direction is hard to assess. The
stated aim of the leaders is to raise the incomes and status of the
80 per cent peasants and workers, but Western observers have
few opportunities to judge the results on the ground.

The leaders have, on the other hand, definitely succeeded in
keeping their country free from the dangerous involvements with
neo-colonialism that have afflicted and threatened neighbours.
For example, although the Burmese Communists have been in
revolt since 1948, and there is a largely uncontrollable common
frontier with China, there has been no evidence of any outside
support to the rebels, or of any great growth of support for them
internally, because the Rangoon government has cultivated good
relations with Peking and refused to become involved in any

respect or to any degree in American designs for the area. Further, by severely restricting foreign aid, the Burmese have escaped the grave disadvantages which dependence on such assistance has brought to other countries in the way of mounting interest payments and loss of foreign policy independence.

In Indonesia as in Burma the nationalist movement in general had a leftist inclination. This was accentuated by the long armed struggle against the Dutch who sought to reimpose their authority after the war. In 1948, the Communist Party of Indonesia, in the midst of the nationalist war with the returning colonial power, staged an armed uprising which was quickly suppressed. One of the Communist leaders, Suripno, later wrote:

> 'The lesson we learned, a very precious one, although very hard, was that *the people did not support us.*'[21]

At that time, although there were good class grounds for doubting whether the nationalist *élite* were capable of generating economic development, the loyalty of the people to Sukarno, Hatta and the other leaders was unshakeable. Moreover, the nationalists suffered from none of the drawbacks that weakened them elsewhere:

> 'The republic was without Western military advisers, without the presence of large Western embassy staffs, without Western programs of economic or technical assistance and without the presence of Western information services. In a sense, the republic was without the elements of Western influence that have often compromised leaders in underdeveloped countries in their struggle against internal Communist machinations. The Communist bid for power in Indonesia, generated from within, was met and defeated from within.'[22]

Having defeated this attempted coup, the nationalists carried their campaign for independence to a successful conclusion. The campaign was waged on two levels—the combat level and the propaganda level. We have seen that one of the reasons for the failure of the Huk campaign in the Philippines was its complete isolation from the outside world. The Indonesian nationalists did not make this mistake; they very shrewdly cultivated contacts

with a variety of sources guaranteeing their case an international
hearing, so that:

> 'The reason that the Dutch were finally willing to withdraw
> their forces from Indonesia was not because they were defeated
> by our army, but because they were weakened and stymied by
> us so that there was no longer any hope for them to destroy
> the Republic. When their efforts to do this were frustrated,
> international pressure hastened the transfer of sovereignty.'[23]

An important part of the international pressure was applied by
the United States; in 1948 and 1949 the U.S. government found
it embarrassing to have a NATO ally, Holland, engaged in such
an unpopular war, waged so ruthlessly. By 1950, American
policy had hardened against Asian nationalism.

Following independence (1949), there was a short-lived period
of multi-party democracy, during which little was accomplished
in the way of improving the economic circumstances of the people.
Comments an astute Dutch historian:

> 'The main factor . . . which accounted for the failure to
> bring about any general improvement in this situation (a steady
> deterioration of general social and economic conditions),
> despite the lip-service paid to the need for it and the partially
> successful reforms which were actually carried out, was the
> failure to put into practice any comprehensive and sweeping
> programme of economic reforms. There were, of course, the
> social revolutionaries—and among them the communists—
> who had their particular ideas on this subject, but the PKI
> never occupied a single seat in any of the seven cabinets of this
> period. The other social radical leftists who were occasionally
> given ministerial posts were never in a sufficiently strong
> position to influence general policy. In all governments between
> 1949 and 1957 the parties who predominated represented what
> might be called the middle-classes—the economic bourgeoisie,
> the Western-educated intellectuals, the civil servants. It is true
> that only a very small minority belonging to these groups can
> be classified as bourgeois-capitalist and, as a result, the major-
> ity were able to adhere to some socialist ideas without embarras-
> sing consequences for themselves. But their socialism was
> directed more negatively against foreign (Dutch and Chinese)

capitalism than positively towards any real programme of socialization. Moreover, whatever disharmony might exist among these parties and on whatever issues they were fighting each other openly or intriguing against each other in secrecy, they were in complete agreement that the proletariat, whether rural or urban, should be kept in its place. This was not easy, however. First, economic conditions were not conducive to preventing social unrest from spreading. Secondly, the masses had been greatly affected by the revolutionary troubles of the previous decade. To a large extent the propaganda of the nationalist parties themselves was responsible for this, for in order to enlist the support of the lower classes, they had promised a better life in the future. Indonesia, they had said, would cease to be a nation of coolies, but this is what it continued to be. After independence, the nationalist *élite* had taken over political control and the direction of economic affairs and the proletariat had been left behind with its expectations unfulfilled. The disappointment of the lower classes was successfully exploited by the PKI and other social revolutionary politicians who were in a stronger position to do so than the middle-class nationalists who were in power, since they were glad to point out the failures of the government. Under Dutch rule the nationalists had done the same, but they could not possibly afford to follow this line once they had become the government themselves.'[24]

The Indonesian Communists had learned their lesson, however, from the disaster of 1948. This time, under the able leadership of Aidit, they strove to build a mass base. Membership of the Party rose rapidly; it was soon the biggest Communist party in the world outside of Russia and China. Moreover, millions more joined PKI-controlled organizations such as SOBSI, the trade union federation, or Barisan Tani Indonesia, the peasant union. Aidit saw that one of the weaknesses of the party earlier had been too great concentration on the relatively tiny proletariat at the expense of the peasants, who constituted 85 per cent of the population. In an important article in 1953 he re-oriented the party with the statement that 'The agrarian revolution is the essence of the people's democratic revolution in Indonesia'.[25] Moreover, there were plenty of grievances upon which to build, for the economic policies of the government, insofar as they existed, failed to halt inflation, falling living standards, unemployment, corruption, land fragmentation, soil erosion and a dozen other circumstances detrimental to the peasant.

These objective economic factors favoured Aidit's waiting game. So did President Sukarno's need to lean on the PKI as a counter-balance to the armed forces, in the upper reaches of which socially conservative figures dominated. Sukarno pressed energetically anti-imperialist policies, with which the PKI could identify, and yet which offered the armed forces a continuing active role in the revolution—as, for example, with his campaign to free West Irian (West New Guinea) from continuing Dutch occupation. Yet Sukarno could not afford to antagonize the *élite* by implementing effective social-radical measures internally, so that PKI backing for him was subject to the drawback that the party itself would be associated with the economic failures of the President.

Moreover, there were other circumstances which militated against the PKI and other left organizations. The United States, alienated by Sukarno's leftist foreign policies and by the political complexion of some of his supporters, had begun casting round for alternative governments in Indonesia before the end of the 1950's. There were a number of possibilities. Not all the islands of the vast archipelago were reconciled to rule from Djakarta—'Javanese imperialism', as they saw it. There were also disgruntled individuals who had run foul of Sukarno or who bitterly disagreed with his policies. The Americans dabbled in these divisive currents right up until 1958, when they changed their tactics. That year saw the failure of the biggest of the regionally-based anti-Djakarta rebellions. A number of dissidents fled to Sumatra, and there proclaimed a

> 'Revolutionary Government of the Republic of Indonesia . . . strengthened by the expectation of considerable outside support',

according to one authority. The latter adds:

> 'It is difficult to ascertain to what extent they indulged in wishful thinking, but in any event foreign agents did make commitments to them and one shipload of supplies reached Padang before the rebellion was launched. Soon afterward considerable

quantities of modern American military equipment were flown to the rebels, mostly from Formosa. . . . American military supplies to the rebels continued to arrive in considerable quantities. . . .'[26]

Intervention became even more direct when

'. . . two B-26s and two Mustangs strafed shipping . . . and bombed Macassar. . . . Doubts about the participation of Americans in the affair . . . were removed on May 18, when a B-26 was downed near Ambon and Allan Lawrence Pope, the aircraft's American pilot, was captured.'[27]

American support for the anti-Sukarno rebels was based on their explicit anti-communism. One of the leaders told a British correspondent to

'. . . tell people . . . we need anti-communist literature which we can translate and distribute in Java. We are alone in this great struggle against communism and we need help.'[28]

However, despite the support of some anti-Communist politicians, military commanders and regional leaders in Sumatra and the Celebes, the 1958 revolt was quickly broken by the loyal forces of the Republic:

'. . . the population of the territories where the dissidents had taken over power hardly lifted a finger to support their régime.'[29]

Those rebels who returned to the fold were accorded extraordinarily moderate treatment:

'They were welcomed as returning prodigal sons rather than rebels, particularly the military men among them, and in several instances they were even permitted to retain their arms and their formations, a leniency typical of the way an essentially rightist government treats its essentially right-wing adversaries, and contrasting sharply with the savage butchery that had followed the suppression of the Madiun (i.e. communist) rising.'[30]

The collapse of the Sumatran revolt compelled the US to change tactics; from that point on all efforts were bent to cultivating close relations with known anti-communists, like General Nasution,

inside the official armed forces, and to building up the fire power
of the Indonesian Army with a view to baulking the PKI. From
this point of view, Aidit recognized that his party was at a grave
disadvantage, for while the Army leaders could fly quite openly to
various world capitals in search of credit for the purchase of military equipment, which could then be openly and quite legitimately
shipped into Indonesia, there were no channels by which arms
could be brought in in any significant quantity for the communists.
Even had the Chinese wished to help Aidit in this respect, they had
no means of doing so. There can be no doubt that any Chinese
ships that had tried to run guns in to Indonesia would have been
blown out of the water by British or American warships before
they ever reached their destination.[31] The motives for thus 'enforcing domination' are candidly exposed by a Conservative M.P.:

'More than other nations in the world Britain depends for
her livelihood on assured access to raw materials and markets.
Some of our most important raw materials—oil, rubber, tin,
copper, jute and wool—come from the arc of countries stretch-
ing round the Indian Ocean. . . . One way and another, the
present and potential British investment east of Suez must be
worth several thousand million pounds. . . . If Communism
came to these countries Britain's investments would be lost.'[32]

In this way, a gross disparity in fire-power grew up as between
the largely conservative social force of the Army and the radical
force of the PKI and sympathetic groups, with consequences we
will have occasion to examine in the final chapter.

But at this point, having looked at a number of the post-war
popular up-risings, it is necessary to come to some general conclusion as to their true roots and nature. The conventional view,
so long accepted in the West, is that these revolts were inspired
and puppet-stringed from outside, as part of the world designs
of international communism. Thus:

'Zhdanov made a speech at a conference in October 1947
which was a veiled order to the Communists of Southeast
Asia to revolt. . . . The new policy was discussed at the Com-
munist-sponsored Youth Conference of South and Southeast
Asia which was held at Calcutta in February 1948. Shortly
afterwards there were Communist revolts in Malaya, Indonesia

and Burma. . . . That is too many coincidences to be a co-incidence.'[33]

However, closer examination of the various insurrections hardly sustains this hypothesis. British repression of their activities had pushed the Malayan Communist Party, for example, into a position where they had virtually no alternative but revolt. The *Times* Far Eastern correspondent wrote at the time that:

> 'An incontestable conviction is growing that the Malayan Communists were compelled to undertake military operations sooner than they were ready for them; that is, they were forced into revolution . . . the murder of the three British planters (on June 16, 1948—the conventional date for the start of the "Emergency") was not part of the plans of the Communist leadership, but an accident.'[34]

Be it noted that the MCP were 'forced into revolution' not by Russian instructions but by British suppression of legitimate organs of working-class representation and struggle. One glaring weakness of the conventional explanation has always been its failure to explain what kind of sanctions Moscow could wield to force parties, with which contact was minimal and to which virtually no economic or military aid was being given, to risk everything—including the lives of their members—by revolt. On the other hand, it is quite understandable that men faced with indefinite imprisonment or deportation by the British should resort to desperate measures in self-defence.

In the case of Indonesia, the accepted Western view has always been based upon the assumption that the Madiun uprising of the PKI was a direct consequence of the return to Java from Moscow of the known communist Musso, who, in this view, brought with him the 'instructions' of the Russian party. Facts, however, make this interpretation untenable:

> 'The PKI . . . had determined to undertake armed struggle, *if all else failed*, a month *before* Musso appeared in Jogjakarta.'[35]

Furthermore,

> '. . . the Madiun rising, according to all evidence, was in-advertent. . . .'[36]

This American author, whose work is based on Russian as well as Western sources, concludes that

'. . . it appears that Moscow and the Indonesian Communists were working somewhat at cross purposes. . . . Emphasis . . . attaches more properly to the likely *absence* of Soviet directives, which might have restrained the Indonesians, than to the probability that any existed to goad them on.'[37]

Finally, Mills (cited above, pp. 171–2) mentions Burma. McLane states that

'No single episode brought the Burmese Communists to the point of openly defying the Nu government. . . . No exclusive significance, at any event, attaches to the Southeast Asian Youth Conference as the source of the Burmese rising . . . the Burmese Communists might well have taken to arms when they did had there been no Youth Conference at Calcutta, or no Burmese delegation present at it.'[38]

The truth is that by 1948 the Cold War was in full swing, and everywhere the Western powers were stepping up repression of Communism and allied political movements that threatened the hegemony of the West. In February, Czechoslovakia had undergone a bloodless coup which put the communists and other left wing parties firmly in power, in order to forestall the fate of the left in countries such as Greece, where massive Western intervention had destroyed the working-class movement and installed reactionary rulers in power. Czechoslovakia hastened the application of the anti-communist policy of the West throughout the globe, and as repression mounted, in South-East Asia as elsewhere, resistance on the part of indigenous revolutionary forces naturally stiffened. In Burma, although already by 1948 an independent country, the presence of British troops was secured by treaty for a period of three years from August 1947; although they were only marginally involved in the civil war which followed the Burmese government's decision to issue a warrant for the arrest of the Burmese communist leaders, they *were* involved. At the same time in Indonesia the communists were struggling against the influence of moderates such as Hatta, who was accused of conceding too much to the Dutch in negotiations, and who was certainly the man in whose leadership

'. . . the Dutch, and the Western powers generally, could be expected to place maximum trust.'[39]

Moreover, there had already been manifestations of spontaneous popular social revolution in Indonesia, notably in Sumatra.[40] It would appear, then, that there is no need and no justification for invoking an international communist conspiracy to account for the varied revolutionary movements of post-war South-East Asia.

It remains to study the fate of the working class of the Indian sub-continent, and the extent of their liberation, in the post-war period. As we have seen, Gandhi and the social forces he represented were essentially conservative, and had acted as a restraint on the development of a militantly revolutionary Indian working class movement. Objective economic circumstances for the mass of the people were no better in India than in China. And indeed there *were* armed up-risings of the Indian peasantry in the post-war years, but for various reasons they were limited in geographical spread and in duration.

Let us look at two major ones, about which information though sparse is not completely unobtainable. The first, dating from 1945–6, occurred in what is now East Pakistan. This was known as the *Tebhaga* movement.

> '*Tebhaga*, the slogan of the movement, was the demand for the reduction of the share of the proprietor from one-half of the crop to one-third . . . the *jotedars*, the proprietors of the land, were in fact "occupancy tenants" (with transferable and heritable rights in the land) who paid a fixed-money rent to the Zemindars, the great landlords. Over the years the fixed-money rent paid to the landlords had become a relatively small part of the value of the crop. Thus it was the *jotedars* who appropriated the largest share of the crop. Their land was cultivated by *ahhiars* or *bhargadars* who were the share-croppers.'[41]

The sharecroppers were in an intolerably dependent position, as the death of three and a half *million* of them in the 1943 Bengal famine tragically shows. The *jotedars* on the other hand stood to gain from rice scarcity, as they had the major part of the crop passing through their hands on the way to hoarders, profiteers, speculators and others with the money to pay.

Hamza Alavi, in the article quoted above, shows that the immediate aftermath of the terrible famine was a growth of contact between the suffering rural peoples and potential leadership. Students and others engaged in famine relief work saw at first hand what the conditions of a dependent peasantry could deteriorate to where the power of the landlords was almost without limit or restraint. For a short period things favoured the peasants. The authorities were alarmed by the Japanese invasion of Assam and parts of East Bengal into taking action against too blatant war profiteering etc., and this weakened the *jotedars*. Moreover, the very magnitude of the famine had produced a temporary labour shortage which transiently strengthened the peasants.

The *Tebhaga* movement was under way by 1945. The Indian Communist Party, however, had to wait until the end of the war with Japan before throwing its weight behind the peasants. By 1946 the situation was, for the landed *élite* and the authorities alike, an extremely threatening one throughout the affected regions, for the peasants were asserting their rights by retaining the crops, setting up peasant committees to administer their own affairs, and resisting attempts by landlords, police and troops to restore 'law and order' (i.e. the division of the harvest in the proportions two-thirds to the non-cultivator, one-third to the peasant cultivator).

In 1947 the *Tebhaga* movement collapsed as quickly as it had arisen. Bigger issues—Independence, Partition—over-shadowed it. Although the revolt had taken place in a largely Muslim area, much of the leadership had been Hindu. The troubles that were to accompany the setting up of Pakistan and India broke this partnership irrevocably:

'It is now twenty years since the *Tebhaga* struggle had begun. But nothing like it has arisen again in areas in which it had been the most powerful.'[42]

The other big post-war revolutionary peasant movement in the Indian sub-continent was the *Telengana* movement. This originated in Hyderabad State, notorious for its 'backward, oppressive and ruthless aristocracy'. Starting with what were, in the circumstances of dire poverty and distress, moderate demands, the peasants were driven by armed repression into armed resistance.

It is important to note the chronology here, and the chronology of the relationship of the *Telengana* peasants with the Communist Party, of which Alavi writes:

> 'By 1947 the *Telengana* Movement had a guerrilla army of about 5,000. The peasants killed or drove out the landlords and the local bureaucrats and seized and redistributed the land. They established governments of peasant "soviets" which were integrated regionally into a central organization. Peasant rule was established in an area of 15,000 square miles with a population of four million. . . . Local communists had participated in the movement vigorously, although it did not receive the official sanction of the Communist leadership until later. By the time of the Second Congress of the CPI in March 1948 the *Telengana* Movement had already entered its revolutionary phase and was one of the factors which influenced the leftward swing in the Communist Party line at the Congress.'[43]

In other words, it was the peasant movement which influenced the Party, and not the Party (under 'instructions' from Moscow) that influenced or instigated the peasant movement.

Factors which had earlier favoured the *Telengana* movement, such as the general political unrest and tide of nationalism sweeping the sub-continent in the wake of war, were later to turn against it. The confusion over the future alignment of Hyderabad state created fatal divisions and about-turns among the leaders, and the Indian Army proved more competent, powerful and successful in repressing the up-rising than the local forces had been. Finally,

> '. . . the movement developed its initial momentum from the fact that its demands were broad-based and it drew in the middle peasant as well as the poor peasant. Later on, when the peasant "Soviets" were set up and land was redistributed, conflicts of interest between different sections of the peasantry came to the surface. . . . The disruption of the peasant base proved disastrous when they were under heavy military attack.'[44]

Heavy military attack alone cannot destroy a revolutionary movement when the people are united and determined in their aims, a fact which is amply borne out by French experience in Vietnam and Algeria and US experience in Vietnam.

Hamza Alavi sums up the lessons of the *Tebhaga* and *Telengana* Movements as follows:

> 'The . . . Movements had both risen from their local roots rather than from any initiatives of the Communist Party. . . . After the Communist Party Congress of 1948 the Party was committed to launch insurrectionary forms of struggle. But it was not able to organize any movement . . . (although) . . . local peasant unrest continued to manifest itself throughout India. But it remained localized and limited in scope. *It was clear that peasant insurrections could not be launched merely by Party decisions, but required certain pre-conditions to exist before they could develop.*'[45]

Conditions for the bulk of the peasantry have not noticeably improved in the years since 1951, when the *Telengana* movement was finally crushed. Land reform carried out under the ruling Congress government has no doubt decisively altered some aspects of the rural scene. An upper segment of the tenantry were enabled to acquire land. Capitalist, as opposed to feudal, methods of agriculture were encouraged. Co-operatives were fostered, too. But the *basic* class structure of the Indian countryside has remained unchanged. The poor remain in a position of dependence and the rich in a position of control. Even in the co-operatives the rich retain effective control, as they do in the village councils. The result is stagnation at best, retrogression too often in practice. The average calorie consumption of the Indian is no better than 1,880 per diem—far below the basic minimum requirement of 2,300 calculated by the Food and Agriculture Organization of the U.N., and not much more than *half* the British figure of 3,270. This spells out a reality of privation and want on an unimaginable scale, with the constant threat of absolute disaster never more than a breath away. The *Daily Telegraph* reported in 1966 that:

> 'India's worst famine is expected to strike the northern plains by January or February and continue until the harvesting season next autumn . . . According to latest estimates *the famine belt covers 100 million people* living in an area stretching

from Gujarat on the West Coast to the borders of Bengal in the east.'[46]

The population grows by nearly 10,000,000 a year, but the crops are not expanding at the same rate. The result is that:

'It is not as though the risks of famine have been slowly shrinking over the years, or the numbers of the starving been significantly diminished. The average Indian in the 1950's was much further from sufficiency than the Indian of the 1870's.'[47]

Shackled by poverty, hunger and dependence upon the rich, the peasants of India can not yet be said to have won their liberation. The *élite* who utilise and manipulate the political structure from village level right up to central government level understand well enough the real threat to their continued exercise of wealth, privilege and power. The real threat is that of a truly radical programme of land reform and socialist planning, a programme capable of liberating the energies of the masses and harnessing them to the tasks of *national* economic development. Peasant discontent, which might threaten to congeal into peasant action on a national scale, must, therefore, be channelled off into safer directions—religion, language, race, caste, local issues of all kinds. The conflict with China over border definition played a useful role in distracting attention from the poverty problem. For

'. . . the aroused peasants possessed the potential to change the basic social structure.'[48]

'Despite the outcry of Bombay businessmen, what Indian agriculture needs is not less "Communism", but more—if the chasm between rich and poor is to be crossed, if a sense of community and so of national effort is ever to be induced, if enough food is to be grown to feed the multitude of starving. . . . To propose . . . that Congress itself should imitate Communist practice, and recruit from the countryside party cadres, with the background, enthusiasm and ability to communicate the purpose of co-operative farming to the peasants, is not to destroy democracy in India, but to develop it . . . it is nonsense to call the securing of privilege the protection of liberty. . . . The alternative, an even further impoverishment of the poor who compose the vast majority of the Indian people, bears no real relation to democracy or freedom. *If a small minority of dissidents must be coerced into co-operative farming, there is coercion on a far greater scale in the very inequalities of present-day rural India.* Are the landless labourers, and the small cultivators sunk in debt and unable to scratch even a subsistence for themselves and their families, not endlessly coerced?'[49]

The inescapable fact of India is that the revolution begun by the achievement of independence is incomplete:

'Indian independence, for so long the promise of the poor, has become instead the reward of the rich.'[50]

The contrast with China could hardly be more complete. The present upheavals connected with the proletarian cultural revolution cannot obscure the underlying economic success of the régime since 1949. Mistakes have been made, but overall progress has also been made. Western observers returning from China, however adverse their comments on the consequences of the cultural revolution, agree that the food-shops mirror a country which is no longer hungry and the streets a people no longer poor in the sense of the age-old poverty of Asia.

To elucidate this matter, and to explore the role of Western capitalism in general and American imperialism in particular in preserving inequalities is the task of the next and final chapter.

REFERENCES

1. C. Buss: *Asia in the Modern World*, London, 1964, p. 302.
2. UNESCO, 18/7/50.
3. K. Nkrumah: *Neo-colonialism: The Last Stage of Imperialism*, London, 1965, p. ix.
4. Cited in W. Miller: *A New History of the United States*, New York, 1958, p. 333.
5. Cited in R. Segal: *The Race War*, London, 1966, p. 137; Segal comments: 'The United States was assuming the right to ensure amenable régimes throughout the continent.'
6. R. Segal: *The Race War*, London, 1966, p. 143.
7. D. Bryan: *China's Taiwan*, London, 1959, p. 8.

8. D. Wurfel: 'The Philippines' in G. McT. Kahin (ed.): *Governments and Politics of Southeast Asia*, New York, 1964, pp. 698–9.

9. W. J. Pomeroy: *Guerrilla and Counter-Guerrilla Warfare*, New York, 1964, pp. 61–3.

10. W. J. Pomeroy: *Guerrilla and Counter-Guerrilla Warfare*, New York, 1964, p. 66.

11. Ibid., pp. 69–70.

12. F. Spencer Chapman: *The Jungle is Neutral*, London, 1965, p. 281.

13. J. M. Gullick: *Malaya*, London, 1963, p. 85.

14. Ibid., p. 96.

15. *Berita Pemuda*, Vol. 3, No. 3, London, 1965, p. 5.

16. H. Miller: *The Story of Malaysia*, London, 1965, p. 176.

17. Cited in Han Suyin: . . . *And the Rain My Drink*, London, 1961, p. 100.

18. See *The Times*, London, 11/8/65.

19. Malayan rubber '. . . saved the United Kingdom from bankruptcy after the war by earning more dollars in the critical five years 1947–51 than all the industries and trades of the metropolitan country put together.' C. A. Fisher: *South East Asia*, London, 1964, p. 610.

20. J. Silverstein: 'Burma' in G. McT. Kahin (ed.): *Governments and Politics of Southeast Asia*, New York, 1964, p. 93.

21. A. C. Brackman: *Indonesian Communism*, New York, 1963, p. 101. author's italics.

22. A. C. Brackman: ibid., p. 99.

23. A. H. Nasutin: *Fundamentals of Guerrilla Warfare*, Djakarta, 1953, p. 15.

24. J. M. Pluvier: *Confrontations*, Kuala Lumpur, 1965, pp. 35–7.

25. D. N. Aidit: 'The Future of the Indonesian Peasant Movement', *Red Star*, July 1953.

26. G. McT. Kahin: 'Indonesia' in G. McT. Kahin (ed.): *Major Goverments of Asia*, Ithaca, 1963, pp. 647–8.

27. A. C. Brackman: *Indonesian Communism*, New York, 1963, p. 250.

28. J. Mossman: *Rebels in Paradise*, London, 1961, p. 70.

29. J. M. Pluvier: *Confrontations*, Kuala Lumpur, 1965, p. 50.

30. J. M. Pluvier: ibid., pp. 50–1.

31. 'Close watch by very high-flying reconnaisance jets equipped with the latest electronic equipment allows Britain to keep a close watch over all Indonesia . . . (and) . . . American F-111 (TFX) will be able to *enforce British domination over the area*.' Air Commodore E. M. Donaldson in the *Daily Telegraph*, 11/8/65. Author's italics.

32. Julian Amery: 'East of Suez: The British Stake', *Daily Telegraph*, 24/1/66.

33. L. A. Mills: *Southeast Asia*, Minneapolis, 1964, p. 140.

34. *Far Eastern Survey*, 22/12/48, cited by C. B. McLane: *Soviet Strategies in Southeast Asia*, Princeton, 1966, p. 395.

35. C. B. McLane: ibid., p. 406; author's italics in first instance only.

36. C. B. McLane: ibid., p. 408.

37. McLane: pp. 404, 409.

38. McLane: ibid., pp. 375–6.

39. H. Feith: *The Decline of Constitutional Democracy in Indonesia*, Ithaca, 1962, p. 23.

40. W. F. Wertheim: *Indonesian Society in Transition*, The Hague, 1956, p. 159.

41. Hamza Alavi: 'Peasants and Revolution' in R. Miliband and J. Saville (eds.): *The Socialist Register 1965*, London, 1965, p. 265.

42. Hamza Alavi: ibid., p. 268.

43. H. Alavi: ibid., p. 268.

44. H. Alavi: ibid., pp. 269–70.

45. H. Alavi: ibid., p. 270; author's italics.

46. 7/11/66. author's italics.

47. R. Segal: *The Crisis of India*, London, 1965, p. 180.

48. R. Segal: *The Race War*, London, 1966, p. 143.

49. R. Segal: *The Crisis of India*, London, 1965, pp. 216–17. Author's italics.

50. R. Segal: ibid., p. 287.

Note (see p. 159): Numerous books have been written about the war in Vietnam, now the classic example of a war of liberation; the following list includes the most valuable works.

W. G. Burchett: Vietnam—*Inside Story of the Guerrilla War*, London, 1965.

D. Halberstham: *The Making of a Quagmire*, New York, 1965.

W. G. Burchett: *Vietnam North*, London, 1966.

M. Gettlemann (ed.): *Vietnam*, London, 1966.

E. S. Herman and R. B. Du Boff: *America's Vietnam Policy*, Washington, D.C., 1966.

D. Pike: *Viet Cong*, London, 1966.

F. Schurmann, P. D. Scott and R. Zelnick: *The Politics of Escalation in Vietnam*, New York, 1966.

D. Duncan: *The New Legions*, London, 1967.

B. B. Fall (ed.): *Ho Chi Minh on Revolution*, London, 1967.

There are several editions in English of General No Nguyen Giap's *People's War and People's Army* (e.g. Hanoi, 1961). General Giap was the victor of Dien Bien Phu, and this account of the war of the Vietnamese people against the French has become a standard text on the subject of liberation.

CHAPTER EIGHT

Liberation and the American Empire

IT is now time to draw together the threads of this necessarily rather diffuse discussion, and in particular to pay attention to the following questions: Is the conventional, received and general opinion in the West about the nature of liberation struggles a realistic one? Does political independence without radical social and economic change liberate the people of former colonies in any meaningful sense? What is the real interest of the West in general and the United States in particular in intervening in the processes of social change in Asia, and the 'third world' generally, in order to stabilize the *status quo?*

It is as well to remind ourselves briefly of what that *status quo* consists. To quote U Thant, Secretary General of the United Nations:

'The harsh fact persists that many of the poorest economies have continued to grow most slowly. The growth in developing countries as a whole slowed down from an average annual rate of 4·5 per cent in 1955–1960 to 4 per cent in 1960–1963. At the same time the growth rate in the economically advanced market economies has accelerated from 3·4 per cent in the earlier period to 4·4 per cent in 1960–1963. The gap between the per capita incomes of the developing countries and those of the developed countries has also widened during the 1960's; between 1960 and 1962 the average annual per capita income in the developed market economies increased by almost $100 while that in the developing countries increased by barely $5.'[1]

And again:

'The misery of much of the developing world is a progressive misery. It threatens to grow worse in the second half of the decade. On present showing the numbers of unemployed and men and women suffering from hunger and malnutrition will be markedly greater in 1970 than today . . . in 1955 the Indian estimate of unemployment was some 5 million. By 1961 it had grown to 8 millions. Even if the planned production targets for 1966 and 1971 are fulfilled, the Indian authorities estimate that unemployment will still rise to 12 million and 14 million in these two years respectively. A particularly disturbing feature in these situations is the degree to which unemployment will fall most heavily on young people. In Indonesia, 50 per cent of the urban unemployed and in Ceylon 80 per cent are under 25 years of age. . . . In a world of hope and upheaval, the young men seize the means of transport designed to open up the countryside to stream away from the farms before there is room for them in the cities and before the farms are producing a surplus of food.'[2]

We may safely conclude from the statistical picture that there are more hungry people in the world today than ever before in history, and add that moreover there are more illiterate and totally uneducated people in the world today than ever before (there are about 373 million children of school age throughout the world, but only 115 million of them go to school—3 out of 10; almost 750 million adults, half the population of the 'free' world in Asia, Africa and Latin America, have had no schooling and cannot read or write): not a *status quo* with any attraction for the vast majority of the world's population.

How has this situation come about? It is not enough to say that the advance of science and know-how in the West has brought falling death rates everywhere, and therefore caused over-population and falling living standards in the less developed lands. How did these countries *come to be* 'less developed'? Why did falling death rates not bring impoverishment in the *West*, but on the contrary can be seen to be an essential integral element in the rising living standards associated with the Industrial Revolution?

Our answer must necessarily be brief. But fortunately the basic components are clear. When the Western countries first started expanding overseas, there was very little to choose between their average overall level of social, economic, political, technological, artistic and scientific—in brief, cultural—achievement and that of the peoples with whom they came in contact. However, once a gap had begun to appear, for whatever reasons (and they are complex), it steadily opened in favour of the West. There is nothing surprising in this: in the circumstances of a more or less free operation of market forces, unimpeded by interventions deliberately contrived by men to right inefficiencies and injustices, 'cumulative circular causation' is a universal phenomenon. Popular lore recognizes this with the saying 'money makes money'. It is self-flattering for people in the West to attribute the gap between living standards in the industrial and the non-industrial countries to differences in inherent racial capacities. But in these kinds of (unscientific) terms how can we then account for such phenomena as the economic growth of the South East of England at the expense of the North West, Northern Ireland, Scotland and elsewhere inside the British Isles? Or the differences between north and south in Italy? Or in the United States of America? No, it is clear that once the gap had opened in favour of the Western world, familiar economic forces conspired to prise it continually further open *in the absence of countervailing forces*. (The complex factors originally responsible for the gap included such capricious items as the shortage of timber in parts of the West—such as Britain—necessitating improved techniques involving coal and iron, which in turn revolutionized military technology, and the circumstance that while Europe desperately needed some products of the rest of the world, the rest of the world was rather indifferent to the products of Europe.)

The consequences of the gap were multiple and self-reinforcing. Bit by bit the colonial powers were drawn or forced into assuming political control of most of the rest of the world. Once this had occurred, political power was used to accelerate and intensify the operation of economic forces. The extraction of capital from the colonies was facilitated by the introduction of new methods and by the implementation of regulations favouring Western enterprise and discriminating against local and competing enterprise. The economic surplus of the colonies—the capital which might otherwise have been invested locally—stoked, on the contrary, the industrialisation of the West. The twin results were rising living standards in Europe and North America and stagnant or falling living standards elsewhere.

The best single indication of the impact of colonialism is perhaps the case of Japan. Japan alone of Asian countries avoided both colonialism and economic imperialism (Thailand and China were in effect economic colonies, the former after 1855 and the latter after 1842). And Japan alone of Asian countries succeeded in industrialising. Why? An answer may be sought in contrasting the success story of Japan with the story of Java, long colonized by the Dutch.

'Both are heavily populated. Both rest agriculturally on a labor-intensive, small-farm, multicrop cultivation régime centering on wet rice. Both have managed to maintain a significant degree of social and cultural traditionalism in the face of profound encounter with the West and extensive domestic change. In fact, in agriculture, the further back one goes toward the mid-nineteenth century the more the two resemble one another. Japanese per-hectare rice yields at the beginning of Meiji (1868) were probably about the same as those of Java at the beginning of the Corporate Plantation System (1870); today they are about two and a half times as high. Between 1878 and 1942 the percentage of the Japanese labour force employed in agriculture dropped from around 80 to around 40; the Javanese . . . had not fallen below 65 percent. And . . . the percentage of aggregate net income contributed by agricultural production in the Japan of the 1880's was of the same general order as that in the Java of the 1950's, by which time the Japanese percentage was only a third as large. . . . Between 1870 and 1940 Java absorbed the bulk of her increase in numbers—about thirty million people—into post-traditional village social systems. . . . From 1872 to 1940, the Japanese farm population remained virtually constant around 14 million people . . . at the same time as the total population grew approximately 35 million . . . Japan increased productivity per agricultural worker 236 percent, Java—the estates aside for the moment—hardly increased it at all . . . where Japanese peasant agriculture came to be complementarily related to an expanding manufacturing system in indigenous hands, Javanese peasant agriculture came to be complementarily related to an expanding agro-industrial structure under foreign management. As labor productivity in the capital-intensive sector in Japan increased, it increased also in the labor-intensive sector; as it increased in the capital-intensive sector in Java it remained approximately constant in the labor-intensive one. In Japan, the peasant sector supported the industrial one during the crucial three decades of the latter's emergence largely by means of extremely heavy land taxation; in Java, the peasant sector supported the industrial one through the provision of under-priced labor and land. In Japan, the industrial sector, once underway, then re-invigorated the peasant sector through the provision of cheap commercial fertilizer, more effective farm tools, support of technical education and extension work and, eventually, after the First World War, simple mechanization, as well as by offering expanded markets for agricultural products of all sorts; in Java most of the invigorating effect of the flourishing agro-industrial sector was exercised upon Holland, and its impact upon the peasant sector was . . . enervating.'[3]

It is impossible to escape the conclusion, which indeed the author cited above comes to, that:

'The existence of colonial government was decisive because it meant that the growth potential inherent in the traditional Javanese economy—"the excess labor on the land and the reserves of productivity in the land" to use the phrase that has been applied to the "slack" in the Japanese traditional economy . . . was harnessed not to Javanese (or Indonesian) development but to Dutch.' The hapless Javanese achieved '. . . the agonies attendant upon industrialization without achieving its cultural, social and psychological fruits. The real tragedy of colonial history in Java after 1830 is not that the peasantry suffered. . . . The tragedy is that it suffered for nothing.'[4]

It would be easy to multiply the examples. A Cambridge-trained Burmese economist, for example, writes:

'. . . unlike Japan, the expansion of imports (into Burma) was accompanied by only a slow development of import-saving light consumer-goods industries. This was partly because of the lack of entrepreneurship and partly because of the free trade policy which failed to give protection to these industries in their infancy. But another important reason was the employment of large numbers of temporary Indian labourers, whose high propensity to save (for remittances to their families in India) damped down the level of internal demand in Burma. Their employment therefore contributed both to the shortage of indigenous savings and to the lack of investment incentives, the result of which was a slow development of domestic industries.'[5]

For both the lack of protective tariffs and the introduction of Indian labour Britain, the colonial power, was directly responsible. The importance of the first point is underlined by the fact that even nations with the advantages of the United States and Germany required initially to shelter their infant industries behind protective tariffs against British competition.

But the significant general point is readily illustrated. The building of the railway network in Britain in the nineteenth century directly stimulated the growth of the British iron and coal industries, the development of a British locomotive and rolling-stock construction industry, and the expansion or inauguration of a host of British subsidiary or consumer good industries to meet the demands of the new mills, mines and factories and of the new skilled workers. When the construction of railways was extended to the colonies, in order to facilitate the extraction of their wealth, it was undertaken by British capital, with British management and British skilled labour; and, because it was accomplished with the help of British steel, coal, locomotives and rolling-stock, and because the British employees disposed of the bulk of their incomes either in the form of remittances to Britain or by importing British consumer goods into the colonies, the stimulating economic impact was again felt in Britain rather than in the colonies. Colonial investments, in other words, result in the development of *enclaves*; these are geographically sited in the colonies but economically are almost as much part of the metropolitan country as domestic investments.

The relevance of this to our study of the national liberation movements of today is as follows. The growing wealth of Western

Europe and North America enabled the governing *élite* to yield,
if need be, to some of the demands of the mass of the people for
a better life and a share in the growing patrimony and its govern-
ance. The world's markets from Alaska to Madagascar and from
Korea to Peru lay at the mercy of the new factory industry and
its accompanying marvels of finance and business organization.
The confident wielders of that power could afford to relax
somewhat the oppression which had weighed so heavily and
inhumanly upon their own labouring classes. There were even
positive advantages in compromising with working class demands
and elevating at least an influential segment of that class to comparative security and respectability, for thereby the frontiers of
revolution were pushed overseas into the colonies: such grievances as remained domestically were either negotiable or could
safely be neglected. Furthermore, in due course the rising pur-
chasing power of the man in the street was perceived to have an
important contribution to make to the stability and viability of
capitalism, whereas earlier it had been regarded solely as deduct-
ing from the stock of capital available for investment. The special
circumstances of the pioneer industrializing powers, in other
words, permitted and facilitated peaceful and piecemeal social
revolution.

If the sun shone on one part of the globe, the other hemisphere
was correspondingly plunged in darkness. Rights grudgingly
conceded to the metropolitan masses were brutally denied to the
unregarded peons, kaffirs and coolies of the colonial world. While
the circumstances of at least a considerable portion of the Western
workers were steadily improving, those of their colonial brothers
were as steadily worsening, pressed down by rising population,
fragmentation of land-holdings, progressive indebtedness, rack-
renting landlordism, and by Western engrossment of the local
potential investible surplus (to the existence of which the very
magnitude of colonial profits testified). In dealing with the
colonial working-class movements, moreover, even the limited
accommodation characteristic of the *élite* in their own countries
was discarded in favour of repression (and one ought not to overlook the steady increase in the fire-power available to the *élite* in
safeguarding their privileges between Peterloo—1819—and
Vietnam today; even in 1819 the established authorities were
obsessed with 'revolutionary plots among the people'). So that

both in terms of the avenues of advance permitted them, and of the strength of the forces ranged against them, the colonial working people had clearly desperately more difficult struggles facing them in their search for liberation than the working people of the West had had (and even their achievement is far from complete). Accordingly, the whole nature and character of the later struggles were likely to differ from the earlier.

It ought to be understood, too, that the whole context of the struggle was—and is—immeasurably harsher in the developing countries than in those that succeeded in industrializing earlier. The presently developed countries had enjoyed political independence and stability for some time before they started industrializing. As far back as the end of the seventeenth century, England had a non-agricultural sector, in terms of the percentage of the working population employed in it, greater than that holding today in the underdeveloped countries in general. Per capita incomes in the present poor countries are only between a third and a sixth of those to be found in the developed countries a century ago. The present rich countries all *started* with small populations (the USA, for example, had only 3 million people in 1780—and a continent the size of China to expand into), whereas many of the presently poor countries have giant populations (for example, China, India, Indonesia, and Pakistan have all nine-digit populations). In the developing countries today, death rates are lower, and birth rates higher, than in the West's industrial revolution. Finally, there is a new factor of conscious emulation; as two economic historians have written:

'In the past social welfare came as a by-product of economic development. . . . At the present time in South East Asia, as in many other under-developed regions, there is a tendency to aim directly at social welfare. . . .'[6]

If one looks in this light at the countries of the developing world today, some understanding of the magnitude of the task facing them must emerge. Since we have associated quite directly the present poverty of the third world with colonialism, it is now necessary to consider the question of the relationship between independence and poverty. But in addition, we require also to investigate the relationship between the *type* of independence and poverty.

There are a number of newly-independent countries which are
generally held up in the West as models of what can be accomplished non-violently and democratically. High up on every such
list stand the Philippines and Malaysia. Yet, as we have seen,
both suffered from left-wing up-risings in the post-war period,
up-risings which were only put down with the decisive help of
the metropolitan power. Perhaps, however, the objective
circumstances have now so changed that there is no further
danger of 'democracy' being threatened? What are the facts?
A distinguished scholar of South East Asia writes of the Philippines:

> 'The statements of Francis B. Sayre, America's last High
> Commissioner to the Philippines before the war, still hold
> true: "The bulk of the newly created income went to the
> Government, to landlords, and to urban areas, and served but
> little to ameliorate living conditions among the almost feudal
> peasantry and tenantry." "The gap between the mass popula-
> tion and the small governing class has broadened, and social
> unrest has reached serious proportions." '[7]

An even more recent witness writes of the same country:

> 'For the tenant farmer . . . life is a cycle of debts. The cycle
> is broken only with the harvest. Within weeks almost every
> tenant farmer is in debt again to the landlord, and there he
> stays until the new harvest brings fleeting relief . . . graft and
> corruption . . . are so highly embedded in the higher levels of
> Philippine society that had (the new President) made the
> arrests the situation warrants it is improbable that he would
> have been able to get a quorum in Congress. . . . The social
> and political consequences of the decline in respect for justice
> and law have been exacerbated by mounting unemployment.
> In 1965 the totally unemployed numbered 950,000, or 8·2 per
> cent of the labour force, and hundreds of thousands of others
> were underemployed. With the population growing at the rate
> of 3·2 per cent, some 400,000 new job-seekers are being
> thrown on the labour market annually and the economy has no
> capacity to absorb them. Since one of the status symbols of the
> rich is a Swiss bank account, it is scarcely surprising that in
> this land of gross inequalities in wealth and opportunity the

Communists have penetrated the universities, organized labour, the Government and the armed forces.'[8]

How is the Philippine Government to tackle its problems? Warner gives some indication in the same illuminating article, by mentioning both 'the promise of a billion dollars in private investment from the United States and Japan' and 'punitive action' ('. . . some of the blunders that marked the early years of the Vietnam war were repeated here. One incident in Darlac Province has been described . . . as a peasant 'massacre', and there have been reports elsewhere of intimidation and unnecessary heavy-handedness on the part of the security forces, along with the all-too-familiar stories of chicken stealing and petty pilfering by troops.') It is interesting to compare these 'all-too-familiar stories' with Eqbal Ahmed's assertion that

> 'An outstanding feature of guerrilla training is stress on scrupulously "correct and just" behaviour toward civilians.'[9]

Behind the facade of political independence and US-type democracy, the realities are gross rural poverty, mounting unemployment, indefensible inequalities of wealth and unending armed suppression of the protest movements of the people.

What of Malaysia? Average per capita incomes are certainly higher here, and the Malayan Races Liberation Army never succeeded in building rural support to the extent the Huks did during their maximum strength. Nevertheless, much of the glitter is ostentatiously paraded in the towns, while tucked away out of sight of the casual visitor lurks real poverty, urban and rural. Even comparatively rich Malaya still consists 60 per cent of peasants, and this peasant sector is

> '. . . an economy of poverty and chronic debt, relieved only in years of exceptional prosperity . . . and normally at levels not much above the appalling poverty of most of Asia.'[10]

The poor rural people have not been as lucky as the rich foreigners in the trends of the economy:

> 'In 1947, total Malayan rice production amounted to 252,000 tons, and the average price of rice per kati was 55 cents, making a total value of about $238 million. Fourteen years later, in

1960, rice production had increased to 560,000 tons, but the price of rice had decreased steadily to 28 cents per kati, making a total value of $245 million. In other words, whilst production had increased by 118 per cent, value in 1960 was only 3 per cent higher than in 1947. Indeed, since the general purchasing power of money in 1960 was about 12 per cent lower than in 1947, in terms of real income the 1947 position was in fact far better than the position in 1960. This is a marked contrast with the situation in the rubber sector, where value increased from $539 million in 1947 to $1,709 million in 1960, a rise, in terms of real income, of 179 per cent.'[11]

Lim Chong Yah adds:

'Generally speaking, in Malaya, to grow nothing but paddy is to ensure relative poverty. This condition is aggravated by the ever-increasing labour/land ratio. . . . Institutional defects, such as landlordism, land fragmentation, and credit indebtedness have exacerbated the situation, and accelerated the poverty-generating process. About half to two-thirds of Malaya's rice farmers do not own the land they cultivate. They are tenant farmers, and most of them have to pay a rent of one-third or a half of their crop to the landlord: some even pay as much as three-quarters of their crop in rent. Nor is there any security of land tenure. In Kelantan State, farm tenancies changing hands in a single year have been known to reach a figure of 47 per cent.'[12]

The Malayan economist concludes that:

'Unless the rural population can participate actively in the whole development process, they themselves will continue to be left out and to remain poor even though the geographical area as such may be well developed. . . . Moreover, an economic upsurge cannot be brought about unless the institutional chains that fetter the energies of the rural people are broken. . . . The Government must act to free the rice-farmers from the grip of landlords, money-lenders and shop-keepers. . . . It is clear that a revolutionary change in land policy, and in the social structure of the countryside, must be brought about. . . . There is no room for conservatism. . . ,'[13]

It should be noted, in considering this excellent advice, that the Malaysian government British troops and British policy put into power and helps to keep in power is composed exactly of very conservative landlords and, in effect, big-capital money-lenders and shopkeepers. It is to be doubted whether they are likely to stir themselves energetically to undercut the wealth and power of the very social classes they represent.

An indication of the drag private foreign investment imposes on the Malayan economy may be had from another economist's calculations of the net outflow of 'investible funds' (that is, potential capital sent out of the country rather than invested in it):

'. . . the net outflow for the five years 1957–61, $3,018 million, was *only slightly less than the total of public investment under both the first and second five-year plans* ($1,007 *million* + $2,150 *million* = $3,157 *million*). If the government had been able to tap *only one third* of the private outflow, and eliminate its own outflow (which is largely under its own control) it would have been able to marshal $1,358 million for internal investment, which would have increased gross domestic fixed capital formation by 50 per cent over the period 1957–61.'[14]

Between them, these two non-political, academic professional economists have effectively demolished the 'progressive' claims of the present Malaysian leaders, and underlined the need for radical land reform and nationalization of foreign enterprises. Unhappily, both the neo-colonial power (Britain) and the Malaysian *élite* derive too much profit from the status quo to make it at all likely that they will yield their mutually beneficial positions without a fight, the superficial appearances of 'democracy' in the country notwithstanding.

A country which is in somewhat similar circumstances is Thailand. Its firmly anti-Communist foreign policy and commitment to development via capitalism and private foreign investment have long been hailed in the West. But what has, in fact, been achieved? There is now an insurrectionary movement among the peasants in the North and North-East of Thailand demanding the presence of 40,000 American troops to help crush it. It is true that there has been economic 'development', but it has been restricted to enclaves:

'. . . the recent increase in income has been too concentrated in Bangkok and has resulted in bigger investment in construction, especially of apartment houses and shopping areas, and not enough has gone into the rural areas and provincial towns in order to increase the productive potential in agriculture and industry to a more satisfactory level.'[15]

Two important sources of demand for apartment houses and all the paraphernalia required to furnish them and service their needs —air-conditioners, imported cars, Scotch whisky, etc.—are 'influential' politicians who own enterprises, and US troops with their high incomes. Income and land tax are ridiculously low, in order not to alienate the powerful interests whom taxation would hurt, and

'. . . the government relies on the rice export premium for 10–12 per cent of its total revenue . . . (and) . . . on foreign aid and loans to a substantial extent in financing the country's development. There are however limits to borrowing from abroad, as the country cannot afford to see its future foreign exchange income always siphoned away in debt service.'[16]

The rice export premium hits the indigenous farmer. Foreign business here, however, as in Malaysia and the Philippines, is offered several kinds of inducements in the way of 'tax holidays' and other such devices. This is palpably the kind of status quo well worth the efforts of the Western governments to preserve.

On the other hand, there are countries which have definitely evolved in ways totally unsympathetic to the needs of Western business. Most important of these, of course, is China. Foreign investment has no opening here for profit. China's raw materials are being used for her own development. Western-produced consumer goods have here no exploitable market. With what success has China defied the economic embrace of the West? The French agronomist Dumont concludes that

'The Chinese peasant has furnished a near superhuman effort—and in some cases, 1958 particularly, the effort required of him has been inhuman—but though the price is very high, the country is well on the road to development.'[17]

Dumont adds:

'. . . there have certainly been food shortages in China, but to my knowledge no one has died of hunger. In India, each year even after the most successful harvests, thousands die of hunger whether in the villages or on the pavements of Calcutta. The Western press has always been distinctly cautious in publishing this side of the story.'[18]

A geographer, having noted the food shortages that afflicted China in the years between 1959 and 1962, comments that the re-organization of agriculture by the Communists, although it could not prevent tightening of belts, prevented the kind of disastrous famine that similar conditions of flood and drought would have brought to the peasant in the past:

'The organization of the commune system gave him the means to fight these problems by mobilizing the rural population (and the Army) to fight drought and flood conditions, by digging new wells and by extending the dyke and water storage systems. . . . Moreover, the Chinese government was able to buy—and to pay for—large quantities of overseas grain; it was also able to do what few Chinese governments could do and that is to see that the country's food supplies were fairly shared. It was a lean period—but there was no starvation and China emerged from it. . . . By 1963 crop output, from all reports, was again moving upwards. By 1964 the grain harvest was described as "one of the most satisfying in China's history", sugar production was two-and-a-half times that of 1963 and there was a glut of fruit and vegetables and a surplus of pork reported in some of the bigger cities.'[19]

The Western press in general reported further improvements in 1965. A recent visitor from the West reported that

'. . . life has become steadily better for the Chinese after the recovery of the economy. They are well fed in both town and country, comparatively well clothed and State social security protects them from the vicissitudes of life. In the shops between 1964 and 1966 (I was there in both years) there was an immense increase in the availability of consumer goods and there seemed to be no shortage of would-be purchasers.'[20]

Moreover, by quite deliberate policy choice, the Chinese rulers have sought to avoid 'enclave development' in any form. It is, of course, impossible for private foreign firms to invest in China and draw out a major part of the investible surplus in the form of dividends, profits, interest, and remittances. But 'enclaves' may also grow up with unplanned location of industry in a number of places, cut off from the countryside and potentially developing interests conflicting with the interests of the rural people.

'One of the distinctive features of China's industrial revolution has been the many-fronted advance of industry. Existing plants are being extended; new large- and medium-scale factories are being established; and alongisde this modern, large-scale, industrial sector the productive capacity of peasant or "native-style" industry is being used to the full. This policy of "walking on two legs" . . . is one of the biggest contributions made by the Chinese to solving the problems posed by poverty and economic backwardness; it is a policy which gives the geography of New China a personality quite different from that of most other underdeveloped countries who have been content to follow Western models of economic development (which involves capital-intensive and geographically highly concentrated industry, in contrast to the labour-intensive and dispersed industries of Chinese planning). . . . It is a policy which has social advantages also. It is easy to see that, in a country the size of China, the creation of a series of giant industrial complexes would have only a limited social and technological effect, for the majority of the rural population would remain cut off from the industrialization and mechanization which are the bases of modern life. The policy of dispersal, of "walking on two legs", avoids the creation of a new "technocracy" in the heart of the countryside and makes possible the maximum diffusion of new techniques and new ideas among the peasant masses. It thus lays a firm foundation on which an accelerating "technical transformation" of rural China can be based.'[21]

It is by means such as those employed in China that what may be called *overall* or *national* economic development is achieved, as opposed to the *enclave* development characteristic of most of her Asian neighbours.

But there is another, and often unfairly overlooked, success story in Asia—namely communist North Korea. Recovering from the awful devastation accompanying the Korean War, the North has hoisted living standards to previously unimaginable levels; one authority in fact states categorically that

'All the economic miracles of the post-war world are put in the shade by (North Korea's) achievements.'[22]

Meanwhile, South Korea under American tutelage continues to languish in poverty, despite huge injections of US aid. The contrast is an instructive one, and Koreans returning from residence abroad have 'voted with their feet' by choosing to go to the North rather than the South.[23]

Burma, another Asian country which has resolutely rejected involvement, both political and economic, with the West, has also significant achievements to its credit. Recognizing that land redistribution was the key to the economic problem,

'. . . the government . . . has initiated such a policy in order to reshape the economic and social structure of the country. In spite of political difficulties . . . the implementation of the programme has been carried on vigorously and . . . with considerable success. The agrarian reform has been closely associated with a gradual expansion of the agricultural area and with an overall educational campaign to awaken the people to their economic and social responsibilities. . . . In spite of all administrative short-comings, political confusion, and deficiencies in planning, the laudable achievement of the Union of Burma lies in the fact that it has vigorously written off the economic concepts of the colonial past and is seriously attempting to remedy the defective structure of its rural society . . . only the generous fulfilment of the promise to redistribute the land enabled the government to confront successfully its external and internal enemies and to mobilize the energies of the nation. The Burmese recovery, indeed, is no miracle and is not even a secret: it is based on the honest implementation of a well-conceived agrarian legislation.'[24]

The contrast with unhappy Vietnam could hardly be sharper; but the Burmese rather quickly saw the disadvantages associated with accepting 'aid' from the United States.

At one time it appeared as if there was a third group of countries, suspended in a separate 'neutral' category between those clearly aligned with the West and those committed to development along communist or socialist lines. However, time has shown that the neutral' countries are in practice simply countries in which a temporary balance has been struck between the internal force pressing for social revolution and the external force of the West pressing for alignment. A few examples will illustrate this point, and lead us into a discussion of the extent of American intervention in the affairs of the 'free' world and its motives.

India is the prime example in Asia, indeed in the world, of a neutral country, supposedly steering an independent path between the rival power blocs, and guiding its policies by the twin beacons of democracy and socialism. Actually, the real conservatism of Congress was always apparent, even in the shadow of Nehru's socialism. And so the superficially 'socialist' aspects of Indian development, such as nationalization, have in practice strengthened private business by their pricing policies, while the private sector has been afforded every opportunity for profit. Tax levels have been low, enforcement lax, and avoidance scandalously prevalent. While inflation has economically weakened officials and politicians in terms of their salaries, it has not prevented business from accumulating great wealth. The result has been, predictably, general corruption.

'More and more it is the businessmen who deserve to be called the ultimate rulers of India today. . . . And these rulers . . . are not for the most part pioneers, ready to risk their resources in exploration determined to develop, in however ruthless a way, the economic strength of their country . . . in general the businessman is more a speculator than a builder, a pirate rather than a pioneer. His base is not in industry, though he will exploit industry to his profit, but in commerce and finance. He has none of that sense of national responsibility which characterized the Japanese businessman in the first flush of his country's economic expansion. Still less has he the moral disposition of the Quaker industrialist. For him the production and sale of goods—within the law if possible, and outside whenever profit demands it—is an opportunity to advance himself, his family, and his caste in an accumulation of alliances and wealth.'[25]

The results of opulence for a relatively tiny *élite* and unchanging misery for the majority ('An estimate that 35 million of the 52 million people of Bihar State, India, are facing near famine conditions was made today by Mr. Jaya Prakash Narayan, president of the Bihar Relief Society.'[26]) are predictable. First, a total gap between ruler and ruled, and, second, a determination on the part of the *élite* to maintain that gap. Professor Gadgil explicitly compared the Indian situation with that prevailing in China:

'Among the special features noted about Communists China by most observers are the plain living of its leaders, the absence of wasteful consumption, the focus of administrative arrangements on helping the poor and the backward, the emphasis on utilizing idle manpower and on the dispersal of industry. I attach importance to all these. It is true that little effective attention is paid to any of them in the Indian Plan.'[27]

Maintenance of the differentials entails two things: the continuing stagnation of the economy due to the absence of incentives for the peasant masses; and preparedness on the part of the *élite* to defend themselves. Of the former there is little doubt. A recent visitor with an extensive and prolonged experience of India wrote bluntly that

'. . . in India little real development has taken place in the past 20 years. . . . Catastrophe could follow, but this cannot be tolerated in the twentieth century; it will be prevented, *revolutionary activity will be suppressed and the disease will not be cured.*'[28]

The tailend of the quotation reveals the true position of the Indian ruling classes. To avert catastrophe in the form of famine, they increasingly rely upon foreign aid. But the richest donor by far is the United States of America, and her government imposes harsh conditions. When Mrs. Gandhi recently joined Tito and Nasser in condemning US bombing of North Vietnam, American food aid to starving India was mysteriously suspended. Moreover, part of the condition of obtaining US aid is that the country will be opened to private foreign investment and that 'stabilization' policies will be carried out. The first entails great loss of potential investible surplus to India, for as an economist comments:

> 'Foreign private investment is expensive. At the very least profits run at 10 per cent per year after payment of taxes; in all probability they are very much more. To this should be added the high cost of know-how, licences, and such-like.'[29]

The second, insisted upon also by US-dominated international agencies such as the International Monetary Fund and the International Bank for Reconstruction and Development, entails in effect stabilizing the income status quo, the undesirability of which we have already commented upon.

Fear of revolution internally also forces the ruling classes of India into feverish arms expenditure. In 1965–66, 17 per cent of all central government expenditures went on 'defence'. This does not yet approach the figures for, say, South Korea (31 per cent) or Taiwan (44 per cent), but the 'threat' of China has produced a common interest on the part of the Indian *élite* and of the governments of America and Russia to help the figure on its way up. In practice, failure of the social revolution to follow political independence in India has remorselessly driven the country into a position of economic and military dependence and left the masses as yet unliberated, in poverty.

In a well-known pamphlet, a group of Pakistani students demonstrated how US economic and military aid has also been a 'burden' to their country. Apart from the obvious point, often significantly overlooked, that loans, investments and US sales (as a result of prior aid) in practice mean in the end a net flow of capital from the original donor to the original recipient, the authors draw attention to a point of extreme importance for our present study, namely that:

> 'In the long run, the worst aspect of military aid lies in the complete change it produces in the balance of social and political forces in favour of conservatism and established vested interests. The dragon seeds sown by military aid have produced a fearful crop of military officers, with their social roots in the most conservative sections of our society, who have learnt to sit in judgement on our people. It is an overwhelming force without any countervailing force to hold it in check.'[30]

At this stage, countervailing power in the form of trade unions and peasant organizations have not had time to develop, nor will the military now permit them to develop. As a Latin American radical bitterly complained, US military aid in practice means that the poor countries are garrisoned by their own armies.

The tactics of US intervention to stabilize the status quo vary from case to case. In Vietnam it has meant massive deployment of overwhelming military might. But in Indonesia, as in India and Pakistan, it has been more indirect (though it should be added that when President Ayub Khan of Pakistan, for reasons connected with his disagreements with India, moved closer to China, the *Daily Telegraph*[31] alleged, in a report never subsequently repudiated, that the American Central Intelligence Agency—CIA—attempted to overthrow and replace him. Indonesia, under President Sukarno, was intent on achieving genuine foreign policy independence. But the realities of the US–USSR *détente*, and the growing realization on the part of Sukarno and those closest to him that the situation in South-East Asia threatened to develop along the same lines as Latin America, in permanent dependence upon the rich countries of the West, drove the Indonesian leadership into a position close to that of China in foreign policy terms. But at the same time, the internal class structure and balance of social forces in Indonesia inhibited social revolution along the Chinese pattern, for the conservative *élite* controlled the overwhelming fire-power embodied in the armed forces, as supplied and aided by the Americans and Russians.

Conditions for the common people were, however, deteriorating alarmingly. Inflation eroded their money incomes. Corruption blocked economic activity of a productive kind. More ominously, in the rural areas the peasantry were sinking more and more deeply into perpetual distress.

'The evils of progressive indebtedness and loss of control over the peasants' land to landlords or creditors have become more and more pronounced. . . . Particularly noteworthy has been the spread of large and absentee landownership . . . (and) . . . the landless peasants live "as serfs . . . and are unable to free themselves" . . . it is indisputable that a polarization of classes, based on the widening distinctions between the

landowning and the landless is . . . a social dynamic of major
importance in contemporary Indonesia.'[32]

Naturally in these circumstances, the Communist Party of
Indonesia (PKI) flourished, attracting millions of members and
millions of further adherents to its various specialized organizations catering for trade unionists, peasant unionists, women and
so on.

Both tendencies, Sukarno's drift towards alignment with
China, and the rapid expansion of the PKI, were thoroughly
alarming both to the conservative *élite* in Indonesia, and to the
US government. A Council of Generals, made up of officers
well-known for their right-wing views, and with long-standing
connections with the United States, planned to stage an anti-
Sukarno and anti-PKI *coup d'état* on October 5th, 1965. Detach-
ments of the US Seventh Fleet proceeded towards Javanese
waters, and US troops in the Philippines were alerted for possible
trouble. Wind of trouble reached the ears of people sympathetic
to the communists, and was conveyed to the PKI leadership. It
was a difficult position, for the fire-power equation overwhelmingly favoured the army. In the end, it was officially decided to
try to sit the trouble out. But some youth and junior officer
elements decided to try to nip developments in the bud by
assassinating the top generals. The attempt failed, and a wholesale slaughter of communists and communist-sympathisers
followed on this pretext. Estimates of the numbers killed vary
from 500,000 to 1,000,000, but whether one accepts the higher or
the lower figure, this was one of the most efficient political
slaughters of all time, and set back the prospects of the Indonesian
social revolution indefinitely. Had at any time the generals been
unsure of victory, they would certainly have called in the American forces hovering nearby in order to crush 'Chinese-inspired
subversion' on the part of the PKI. The actual result, placing a
government of anti-communist military men and landlords in
power, gratifyingly assured Western objectives in the region.
The 'confrontation' with Malaysia was called off. Assurances
were given of the un-freezing of long-blocked Western profits in
Indonesia and of good prospects for Western private investment
in Indonesia in future. In return, a Western consortium promised
to bale Indonesia out of her immediate economic problems, such

as her shortage of foreign exchange. Where Sukarno had been pro-Chinese in foreign policy, the new rulers were violently anti-Chinese, with strong racist over-tones (evidenced by the persecution of Indonesia's 2½ million Chinese which ensued).

Two interesting speculations must conclude this brief discussion of the sudden end of Indonesia's experiment in neutralism. One is this. What would the reaction have been in the Western press if the Indonesian communists had taken power and slaughtered several hundred thousand landlords and their wives and children? Huge headlines would have advertised 'Red Terror Sweeps Indonesia', and the story would have been pursued relentlessly for months if not years. As it was, the Western press hardly thought the barbarically-executed deaths of several hundred thousand human beings, men, women and children, worth a mention (though much space was given to the deaths of the six generals caught by the communist sympathisers). Moreover, had the trial of strength gone the other way, readers in the West would have learned that it was because of Chinese subversion and Chinese aid to the PKI. As it was, few papers pointed out the known links between the US government and men like General Nasution and General Suharto, and the fact that their followers were heavily armed with US equipment, so that the Indonesian army was, on paper, the most powerful in Asia.

The other is this. No doubt there will now ensue in Indonesia 'enclave development' of the type familiar in American neo-colonies in Latin America and South-East Asia. But is it likely that the *élite* of Indonesia will show themselves any more keen for suicide than their counterparts elsewhere in the 'free world'? That is, is it conceivable that the oligarchs will sign their own death warrants by authorizing measures of land reform and taxation of high incomes sufficient to start the process by which the peasant 80 per cent of the population might share in both the process and the proceeds of economic development? Surely not. One can, I think, safely speculate that, unless there occurs in the meantime another, more radical, revolution in Indonesia, the peasants will be as poor, illiterate and desperate in twenty years time as they are today. Their liberation has been postponed. But the geographical area available for Western business in its search for markets, raw materials and investment opportunities has been enhanced by some three-quarters of a million square miles, housing over 100 million people.

Although we have devoted our attention to Asia, the interventions of the West in general and the United States in particular have been world-wide—from Guatemala and the Dominican Republic in Latin America, to Suez and the Lebanon in the Middle East, and to the Congo in Africa. And in each and every case, the objective has been the same—to stabilize the status quo, a status quo which we have seen to be so disastrous for the majority of the human race. This is Peru, for example:

'The peasants . . . live a miserable existence. Out of 9 million hectares of arable land and natural pastures, 3 per cent of the owners possess 83 per cent of the farm area, and 97 per cent of the owners possess 17 per cent of the remaining area. There was no real progress towards agrarian reform and the peasants, organized in unions, under the inspiration of Hugo Blanco and his group, oppose the tenant system, demanding direct ownership of the land. They live in very bad conditions, with a daily intake of less than 1,200 calories, a diet similar to that of a concentration camp. They face virtually the highest infantile mortality rate in the world, and smallpox, tuberculosis, whooping cough and dysentry are endemic. Three million peasants live on the margin of society with a maximum wage of 8 soles (about 2d.) a day.'[33]

The picture could be duplicated for the rest of Latin America, even for those countries, like Brazil, with impressive capital cities and limited enclave development. The distinguished French agronomist Dumont writes of two Brazilian lads, aged 18 and 11, working in the cane fields:

[they] 'look hardly 14 and 8. They are obviously rickety; probably for lack of milk since their weaning, and, because the mother was short of protein, weaning was probably finished at six months, far earlier than in Africa. I come closer: and I am overwhelmed by the look of the younger: sweat runs down a face thinned by physical misery. Clearly he will not be going to school, since . . . he has had to start work before 10 years of age in order to eat—and "to eat" is an overstatement. That is unbearable, and even more unbearable

are the frightened eyes of a little martyred animal with which he looks at the manager who is taking us around.'[34]

Of India, Dumont caustically observes that matters have steadily worsened secularly:

'In the eighteenth century, the landlord claimed in return for the use of his land one third of the total crop; the serf received one third of the crop in return for his labour, and the final third went to whoever provided other factors of production (horses, plough, seeds, manure, water, etc.) At present in India (Jan. 1962) the property owner furnishes nothing but his land, with no additional capital of any sort, and receives on average 50 per cent of total production. There are cases in the Cavary Delta near Tandjore where the landlord receives as much as two thirds of the total crop. Not only is the rent burden imposed upon the labourer higher than in the eighteenth century but the social situation is generally worse than that which existed before British colonisation.'[35]

In contrast, the peoples of the West have made unbelievable economic progress since the eighteenth century. Calorie intake per capita per diem averages circa 3,000 instead of 2,000 or less. Literacy is nearly universal. On every index of material welfare, the minority of Western people stand head and shoulders above their poor relations in the third world. As we have seen, the colonial period was responsible for first opening up this gap. Neo-colonialism today ensures that this gap will remain, and indeed continue widening. This is a harsh judgement, but essentially a correct one, and its very harshness explains why it has been necessary for the Western powers to create a rationalizing and legitimizing myth to hide the true nature of the present world struggle.

The struggle is conceived of in the West as essentially a power struggle between two blocs and two rival ideologies, West and East, 'democracy' and 'communism'. In this titanic contest, the communists employ an insidious tactic of 'unconventional aggression' disguised as people's wars or wars of national liberation. Let us just recapitulate at this point the orthodox position on 'unconventional aggression':

'The official American interpretation of revolutionary war can be summarized as follows: (1) It is essentially a technical problem i.e., a problem of plotting and subversion on the one hand and of intelligence and suppression on the other. As the chief conspiratorial group, the Communists are believed to be the most likely initiators and beneficiaries of revolution. It was this attitude which led to the recent attempt to nip in the bud what was construed as the Dominican Communist conspiracy. A logical extension of this theory is the belief that any revolutionary movement is inspired, directed, and controlled from abroad. (2) The active sanctuary—from which guerrillas can smuggle supplies and train their troops—is considered the primary factor in their success. (3) The guerrilla movement is believed to enjoy considerable advantage because, in the words of W. W. Rostow, "its task is merely to destroy while the government must build and protect what it is building." (4) The civilian population is considered important for providing information and protection to the guerrillas; it is believed that civilian-guerrilla co-operation is enforced by terror. . . . Serious inquiry into other bases of guerrilla support and mass mobilization is therefore deemed of no great importance.'[36]

Note that Eqbal Ahmad in his summary uses the term 'revolutionary warfare'. This phrase is in fact eschewed by the Americans, since they wish to overlook the differences between people's war and other forms of guerrilla warfare. One further point of information: the US landed 22,000 troops in the Dominican Republic ostensibly to stop a Communist 'take-over' in 1965; but, by their own admission, there were only 53—fifty-three—'known' communists in the country, of whom the American troops killed 4,000. The real reason was 'to save the military caste at all costs.'[37]

In effect, this section has been an extended refutation of the orthodox position as summarised by Eqbal Ahmad. Before summarising the alternative position, however, it may be useful to point out certain parallels in British social history. During the period of maximum exploitation and repression of the British working classes, during the early years of the industrial revolution at the end of the eighteenth and beginning of the nineteenth centuries, when on the face of it no other explanation of working class protest and discontent need have been sought beyond the brutal and barbaric conditions of their daily life, the ruling classes in fact sought quite other explanations. The Home Office employed secret agents to seek out the 'subversives' who were stirring up trouble among the otherwise satisfied workers (how they were supposed to be satisfied when starving and working 12 or 14 hours a day in appalling conditions did not seem to call for explanation). It was considered that the primary cause of the trouble lay across the Channel in revolutionary France: French agents were allegedly responsible for instigating discontent among the British masses. Early attempts to form unions were regarded as illegal and destructive of legitimate trade and prosperity. Luddism, the smashing of machines, was taken as evidence, not of the desperation and misery of starving people, but of the purely destructive nature of the working-class movement 'while the government must build and protect what it is building'—but for the benefit of whom? It is easy for us now to adopt some historical perspective in this case, and to see that the mass of the people were right to reject a system of society which enriched a tiny minority and kept the majority in conditions of insupportable poverty. But it was no doubt extremely difficult for the rich at the time to reconcile themselves to the idea of surrendering their exclusive privileges. Indeed, they rationalized their privileges by arguing that only by preserving the system would economic progress be possible. We in the West now occupy an analogous position vis-à-vis the vast majority of mankind.

Now let Eqbal Ahmad summarize the alternative hypotheses concerning revolutionary war:

'Revolutionaries consider mass support the primary condition for their success; winning and maintaining popular support remains their central objective throughout the struggle. (2) The requirements of guerrilla war, as well as the history of its failures and successes, confirm the primacy of political factors in such a conflict. (3) Popular support for the guerrillas is predicated upon the moral alienation of the masses from the existing government. The revolutionaries' chief aim is to activate and perpetuate the moral isolation of the enemy régime until such isolation has become total and irreversible.

(4) The conditions leading to revolutionary wars are not created by conspiracy. They are partly inherent in a situation of rapid social change, but the outbreak normally results mainly from the failure of a ruling *élite* to respond to the challenge of modernization. (5) A revolutionary guerrilla movement concentrates on "out-administering," not on "out-fighting" the enemy. (6) The use of terror by guerrillas is highly selective; it does not constitute the main reason for the favourable reaction of the masses to their cause. (7) The external sanctuary has greater psychological and diplomatic than military or political value to the guerrillas.'[38]

These theses, amply borne out by the evidence of recent history, and substantiated by that segment of it recorded here, effectively, of course, demolish the legitimizing and rationalizing ideology and myths promulgated by the Americans in defence of their world-wide military-economic empire. It is time, therefore, to turn to examine the real roots of their conduct and the true nature of the tumultuous social upheavals characteristic of our time.

America has always been economically expansionist and potentially expansionist in the territorial sense. The peculiar circumstances of America's position vis-à-vis Latin America helped mask this, but even so, one ought not to overlook the fact that when it was found necessary to take over new territory, the US took it. The adventures in Cuba and the Philippines took place significantly enough when the impetus from one epoch-making innovation (the railways) was petering out, and the innovation which was to take its place as the thrust sector of the economy (cars) was as yet in its infancy. The necessity of imperialism in these circumstances was brashly announced and justified:

'. . . we are a conquering race . . . we must obey our blood and occupy new markets, and, if necessary, new lands. American factories are making more than the American people can use; American soil is producing more than they can consume. Fate has written our policy for us; the trade of the world must and shall be ours . . . American law, American order, American civilization, and the American flag will plant themselves on shores hitherto bloody and benighted, but by those agencies of God henceforth to be made beautiful and bright. In the Pacific is the true field of our earliest operations. . . .'[39]

The crash which hit the American economy in 1929 marked an important turning point. From that time on, it became increasingly clear that the American capitalist system was no longer viable without massive government intervention. Recovery did not occur naturally, and business bitterly resisted attempts to stimulate recovery by government welfare programmes ('creeping socialism'). The Second World War brought an abrupt end to the period of mass unemployment, and the wheels of industry once again started turning at full speed and capacity, powered by massive governmental demand for war material.

In the immediate post-war period, pent-up consumer demand, which had been partly frustrated during the actual hostilities, helped to buoy the economy over the period of military rundown. When signs of unemployment and excess capacity again began to appear—unemployment in America rose from 1·9 per cent of the civilian labour force in 1945 to 5·5 per cent in 1949— the Korean war fortuitously intervened to justify a rapid and colossal arms build-up, the foundations for which had in fact already been laid as part of the 'cold war' launched by the American President's 'Truman Doctrine' speech of March 1947.[40] From that point, the American economy has been on a permanent war footing. Arms spending soared from $11·4 billion in 1947 to $55·2 billion in 1963; estimates for fiscal year 1966–67 give $58·3 billion. To put this into perspective, the US defence spending estimated for 1966–67 is vastly in excess of the total planned defence of *all the other countries of the world put together*, including in this total such giants as China and Russia, but also such major allies of America as the UK, whose spending ought properly to be included with that of the US. China, with a population three times that of the US, and surrounded by hostile bases and unfriendly powers, spends about a tenth of what America spends (yet America is singularly fortunate in bordering no hostile powers). The Soviet Union, whose alleged 'aggressiveness' served to justify the American arms build-up in the first place, spends barely a quarter of the US defence total. In terms of percentage of Gross National Product, American defence expenditures take 8 per cent, Russian 4·6 per cent; in terms of percentage of total central government expenditures, the comparative figures are 51 per cent and 13 per cent.

To put the matter in a different light, *the US defence budget is bigger than the combined national incomes of all the countries of 'free' Asia taken together.* Yet these countries have some 1,300 million people to feed, cloth, house and otherwise provide for. It ought also to be recalled in this context that such US client states in Asia as Taiwan and South Korea themselves devote quite disproportionate resources to military purposes—at America's behest and on her behalf.

The key to these gigantic arms expenditures is certainly not to be found in the overt belligerence or war preparations of the communist powers. On the contrary, the so-called 'arms race' has been largely one-sided, with the US racing against herself (that is, basing future estimates of defence needs on what the situation *would be if* the USSR were ever in fact to catch up with the US present). Nor surely is it to be found in the fire-power of the revolutionary guerrillas of countries like Peru and the Philippines, with their improvised fire-arms and home-made mortars. Actually, however, as we shall see shortly, both play their part in the rationalizing and legitimizing ideology erected by the US leaders to justify their unheard-of peacetime war preparations. But the true explanation is to be found in the realm of America's own economic needs.

The American economy cannot now operate without bolstering government expenditures of one kind or another. For political reasons, rational government outlays are circumscribed by the prejudices of the voters and, more significantly, by the opposition of powerful business interests. America needs more hospitals, better schools, extensive re-training of the unskilled labour force, millions of new houses and a host of other social amenities. Government intervention in the economy in order to provide such facilities is, however, held to be 'socialistic' and is therefore violently opposed. The real objection of those economically and politically strong enough to count is that such rational governmental interventions compete with and hurt private business interests—such as the real estate interest, for example.

One kind of government spending is, however, free of all the objections that block the others: namely arms spending. People who raucously and effectively object to paying taxes for 'handouts' (that is, for unemployment benefits for those rendered redundant by the irrational operation of the 'free' economic system; for higher teachers' salaries; and so on), have nothing of the same reaction when faced with demands for bigger bills for 'defence'—it is a patriotic duty to meet these. Moreover, far from defence spending conflicting with private business interests, it positively interlocks with them at a variety of levels. For example, there is a limit to the amount of obsolescence you can build in to a car or a house; the consumer would eventually start boycotting your article. But many military products have obsolescence as their very purpose and justification! Further, the consumer of military products is uncritically lavish, his funds being limitless, and his appetite boundless. Military contracts with a total value well in excess of the entire national income of Denmark were handed out to five of the top US corporations alone in 1959.

That military spending is an effective boost to the US economy may readily be shown. Professor Joan Robinson of Cambridge University, an authority on the theory of employment, notes that the 'military-industrial complex'

'. . . have found that expenditure on armaments keeps the system running and fends off stagnation.'[41]

Two other economists point out that

'. . . the difference between the deep stagnation of the 1930's and the relative prosperity of the 1950's is fully accounted for by the vast military outlays of the 50's . . . the percentage of the labour force either unemployed or dependent on military spending was much the same in 1961 as in 1939. From which it follows that if the military budget were reduced to 1939 proportions, unemployment would also revert to 1939 proportions.'[42]

The US government has no need to 'sell' huge military budgets to the business élite. As we shall shortly see, this unparalleled level of arms spending has significance for the American business community in so many respects that the interests of the military part of the ruling élite may be said to be, to all intents and purposes, identical with those of the business élite. But it is necessary to show to the public at large and to world opinion that such outlays are rational and justified.

This is done by charging that the communist powers are liable to advance beyond their own frontiers in order to over-run the 'free' world. Moreover, it is further alleged, as we have seen, that if the communist powers *are* successfully penned within their own frontiers by the overwhelming threatening might of the US they nevertheless succeed in 'seeping' through to the free world to instigate subversive insurrections. To cope with both perils—that of direct and that of indirect (or unconventional) aggression—it is necessary to ring the communist bloc with hundreds of bases, and to keep American troops and military hardware stationed at thousands of spots around the non-communist world. Actually, there is little, if any, evidence that Russia seriously contemplated invading Western Europe at the conclusion of the Second World War[43] even if she had had the capacity to do so, while China's military capacity is almost entirely defensive,[44] and we have seen that there are ample grounds for the poor people of the earth to rise in revolt against their deprivation without the machinations of revolutionary 'terrorists' trained in Moscow or Peking.

But the fact of China's existence and the rising tide of dissatisfaction in the third world *is* related to America's war economy. The success of the Chinese revolution in 1949 and the clear crumbling of European colonial authority in the rest of post-war Asia greatly alarmed America's rulers. From 1949 the whole vast extent and population of China was closed to economic exploitation by the West. Were the rest of Asia to follow China's example, the impact on the economies of the West in general, and of the US in particular, as presently constituted, would be catastrophic. There are several reasons for this.

First, the high and rising living standards of the West are reflected in rising per capita consumption of certain vital raw materials such as oil, steel, aluminium and a host of others. Now it is quite true that there are probably adequate resources of all the essential ingredients for industrialization to guarantee acceptable living standards for all the people of the world for the foreseeable future. But at the moment there does not exist a rational international machinery for prospecting, rationing, pricing and allocating this wealth. It is therefore incumbent upon the strong each to guarantee its own access to that quantity essential for the maintenance and elevation of living standards. If all countries were economically independent it would of course be possible to obtain requirements by bargaining and normal buying and selling. But there are two points to observe here. First, countries as economically independent of the West as China would certainly initiate national economic development and in the process start to use up their own resources in raw materials instead of selling them to the West in order to buy back the manufactured commodities of the West. Second, at the moment the dominance of the West over the international economy enables the rich countries to obtain access to raw materials at highly advantageous prices—for them. What this means in practice is that the poor countries currently dependent—as a result of colonialism—upon the sale of primary produce do not obtain in return for their labour and sacrifice a fair reward. Moreover, the situation shows a secular tendency to worsen—that is the terms of trade tend to move against the poor countries, the prices they have to pay for their manufactured imports rising while the prices they obtain for their exports are falling. In the course of a year this may negative the total net inflow of foreign aid of all kinds—this has happened in certain years since the war. Of course, from the point of view of the other side, that of the industrialized Western nations, this is an excellent arrangement. At present, Britain is enduring an economic crisis originating from a persistent balance of payments gap in the region of several hundred million pounds a year; yet,

> 'Had Britain's import prices moved in line with export prices since 1954, [1962's] import bill would have cost about £800 million more than it did, a saving equivalent to about 4 per cent of consumer spending. Britain has benefited in this way for some years now. . . .'[45]

Since 1952, the businesses of the Western world have annually received in this way a 'bonus' of over one billion dollars, in addition to their usual profits. How deeply this gross injustice is felt in Asia may be judged from the following letter from an Asian which appeared in the London *Times*:

> 'From an Asian point of view the battle for Asia is not an ideological battle. It is a battle for bread, rice and shelter. Asia has nothing to offer but her jute, oil and tin to sell. Infinitely more valuable than any assistance would be a decent price for its commodities. It is time someone as great as Keynes proclaimed that pricing by the "interplay of free trade" is

nothing but organized loot when the trade is between economic unequals, and that, as within any single nation, so between nations, isolated prosperity cannot survive long. The battle for Asia will be won by whichever world bloc realizes this truth first.'[46]

America exerts tremendous power in maintaining this injustice through her huge stocks of raw materials, the release or even the threat of release of which quickly checks rising prices; through her control over international economic agencies such as the International Monetary Fund and the World Bank whose policies impose deflation on the poor countries as a condition of receiving economic aid; and through her long-standing veto on efforts to set up effective international bodies to support commodity prices.

Alongside access to raw materials, the rich developed countries require of the poor developing countries opportunities for lucrative investment and marketing. The degree to which the United States has become dependent upon her overseas trade and investment in recent years has been noted by many economists. From 1950 to 1963, US total direct foreign investment rose from $11·8 billion to $40·6 billion, and during this period profits flowing back from these investments totalled $12 billion—a healthy return, which excludes a variety of hidden remittances, such as patent and copyright fees and royalties.[47] As may be guessed from the foregoing, profit rates on overseas operations of US companies are running at a level twice as high as those to be obtained on purely domestic operations.[48] As a result, the importance of American foreign activity is increasing relative to the domestic market, so that now

'. . . we arrive at a conservative estimate that the size of the foreign market (for domestic and United States-owned foreign firms) is equal to approximately two-fifths of the domestic output of farms, factories and mines.'[49]

This huge and constantly swelling overseas economic involvement predicated on the 'saturation' of the home market and the tax, labour cost and other advantages of operating abroad, is related to what we have already seen of militarism in a variety of ways.

First, an important part of overseas sales are of arms:

'The Defense Department is starting an intensive information program to interest more companies in participating in the military export sales program and to spur those already participating to greater efforts. It plans to conduct a series of briefings for industry and labour groups this fall in cooperation with the National Security Industrial Association.'[50]

So great is this sales effort already that for the foreseeable future any armed clashes anywhere in the 'free' world will be fought predominantly *on both sides* with American weapons, as Senator Fulbright has pointed out.

Second, there has arisen this immensely powerful military-industrial complex between which circulate breath-taking sums of money and lucrative business of all kinds. The personnel of the civilian part merge imperceptibly into the personnel of the military part, so that there is an intricate net-work of shared experience, mutual acquaintances and common ambitions and aims. General Eisenhower in his last speech as President delivered a grave and measured warning about the growing power of this complex, whose material interests dictate 'controlled' tensions (through the CIA, they organized the U-2 flight which sabotaged the promising 1960 summit arrangements) and 'limited' wars— 'limited' only in geographical extent and in the number of participants; US forces in the 'limited' war in Vietnam are currently using

'. . . at least 83 million rounds of small arms ammunition per month, and, per year, 10 million mortar and artillery rounds, 2 million bombs, 4·8 million rockets, 6·8 million grenades . . . these figures . . . are certain to increase.'[51]

Secretary of Defence Charles E. Wilson told a House Subcommittee in 1957, before the complex had become as rich and entrenched as it since has:

'I have said to a number of my friends that one of the serious things about this defense business is that so many Americans are getting a vested interest in it; properties, business, jobs, employment, votes, opportunities for promotion and advancement, bigger salaries for scientists, and all that. It is a troublesome business.'

Taken together, the military sector and the overseas sector dominate the most sensitive areas of the US economy:

> '. . . for many of the firms in the capital goods industries, the overlay of 20 to 50 per cent of demand from military purchases and exports probably accounts for the major share of their profits, and in not a few firms perhaps as much as 80 to 100 per cent of their profits.'[52]

The sheer magnitude of the stake of this relatively small number of people, possessed of scarcely imaginable military and economic power, ought in itself to give an indication of their conservatism and the lengths to which they will go to preserve the status quo— a status quo as lush for themselves as it is crushing for the needy two-thirds of the world's population.

The third inter-relation of the growing overseas economic interests of the US and the permanent war economy is, in fact, the need to protect the far-flung empire by military might if necessary. When investments are threatened by radical nationalist movements intent on ending neo-colonial economic domination, troops and tanks and planes must be at hand to intervene decisively to restore the status quo ante. In recent years there have been typical interventions in Guatemala, the Dominican Republic, the Lebanon, and mainland South-East Asia generally. But intervention, as we have seen, has several dimensions. At one end of the scale it may be sufficient to train, arm and finance local reactionary groups, as in Indonesia in 1965. At the other, it may be necessary to undertake a direct commitment at colossal cost, as in Vietnam. There the war is now costing the US, directly or indirectly, some £700 million a month—about as much as it would take to support the entire population of Vietnam in peacetime for one year. It costs the American armed forces roughly £83,000 to kill a single Vietnamese—or sufficient to feed, clothe, house and otherwise provide for sixty Vietnamese peasants throughout their full life spans. If the cost does not deter the American military-industrial *élite*, neither do the means they must employ. So far something like a sixth of the South Vietnamese people—2·6 million—may have been casualties of US aggression, and the scale of slaughter is being steadily stepped up to the point of genocide.[53]

To understand this frantic indiscriminate killing is to understand what is today entailed in the process of liberation. The great cold fear of the US leaders is that the heroic people of tiny peasant Vietnam will prevail. For, if they do, they will show the world that not all the bribes in the way of 'aid', nor all the military might in the way of napalm, white phosphorus, lazy dogs, gases, poisons, bombs, bullets, missiles and defoliants, can in the end crush the aspirations of the poor and the deprived for independence and a better life. Were Vietnam to prevail, the people's liberation struggles presently smouldering throughout Asia and Africa and Latin America would burst into fire. That is why the greatest military power in the history of the world is seeking so desperately and by such despicable means to extinguish the flame of the Vietnamese people.

To argue, as I have done, that America's interest in halting the revolution of the 'damned of the earth' is to preserve the wealth and privileges of her own ruling *élite* is in itself to argue that her motives, far from being the altruistic support of 'freedom' and 'democracy', are base, material and selfish. But one can be much more positive than that. The kind of living standards to be found among the peasant peoples of the world today are absolutely incompatible with any definition of freedom whatsoever, and it is American aid and military backing which keeps in power the most reactionary ruling groups throughout the third world, *élites* totally and implacably opposed to that land reform which alone can liberate the rural masses and launch them on the path to better living standards and better opportunities in life. A recent international Christian convention, surveying the poverty of the underdeveloped world, seriously debated the concept of 'just revolution', querying

'. . . whether [our brethren in South America] are permitted —indeed whether they are not even positively commanded— to take parts in violent attempts to overthrow the Government. They point out that in most South American States the ruling system results, on a yearly average, in more deaths through hunger or inadequate medical care than was the case in the Second World War.'[54]

Such a 'just revolution', wherever it took place in 'free' Asia, Africa or Latin America, would be a revolution against imperialism and neo-colonialism.

But there is another point. By the Western definition of democracy—rule by the majority—there must logically come a time, if nuclear holocaust is averted, when the peoples of Asia —much more than half the world's population already—will exercise the determining say in all major international decisions, much as the US exercises it at present. Do we in the West seriously consider America's use of her present power a good 'democratic' model for the future? What kind of society, which sets itself up as monitor and policeman of the world, is reflected in such recent random press reports: that when Wall Street tickers carried news of a North Vietnamese peace feeler to India it precipitated a 'peace panic', hitting aircraft shares particularly hard (8/2/66); that 'Copper prices picked up yesterday as *fears* of a quick peace in Vietnam receded';[55] or that the barbarous slaughter in cold blood of some 500,000–1,000,000 men, women and children in Indonesia in order to install leaders favourable to Western business interests was 'The West's best news for years in Asia.'[56] In truth, 'democracy' is not the victory America aspires to throughout the world today, for war itself has become the victory.

This picture may seem altogether too depressing a one. But it is one widely held among Western intellectuals. The British historian Arnold Toynbee has said, for example:

'. . . America is today the leader of a world-wide anti-revolutionary movement in defence of vested interests. She now stands for what Rome stood for. Rome consistently supported the rich against the poor in all foreign communities that fell under her sway; and since the poor, so far, have always and everywhere been far more numerous than the rich, Rome's policy made for inequality, for injustice and for the least happiness of the greatest number. America's decision to adopt Rome's role has been deliberate, if I have gauged it right.'[57]

And, again,

'By far the greatest and most significant thing that is happening in the world today is a movement on foot for giving the benefits of civilization to that huge majority of the human race that has paid for civilization, without sharing in its benefits, during the first five thousand years of civilization's existence.'[58]

During the industrial revolution, the new middle classes seized a measure of power and wealth from the traditional feudal and landed *élite*, but they failed to extend the benefits of the new technology to the rural masses of the world. Now the peasant poor are demanding their rights:

> 'The true proletariat of the mid-twentieth century consists of the poor peasants of the underdeveloped countries, and it is only on the basis of their mobilization . . . that revolution in these countries can succeed.'[59]

But what power America ranges against this peasant revolution! The situation is a profoundly corrupting one. In looking at history and the present, we in the West tend to take a pride in the real and genuine accomplishments of our culture, and to gloss over or ignore the dark side of the coin. As America constantly increases her power and her dominion throughout the globe in order to halt the rising tide of peasant liberation movements, we may be tempted to take comfort from the supposed restraint of the 'democratic' countries as compared with the 'socialist camp'. But this is a misleading dichotomy and a false comfort. The fact is that Western civilization has pioneered the perpetration of previously unheard of levels of violence and mass murder. The tradition runs through from the crusades and religious wars to the First World War, the elimination of the kulaks and the slave labour camps in Russia, the extermination of the Jews in central Europe by the Nazis, the Second World War, Dresden, Hiroshima, Nagasaki, the Korean War (5 million casualties) and now Vietnam:

> '. . . . the crimes are ours, arising from our culture, our West, the same society which today is essentially unchanged from what it was those few years ago when it originated these convulsions, these self-mutilations. . . . There is a tradition of excess—of violence for transcendental and essentially unattainable goals—that is as much a part of the West as is our tradition of regard for individual destiny and worth.'[60]

The unprecedented violence being deployed today by the West, and the sordid and selfish motives for which it is being deployed—to halt the social revolution at the point which maximised the benefit of the rich white minority at the expense of the poor coloured majority—is slowly but surely eroding what resistance the Western regard for the individual put in the way of the use of violence. In the Vietnam war, as American psychologist Erich Fromm points out, for the first time victories are announced not in terms of territory gained but in terms of the number of human beings hunted down and killed. In 'VC' (Vietcong— National Liberation Front; note the dehumanization) areas, which constitute perhaps four-fifths of all South Vietnam, American troops are told that 'all that moves must be considered as Vietcong.'[61] The simple statement conceals a commitment to mass murder of civilians on a scale unattained even by Hitler.

The situation corrupts the oppressor and cruelly enslaves and tortures the oppressed.

'All men are in chains. There is the bondage of poverty and starvation; the bondage of lust for power, status, possessions. A reign of terror is now perpetrated and perpetuated on a global scale. In the affluent societies, it is masked. There, children are conditioned by violence called love to assume their position as the would-be inheritors of the fruits of the earth. But, in the process, they are reduced to little more than hypothetical points on a dehumanized co-ordinate system. For the rest, terror is not masked. It is torture, cold, starvation, death. The whole world is now an irreducible whole. The properties of this whole system force us to submit to the fatality of Vietnam, the starvation of the third world, etc. In total context, culture is against us, education enslaves us, technology kills us. We must confront this. We must destroy our vested illusions as to who, what, where we are. We must combat our self-pretended ignorance as to what goes on and our consequent non-reaction to what we refuse to know. We experience what is and what is being done through the filter of our socially approved lies. But what is, is not the limit of what is possible.'[62]

'But what is, is not the limit of what is possible': it is with this affirmation that we must end this consideration of liberation. The earth has its riches and Man has the talents to make of human life something good and fruitful. If despair is becoming the normal state of mind in the West, a great surging wave of determination and confidence in the future is welling up in the other world of Asia, Africa and Latin America, for liberation can and must be achieved—for the sake of all.

REFERENCES

1. U Thant: *United Nations Development Decade at Midpoint*, London, 1965, p. 3.
2. U Thant: ibid., pp. 5–6.
3. C. Geertz: *Agricultural Involution*, Berkeley and Los Angeles, 1963, pp. 130–3, 135.
4. C. Geertz: ibid., pp. 141, 143.
5. Maung Shein: *Burma's Transport and Foreign Trade*, Rangoon, 1964, p. 195.
6. G. C. Allen and A. Donnithorne: *Western Enterprise in Indonesia and Malaya*, London, 1962, p. 285.
7. E. H. Jacoby: *Agrarian Unrest in Southeast Asia*, Bombay, 1961, p. 210.
8. Denis Warner: 'Mr. Johnson's "Summit" Host', *Daily Telegraph*, 29/10/66.
9. In M. E. Gettleman (ed.): *Vietnam*, London, 1965, p. 375.
10. T. H. Silcock: *The Economy of Malaya*, Singapore, 1957, p. 1.
11. Lim Chong Yah: 'Malaya' in C. Onslow (ed.): *Asian Economic Development*, London, 1965, p. 113.
12. Lim Chong Yah: ibid., p. 114.
13. Lim Chong Yah: ibid, pp. 116–17.
14. E. L. Wheelwright: *Industrialization in Malaysia*, Melbourne, 1965, p. 106.
15. Dr. P. Ungphakorn: 'Thailand' in C. Onslow (ed.): *Asian Economic Development*, London, 1965, p. 173.
16. Dr. P. Ungphakorn: ibid., p. 173.
17. R. Dumont: 'Agrarian Reform' in *Views*, No. 11, Summer 1966, p. 29.
18. R. Dumont: ibid., pp. 30–1.
19. K. Buchanan: *The Chinese People and the Chinese Earth*, London, 1966, p. 47.
20. B. Hook: 'The Red Guard Enters the Scene', *Daily Telegraph*, London, 24/9/66.
21. K. Buchanan: *The Chinese People and the Chinese Earth*, London, 1966, pp. 61–2.

22. Professor Joan Robinson: 'The Korean Miracle', *Monthly Review*, January 1965, cited D. Horowitz: *From Yalta to Vietnam*, London, 1967, p. 136.
23. See D. Horowitz: ibid, pp. 136–7.
24. E. H. Jacoby: *Agrarian Unrest in Southeast Asia*, Bombay, 1961, pp. 107–8.
25. R. Segal: *The Crisis of India*, London, 1965, p. 304.
26. *Daily Telegraph*, London, 22/10/66.
27. Cited in R. Segal: *The Crisis of India*, London, 1965, p. 295.
28. Donald Groom in *Peace News*, 10/2/67; author's italics.
29. M. Kidron: *Foreign Investments in India*, London, 1965, pp. 305–6.
30. Khusro': 'The Burden of US Aid', *Pakistan Today*, New Series, No. 1, Autumn 1961.
31. (15/9/65).
32. J. M. Van Der Kroef: *The Communist Party of Indonesia*, Vancouver, 1965, pp. 193–4.
33. C. Van Gelderen: 'Save Hugo Blanco', *The Week*, 12/1/67.
34. R. Dumont: *Lands Alive*, London, 1965, p. 32.
35. R. Dumont: 'Agrarian Reform', *Views*, Summer 1966, p. 29.
36. E. Ahmad: 'Revolutionary Warfare', in M. E. Gettleman (ed.): *Vietnam*, London, 1965, pp. 369–70. That this is an accurate summary of the American administration's position may readily be verified; see, for example, Secretary of State Dean Rusk: 'American Foreign Policy and International Law', pp. 348–54 in the same volume.
37. See D. Horowitz: *From Yalta to Vietnam*, London, 1967, pp. 231–5.
38. E. Ahmad: ibid., pp. 370–1.
39. Senator Beveridge in a speech of 1898, cited in L. Wolff: *Little Brown Brother*, New York, 1960, p. 63.
40. Responsibility for the outbreak of war in Korea is still—or, perhaps, is increasingly—the subject of debate; see, for example, D. Horowitz: *From Yalta to Vietnam*, London, 1967, pp. 110–37.
41. *The Marxist*, Vol. 1, No. 2, Jan-Feb., 1967.
42. P. Baran and P. Sweezy: *Monopoly Capital*, New York, 1966, p. 176.
43. See, for example, D. F. Fleming: *The Cold War and its Origins*, London, 1961, p. 252 et passim.
44. See, for example, The Institute for Strategic Studies: *The Military Balance*, London, annual.
45. *Barclays Bank Review*, November 1963.
46. 17/1/59.
47. P. A. Baran and P. M. Sweezy: *Monopoly Capital*, New York, 1966, pp. 106–7.

48. Baran and Sweezy: ibid, pp. 196–7, 199.
49. H. Magdoff: 'Aspects of US Imperialism' *Monthly Review*, November 1966, p. 15.
50. *Washington Newsletter*, 11/7/66.
51. E. S. Herman and R. B. Du Boff: *America's Vietnam Policy*, Washington, 1966, Appendix 4.
52. H. Magdoff: 'Aspects of US Imperialism', *Monthly Review*, November 1966, pp. 27–8.
53. See E. S. Herman and R. H. Du Boff: *America's Vietnam Policy*, New York, 1966, Appendix 4.
54. *Frontier*, London, February, 1966.
55. *Daily Telegraph*, 10/1/67; author's italics.
56. *Time*, 15/7/66: of this last, the *New York Times* correspondent wrote that it was 'hopeful' and that it was '. . . doubtful if the coup would ever have been attempted . . . or been sustained . . .' without US aid; 19/6/66.
57. A. Toynbee: *America and the World Revolution*, 1961, cited D. Horowitz: *From Yalta to Vietnam*, London, 1967, p. 15.
58. A. Toynbee: *The Economy of the Western Hemisphere*, 1962, cited D. Horowitz: ibid, p. 209.
59. R. Dumont: 'Agrarian Reform', *Views*, Summer 1966, p. 32.
60. E. Stillman and W. Pfaff: *The Politics of Hysteria*, London, 1964, pp. 8, 13.
61. J. Lacouture: *Vietnam between Two Truces*, London, 1966, p. 163.
62. Programme for a seminar on the 'Dialectics of Liberation', July 1967.

Index